ESSENTIAL

Diary of a Public Transit Bus Operator Volume 1

ISIAH GREENE

Copyright © 2025 by Isiah Greene
All rights reserved.

No part of this publication may be reproduced, shared, stored in a retrieval system, or transmitted in any form or by any means electronic, mechanical, photocopying, recording, or otherwise without prior written permission from the author, except for brief quotations used in reviews, articles, or academic works, as permitted by law.
This is a work of nonfiction. Names, places, and events are presented truthfully to the best of the author's memory and perspective. Some identifying details may have been changed to respect privacy.

ISBN
Paperback: 979-8-9995668-0-5
Hardcover: 979-8-9995668-1-2

Printed in the United States of America

Published by New Greene Era
www.newgreeneera.com

DISCLAIMER

This book is the first installment of my personal diary as a public transit bus operator, covering the period between April 2020 and January 2022. It represents my own thoughts, memories, and opinions from that time and may contain errors, omissions, or inaccuracies. Policies, procedures, and working conditions may have changed since these entries were written, and I acknowledge that improvements may have been made.

Nothing in this book should be taken as advice, official policy, or a current reflection of any organization. I am not responsible for any actions taken or decisions made based on what you read here. This book exists solely to share my journey, not to guide yours.

All illustrations in this publication are original works created specifically for this book and are used with proper authorization. These depictions are artistic interpretations intended only for illustrative and storytelling purposes. Any resemblance to actual persons, organizations, or events is purely coincidental unless explicitly stated.

No official affiliation with, or endorsement by, any public or private entity including the Los Angeles County Metropolitan Transportation Authority (Metro) is implied or intended.

Bus Routes Operated from the Start of the Pandemic until My Resignation

Line 2   Sunset boulevard

Line 14/37   Beverly Boulevard and Adams Boulevard

Line 28   Olympic Boulevard

Line 35/38   Washington boulevard and Jefferson boulevard

Line 217   Fairfax Avenue and Hollywood Boulevard

Line 705   Rapid to Line 105, La Cienega Boulevard, Vernon Avenue

*Line 20   Wilshire Boulevard

*Line 534   Pacific Coast Highway

*= Lines performed outside of original assignments

Dedications and Acknowledgments

This diary is dedicated to my wife Denia, who held me accountable on days I wasn't in the mood to type after work. She never allowed me to miss a day, and if I did, she reminded me to make it up, even on days that weren't all that interesting or when I didn't "feel like it." Thank you so much I love you.

To my neighbor, Dr. Sharma Henderson, who helped me with the initial edits and provided insights on my book layout, thank you so much, big sis.

This is also for all my former co-workers, past and present, who showed up every day and gave their all despite the trials and tribulations that the job and their personal lives threw at them, and to those who made the job much easier with their great energy and team-oriented mindset.

Last but not least, to all the passengers who helped make my days operating buses on Los Angeles city streets so much smoother, thank you dearly.

Illustrations courtesy of Dian Triyasa, used with authorization for unrestricted commercial purposes.

ESSENTIAL: Diary of a Public Transit Bus Operator Volume 1

Preface

This diary came about as an outlet, a form of therapy to release the stress that I had from working in the city of Los Angeles, driving public transportation for the Metropolitan Transportation Authority. I had been driving for twelve years. When I first started working in June of 2009, I didn't really experience stress of any kind, but as the years behind the wheel continued, it seemed as if every year gradually got worse. I would get off work, and my head would feel really warm, like I was in a sauna or something. My neck and ears would be boiling hot at the end of the workday.

Then came the weight gain from all the "stress eating." A handful of my coworkers would go out of their way to express how fat I was getting and how "concerned" they were, but little did they know the why and what led to it. Afterward came the body aches, joint pain in multiple areas of my body, including my lower back, and occasional heartbeats that caused me to cough or gave me extreme worry. As healthy as I appeared on paper medically, you would have thought otherwise.

Further into my employment, I often found myself consuming alcohol on Sunday evenings right before going back to work on Monday afternoons. I was in denial, thinking that I was just having me a drink real quick, but as time went on, Sundays turned into having a drink after any hard day of work. I had to take accountability and acknowledge that I was becoming an alcoholic. I had to take a long-ass look in the mirror, realizing that if I continued on the same path, things would get much worse. I came to the conclusion that I was trying to escape stress due to my job but wasn't going about it the right way. The stress caused anxiety, and not being able to manage the two caused me to drink.

I always thought about taking time, such as a stress leave or some type of leave of absence, away from work, but I always thought, *What about when I come back afterward?* I'd be back to square one. I felt using the company's services wouldn't of ruled in my favor or worse case scenario, be used against me. I also didn't want to become the next operator with his photo at the sign-on window, a five-gallon empty water jug under it for operators signing on to make funeral donations.

On occasion, there were days when I drank a little more than usual, and when that occurred, I always took the following sick days from work. I realized that I needed an alternative, and it dawned on me that maybe I could start writing about my daily experiences being on the L.A. city streets as opposed to bad eating habits and downing multiple pints of liquor at the end of really tough working days.

With all that being mentioned and the interference of COVID-19 disrupting our normal everyday lives, I figured this would be the perfect moment to document my life as a bus operator, which eventually would be my final days with the company.

Driving had its good, bad, and ugly moments, but I'm grateful and thankful for the overall experience. This was not published to "expose" or make the MTA look bad, nor should it be used for religious or political advances. It's simply to show you, the reader, what plenty of transit bus operators go through on the regular and also what a lot of us dealt with as we were considered one of many "Essential Workers" during the pandemic.

Some of the things you'll read might make you feel as if I'm being unappreciative or complaining. Some moments will make you mad, happy, or sad. Some days will be boring, and others entertaining, but I'm sharing with you the raw truth and the emotions that came with it that same day.

I pray that this diary can shed light on the multitude of things that a lot of us deal with daily as public transit bus operators— not only in the city of Los Angeles but throughout the nation and abroad. This diary is strictly my personal experience. Outside of those who appeared in the public eye or work for the higher-ups who have made public appearances, I've concealed the names of those who still work for the company while this diary was written. I shouldn't have to go into detail as to why.

Last but not least, this diary ain't for folks who live "perfect lives" or think they're "holier than thou." If you're sensitive to graphic language or explicit content, you might want to skip this one. This diary is published exactly how it was written—so if you're the grammar police or get ticky-tack about every little thing, this probably ain't for you.

So with all that being said—enjoy the read. You're in for a world of emotions.

ESSENTIAL: Diary of a Public Transit Bus Operator Volume 1

Thursday, April 2, 2020

It was a normal day today, well sort of. Sun was out, it's only a handful of individuals riding. I was doing Line 14 going eastbound on Beverly Boulevard, and when I arrived to Alvarado Street, there's this dude with blonde hair wearing a leather black coat with blue jeans and black boots running toward my bus. The light just turned red, so I'm still parallel to the curb after boarding and alighting passengers as he's crossing the street. I crack open the rear door for him to get on. A homeless-looking woman begins jaywalking across the street after just getting off the same bus he just came from (Line 200) that he was on heading northbound. As of right now, MTA is only allowing passengers to board through the rear door. He is standing in the rear doorway yelling in my direction but looking toward her.

"Hey hold up, driver! The lady wants the bus!" he shouted.

I look in the passenger mirror perplexed. "Who?" I asked.

The man is still standing in the doorway preventing me from closing it. The lady steps up on the sidewalk after jaywalking into oncoming traffic to feed some muthafuckin' birds. Yeah, you heard that right, she started feeding pigeons to be exact, near the parking lot exit of the shopping center adjacent to Winchell's Donuts.

"Who exactly were you waiting for, sir?" I asked out loud.

He depressingly tells me, "Never mind." The light turns green, I close the door and continue in service. He grabs a seat across from the exit door. Once he sits down, dude just goes off on a tangent, talking mad shit.

"If you mutherfuckers don't want to do your fucking job, you should get out the fuckin' seat. All you mutherfuckers with these city jobs, y'all treat the public like shit! You guys, the mutherfucking LAPD, and all you other mutherfuckers that work these public jobs in the city—all you mutherfuckers are ungrateful and treat the citizens of L.A. like pieces of shit!"

Subconsciously, I think he felt crunchy for holding up the bus for that woman and decided to take out his frustration on me. He talked shit the whole time, occasionally raising his voice and using profane language. In the back of my mind, I was thinking, *So much for people handling essential business.* Despite how worried everyone is at this moment in time, Metro stated that they would keep service running for passengers who needed to handle essential duties during this pandemic such as going to the grocery store, going to doctor appointments/hospitals, and for people who still needed to get to and from their jobs that performed what the government considered to be essential duties.

Line 14 turns into the 37 at Hope and 1st Street going into downtown Los Angeles (Beverly turns into 1st Street at Beaudry in the eastbound direction). This dude bad-mouthed me all the way from Alvarado to 6th Street and Grand Avenue, which was his stop. Imagine a skinny guy that looks like former NFL quarterback and Fox NFL analyst Terry Bradshaw with a meth mouth. I'm not over-exaggerating, that's exactly what he looked like. He hit the stop request as I was traveling south down Grand Avenue and walked to the backdoor right as I was approaching 5th Street. He had some final words for me.

"Hey mutherfucker, remember, mutherfuckers get killed out here all the fucking time, and you're no fucking exception. Bus drivers get dropped just like civilians do, brother. Remember that shit the next time you want to treat your citizens like shit!" he shouted.

He finally gets off the bus and gets to the northwest corner with his body facing eastbound but looking at me, yelling obscenities. I just threw my hands up like an NFL player getting flagged for nothing. I didn't disrespect this man in any way, shape, or form, I was relieved that he was off my bus.

My next trip leaving the layover at the Washington Boulevard/Fairfax Avenue terminal going to the Beverly Center was cool, I didn't have no issues whatsoever. But the trip after that, lord have mercy.

I was going eastbound on Beverly Boulevard approaching the stop at Vermont Avenue, and there was an older middle-aged woman with a standing grocery cart, or as I like to call them, "granny carts." She was wearing a long-sleeve dark green shirt with a green skirt of the same hue, white socks, and black slip-on shoes, the ones you would see Bruce Lee wearing in his movies. She appeared to be an Asian woman in her mid-to-late 50s. She wanted to get on through the front door, but Metro was only allowing people to board through the back door at this time. She had a TAP card ready to pay at the fare box, but fare was free. It was about 7:13 p.m. She continued to stand at the front door while I was boarding passengers through the back. I yelled at her through the closed front door with my hands cupped at the sides of my mouth.

"Backdoooor! Backdoooor! Backdoooor!"

She finally realized what I was saying and got on through the back door, occupying the seats on the far side of the rear door. There was a younger girl sitting in the back past the staircase that shouted out,

"Metro is only boarding passengers through the back door due to the Coronavirus, ma'am."

The young lady was professional with what she said and was just being informative, but the older woman got mad and aggressively asked the young woman in a snappy reaction, "Why are you talking to me!? Also, why are you riding public transportation with no mask!? Don't talk to me!" she replied as she flung her right hand up in disgust.

"Well, fuck it then, I just was trying to help you out," the younger woman replied.

She had the appearance of a chola—brown-skinned Hispanic girl with her hair down to her shoulders, wearing a white/light gray sweatshirt and creased khakis, rocking black Chuck Taylors. She had boarded at the Beverly Boulevard and Kenmore stop. An argument broke out between the two, but the younger lady got quiet after the older woman kept chastising her, going off at the mouth with no filter whatsoever.

"Okay ma'am, that's enough, leave it alone, please!" I yelled out to the older lady.

She was adding fuel to the fire with her extreme verbal disrespect toward the young woman. For the life of me, I didn't understand why she was so upset about that. The young lady was quiet but not for long.

I was heading eastbound, approaching the curve after Westmoreland before the Council Street stop. The young woman told the older lady from the area she was sitting,

"Keep talking shit, and imma knock your ass out."

The older lady didn't take heed to her words because she continued to talk in the same manner. I was slowing down to make a stop at Council Street when the younger Hispanic girl began walking down the rear steps toward the rear door. Before doing so, she pulled her pants up and put her hair into a ponytail. Me growing up in South Central, I'd seen that gesture one too many times and knew what would occur next.

The older woman took it upon herself to get up from her seat and argue, getting close to the young woman. They were both in each other's faces in the rear door area, exchanging words. Next thing you know, the younger lady reached back and threw a straight right fist, which connected to the chin and lip area of the older lady, knocking her back into the seat she had just gotten out of. The young woman got off the bus and walked southbound on Virgil Street, very casual. The older woman began crying from the seat she just got knocked into, holding both her hands to her face, and then she started yelling at me.

"You need to call the police!" she shouted as she had tears in her eyes.

"I'm not calling shit!" I replied. "I told you to leave it alone, ma'am. As a matter of fact, get off and call them yourself!"

She stood up, now occupying the aisle area near the exit of the bus, pointing and shouting at me in the space between the rear door and the seat she was originally sitting in.

"I'm not going nowhere until you call the police!" she shouted.

I was furious at this moment, and I could literally feel my blood pressure rising. This was my last trip, and here this woman got mad at that young woman for explaining to her the current rules for boarding an MTA bus. I had to call BOC (Bus Operations Control Center), which is our dispatcher. I got a call back and informed him of the incident. He asked if the lady needed medical help. I yelled to the back while I was on the phone.

"Hey, you need paramedics?"

"Yes, and LAPD too," she yelled in return.

I informed the controller of her wishes, and he told me to hold tight at the location. I was fuming, gripping the phone with frustration. I sat at the bus stop with my hazards on. I still had a bus full of passengers—about twenty of them. The older lady started talking shit to me some more, still standing in the same area.

"I no understand why you want to kick me off bus? I've done nothing wrong, she hit me, she punch me," she griped.

I yelled back while hitting the backside of my right hand onto the palm of my left, now still in my seat but facing the mirror.

"All muthafuckas have to do is get on the bus and ride. Right now is not the time to be confronting people about ANYTHING! You took it upon yourself to have an attitude with her after she politely informed you that there was rear door boarding only!"

"You make me get on through back door, this would have never happened if you would have let me get on through the front," she replied.

I had a huge ass frown on my face as I was beginning to develop a headache. I took the deepest breath before replying. I was still hitting my backhand across the palm of the other with every word.

"Right now, we are not boarding passengers through the front, ma'am, what's so hard for you to understand? If you're not in a wheelchair, not using a walker that requires the ramp, using a cane, barely capable of walking, or a visually impaired individual, you are not allowed to board the front! How hard is it for you to get your ass on the bus and ride? Got damn it! It wasn't that big of a deal!"

The passengers on the bus began bombarding me with questions, asking me what time the next bus came, how long I'd be there, etc., disrupting my train of thought as I was looking for the necessary paperwork for my incident report. With all the questions and concerns coming at me all at once, all while I was trying to mentally process what happened, I ended up getting angry at those passengers.

"If you are not going to fill out any witness cards, get your asses off the bus and wait for the next one, please! This woman already got me pissed off!" I suggested.

I didn't mean for that response to come out like that, but at that moment, I was extremely upset. Those passengers got off and waited for the next bus. Out of those who were initially getting off, a young male passenger was kind enough to stay long enough to fill out an incident report card before going on about his evening. A few minutes later, another bus pulled up and boarded the remaining patrons that were on my bus, leaving me and the older female passenger as the only two people on board. A few minutes after another bus pulled up and boarded the remaining patrons, paramedics showed up, parking right behind my bus. It was about five of them—three in an apparatus truck and two more in an ambulance. One approached the front door while the others went through the back. At this moment, I was standing in the front doorway close to the driver's seat.

"How's it going, operator? Is it the lady back here that needs assistance?" one of the ambulance paramedics asked as he stepped up at the front door entrance.

"Yes, sir," I replied, my arms crossed in frustration. He walked to the back where the other four of his coworkers were already standing. They surrounded her as he began asking questions and sat his medical equipment on the ground.

"How's it going, ma'am? What happened?" he asked.

"I get attack by another girl, and driver trying to kick me off bus. I've done nothing wrong," she replied.

"Ma'am, that's irrelevant to us. Take that up with law enforcement," he said before continuing his assessment.

"Are you hurt?"

"No," she said, shaking her head.

"Okay, are you feeling disoriented, woozy, or lightheaded?"

"No," she answered.

They inspected the area where she was punched on her face, checking under her chin and other areas.

"Okay, you show no signs of major injury, no contusions of any kind. Would you like to go to the hospital?"

"No need, sir," she replied.

"Okay, ma'am, our job here is done. Have a good day! Stay safe!"

They packed up their medical equipment and left, providing me with their unit number for my report. After they drove off, I stood outside the bus, close to the fence of the parking lot next to the public storage, my hands extended at my sides like a pimp ready to slap one of his hoes for being disrespectful.

Shortly after the paramedics left, LAPD and an MTA road supervisor arrived about three minutes apart, both parking behind the bus. LAPD arrived first, and both officers approached me, questioning exactly what happened. I informed them of the situation, and as I was explaining, the road supervisor pulled up. After telling the officers what occurred, they both boarded the bus through the back door to talk to the lady. As they entered, the road supervisor walked up to me after stepping out of her vehicle to ask about the same thing. I gave her the same details I provided to LAPD, and afterward, she got on the bus to talk with the lady as well.

I stood at the front entrance near the driver's barrier, but my supervisor saw this and ordered me to wait outside while she spoke to the woman along with LAPD. After a few minutes, my road supervisor came back to me.

"The lady stated that you tried to kick her off the bus. Is this true?" she asked.

"I told her to get off and call law enforcement herself. She got mad at a girl for telling her to board through the back door, and it escalated into an altercation. I politely told her to leave it alone before she got punched, but she wouldn't," I replied.

"Okay, wait here. Let me get back on and have a word with her," she said.

The supervisor got back on the bus to talk to the lady while LAPD was still present. A few minutes later, LAPD exited the bus, and both officers handed me their card with their badge numbers. They were professional but recognized the silliness of the situation, laughing with each other before going on about their evening.

As soon as LAPD left, I got back on the bus through the front door. The lady and my supervisor were still conversing.

"I want his badge number," the lady told my supervisor.

My only guess was that she wanted to file a complaint against me or pursue some type of legal action. The coldest part of this whole situation was that my supervisor made me take this woman to her stop at Union Avenue. She bad-mouthed me so bad to my supervisor, the paramedics, and LAPD that you would have thought she was talking about a fugitive wanted for murder, but despite all that, she still used my bus. If it was left up to me, her ass would be riding the next bus.

On Beverly Boulevard, Union Avenue is literally a seven-minute drive from Vermont Avenue. This woman wasn't even going to be on the bus that long. My supervisor also instructed me to deadhead back to Division 7 after dropping her off and to report to the window afterward to fill out an accident report. Any of my coworkers will tell you, an accident report is a bus operator's worst nightmare. I really didn't want to have shit to do with this woman, but I had to follow my supervisor's orders. I continued in service, and it was just me and the lady on the bus—no other passengers. I was driving down Beverly Boulevard eastbound, occasionally mean-mugging the woman in the mirror and shaking my head. When we got to Union, she got off and walked to the front door. She stopped and looked at me before approaching the crosswalk.

"Now I have to take a test to see if I have Coronavirus because I don't know if that girl is sick or not," she said.

Was this woman serious!? That should have been a concern before her ass started getting mouthy with the younger woman. I gave her the look that Ken from Street Fighter 2 gives his opponent on the versus screen before the match as she walked across the street northbound on Union Avenue. The nerve of this damn woman!

After dropping her off, I pulled into Division 7, making a left on Alvarado Street heading north to Temple Street, continuing westbound until Beverly Boulevard, making a right turn onto San Vicente, and a right onto Santa Monica Boulevard.

I went to the lobby behind the supervisor's window to fill out a report, which took me about forty-five minutes. The supervisor on shift asked, "What, you writing a book?" because she felt I was taking too long. When you write fast reports, you run the risk of fuckin' up and giving the company a loophole to find a way to blame you for something. To eliminate that, I made my report as detailed as possible and took as long as I could. Those reports ask for everything—from the weather to the type of neighborhood you were driving in. I'm surprised they don't ask what color underwear you had on at the time of the incident. She told me if I took too long, I'd get booted out of the system. I'd rather get booted out the system than sit inside an Accident Review Board (*better known as an ARB*) trying to explain myself due to a mishap on my report. The company will charge you with some bullshit so fast if you're not thorough—fuck all that.

I couldn't wait to get home afterward. I was hungry and stressed out.

Monday, April 6, 2020

Coming off of a great weekend, and it started off great coming from Friday. I figured I'd get my weekend going with some pizza right after getting off. I went to Big Mama's and Papa's up the block to satisfy that craving.

As of right now, there are plenty of places to park along Santa Monica Boulevard and other parts of nearby cities due to the coronavirus. Places where you would spend fifteen to twenty minutes driving around looking for parking isn't even a thing now, and to be quite honest, the shit is real sweet. I'm going to enjoy it while I can because I'm sure this shit ain't gone last long. There are plenty of places to eat near my job and in the surrounding areas that got great food, but I don't fuck with them because of how sketchy it can get after a certain time and how fucked up parking is. During the weekend, I binged-watched the HBO TV series The Wire season one (*yes, I never watched the show*). I was able to catch up on some well-needed sleep, had been using Zoom to FaceTime friends I work with, had some soul food, and got well-needed rest both physically and mentally.

It was a rainy day today, it was not so bad, but it had its issues. Every Monday, I have a coworker on the same line as me doing the 14/37 that doesn't like to work. He is my follower on the bus run behind me. He'll leave the layover at the same time as I do, ride the bumper of my bus up until he gets a stop before our time points, then waits until he gets back on time after running nine to ten minutes early. Dude is lazy as fuck, and it's operators like him that make all of us look bad.

He's the type of person that no matter how much paperwork his colleagues submit to the company in regards to his insubordination, for some apparent reason, he'll still have a job at the end of the day. Truth be told, people like him will get promoted to a higher-paying position before anyone else. A lot of operators get along with him at the division and aren't aware of the type of driver he is when he's out on the road. Surprisingly, he's not the only operator that smiles in his coworkers' faces but dogs them out on the line. We work with plenty of operators that have the same sentiments.

He has bumped heads with a few operators; I bumped heads with him back in January on Martin Luther King Jr. Day. He thought he was getting a taste of his own medicine, accused me of doing what he regularly does to his fellow coworkers, and threatened to report me to the company. That day in particular, I had been running early on all my trips because my leader was leaving a little later than usual, and with it being a holiday, there was no traffic.

We were at the West L.A. Transit Center layover. I left a few minutes after my pull-out time so that I didn't run early. When I got to Adams Boulevard going eastbound, I saw my leader about a mile up the road, but as I was traveling down the boulevard, there was nobody to pick up at any of the stops, so I was cruising. I didn't pick up anyone until I got to Crenshaw Boulevard. As I continued in service approaching the Western stop, I pulled over because I ended up running three minutes early. While sitting at the bus stop, I saw my follower in the mirror in the number one lane flying like a bat out of hell. He caught my eye from my peripheral vision.

He rolled up and opened the front door. I cracked open the driver-side window to see what he needed.

"Say man, you out here passing people up, I'm going to report you to the company," he said.

"Um... whaaat?" I replied, shocked at what I was hearing.

"Yeah man, you out here passing people up, imma report you," he responded.

In the midst of this, a dude that I see regularly hanging out with crackheads on Adams Boulevard between Mont Clair Street and Buckingham Road was on his bus. He walked up to the front, yelling at me while the operator had his door open.

"Yeah, you be passing up people!" he shouted.

The operator waved for him to go sit back down, and he eventually did after a few seconds.

"I don't know what the fuck y'all talking about," I replied with a frown, irritated.

The light turned green, and he reiterated the "write-up" he was going to submit to the company. Then, he crossed to the far side of the intersection, parking his bus adjacent to the parking lot on the corner and turning on his hazard lights. Now that I think of it, I wonder if that dude gas lit him into thinking that I purposely passed him up? When that occurred that day, that initially put him on my shit list. Out of ten years that I've operated public transit buses with the MTA, I've never really had any problems with other operators. I had a minor itch with a few old-timers, but it wasn't nothing major.

One thing I would like to mention that I've taken notice of since the pandemic occurred is that new homeless tents are popping up all along Beverly Boulevard. Since this pandemic, I'm starting to see new tents in places I would never imagine. L.A. already has a ton of tents. Businesses that aren't considered essential had to close down, and homeless people made real estate on the surfaces right outside the entrances and exits of multiple locations.

When I was heading eastbound on Beverly, I picked up a guy who had three roll-away bags and two duffle bags of stuff. They were real huge bags, the ones people use to travel with that weigh damn near 100 lbs, depending on what you put in it. It becomes a bit of a hassle dealing with people who travel with so much stuff because they take up so much space, making it hard for people to come to and from. I'm not one to assume, but he looked like he had just encountered homelessness.

It seems as if you see a new homeless person or people every single day. Whether it's an individual or a family, you just can't avoid seeing it. Regardless of how someone encountered homelessness, I must admit, it is becoming overwhelming to bear witness to.

Tuesday, April 7, 2020

It was pouring rain earlier. Today, I decided to wear a different mask, one different from the one the company gave me. I have a beard, and the one the window provided isn't all that great. It's made of a cotton/napkin material, moves too easily, and is uncomfortable. I wore one that was firmer on the exterior and stayed in place, but the portion that holds onto your nose was itchy and extremely uncomfortable, and it had my beard sweaty.

On my first trip going westbound on Adams Boulevard as Line 37, when I got to Western, there was a lady and her older daughter waiting at the corner for the light to cross the street westbound. The older lady had a walker. I guess they had a change of heart because they started walking toward my bus, flagging me down. I cracked the doors open for them.

"I need the ramp," she requested.

I deployed the ramp for her, and her daughter got on through the rear door. I continued in service after they both boarded. When I arrived at the Crenshaw Boulevard stop, I heard the lady with the walker yell out,

"Walker coming out!"

I hit the parking brake and waited for all the passengers to exit the bus after opening both doors. A few elderly and disabled passengers requested to exit through the front door, so I had to wait a little longer than usual.

"Walker coming out!" she yelled again.

She was talking to another passenger and taking her time making her exit. Then she yelled a third time while still conversing with the same person.

"Walker coming out!"

"Yes, ma'am, I heard you the first time. I got you," I politely replied.

After the remainder of the elderly passengers exited through the front door, I deployed the ramp. I was sitting at the light waiting for her to get off. Her daughter was already outside waiting. It seems like my reply pissed her off, even though it wasn't in a disrespectful manner. As she was getting off, she stopped, turned around, and looked me dead in my eyes.

"WELL, AT LEAST YOU'RE STILL ALIVE!" she shouted before walking off the wheelchair ramp.

I sat there frowning with my head slightly turned to the side, looking like Robert De Niro with that confused and irritated expression. At that moment, I was thinking, *Bitch... what the fuck do you mean by that? What would make you say some shit like that, especially at a time like this?* How the fuck she gone get mad at me because she bullshittin'?

It's things like this that make us pass some of these people up. People think we're just being mean to random passengers when in reality, we've had run-ins with them before, and we remember the inconvenience they gave us last time they rode. Sometimes, as bus operators, we just don't feel like dealing with it. I'll remember her ass, and if I catch her at one of these bus stops solo in the future, I'm passing her ass up.

The rest of the day was smooth. Then, on my last trip, I picked up a crackhead couple heading westbound at La Brea. The area between Harcourt and La Brea Avenue on Adams Boulevard has a heavy presence of drug users. They got on through the back. The lady with the man could barely walk and required his assistance. It was quite evident they were under the influence of something.

He spoke in that mush-mouth crackhead tone as they both boarded.

"Cuh mon beh beh be cool, just come on," he said.

They both sat down and started arguing. What they were arguing about, God knows what. I would have needed the help of Sesame Street utilizing a bouncing ball on each word to understand what the fuck they were saying. The woman became angry and sat on the opposite side of the far rear seats. Then she started fighting the air, looking like Tre from *Boyz n the Hood* after the cop situation. A few times, she fucked around and punched the poles while doing so. She hit them so hard I'd be surprised if she didn't crack a bone in one of her knuckles. The man kept telling her to calm down in that signature crackhead voice.

I didn't feel like dealing with that. As aggressively as she was swinging at the air, I swore up and down they were going to end up fighting each other. She was real upset at dude. I hit the gas hard as hell, damn near rupturing my right achilles. I flew from Hauser to Washington Boulevard and Fairfax Avenue with the quickness. They got off, and I went on about my night. Felt like I dodged a bullet there. Last thing I need is to be dealing with madness after my last trip. Lord knows I'm not trying to fill out another accident report.

Wednesday, April 8, 2020

Earlier today, the Board of Supervisors for the County of Los Angeles held a press conference. David Goldstein, a journalist for CBS 2 Los Angeles and KCAL 9, asked board member Hilda Solis what they are doing to protect MTA operators from exposure to COVID-19. Over the past few weeks, MTA has been running commercials online and statements from the CEO, telling the public what preventative measures they're taking to protect bus operators from catching the virus. But me being on the front lines? Unfortunately, that's not the case. Solis repeated everything the CEO said regarding PPE and the cleanliness of buses. Meanwhile, one of our coworkers, Jay Bohanan, recently died from the virus. A bus driver in Detroit, Jason Hargrove, made a video on his Facebook talking about how a lady in the back of his bus was coughing without covering her mouth—he literally died two weeks later from the coronavirus. I heard through the grapevine that he wore gloves and a mask.

At this moment, we don't know what the future holds or if the preventative measures in place will be enough to stop anyone from getting sick. I'm curious to see how they'll enforce safety for us when there are plenty of disrespectful-ass passengers out here who don't abide by any rules or regulations. Our safety was already a major concern long before COVID was a thing, and there was a clear lack of care about that. It'll be interesting to see how things unfold in the coming days. It's not like they have law enforcement riding each bus run from the beginning of the line to the end, and it's not like they have service attendants at the end of every route ready to clean these buses. I stole some Maintex Turbo Kill spray from the service area at work that was just laying around. On the back of the bottle, it says it kills coronavirus. I do my best to spray my bus back and forth at layovers.

On my first trip, I had to use the restroom once I entered downtown. I pulled my bus over at the hospital I was born in (California Hospital) to handle my business. Three nurses were at the front. Couldn't nobody just walk past them—you had to get your temperature taken. I informed them that I had to use the restroom, but they could barely hear me because I had on an N95 mask. Before I could go any further, they said they had to check my temperature. One of the nurses held a digital thermometer to my forehead, and it showed 95.8 degrees.

"You're a cool guy," she said, and we both laughed.

She told me to let security know because the restroom required a buzz-in. I handled my business, washed my hands like a surgeon, and went back to the bus to continue in service.

I had a decent day. On my second trip, I picked up a guy yelling on the phone about some young Hispanic kids that banged on him. For those who aren't familiar with gang lingo, "banged on" means when a gang member approaches and questions you, basically testing your manhood. He said the kids looked like they were still in high school. Dude had a red bandana across his face and was flamed up in all red clothing. While talking on the phone, he said that back in the day, if you approached someone like that, you had to be ready to die. He said these kids nowadays are perpetrators and don't have the heart they claim to. Man, was he loud as fuck on the phone—I couldn't wait for dude to get off. He called them millennium gangbangers. Bro was looking like Tray Deee from The Eastsidaz but dressed in all red from head to toe.

I get it—I drive public transit for one of the top agencies in the nation, so I'm always going to deal with noise. But some people be so damn loud, you'd swear they were in their own living room on a Saturday night. The loudness of his voice gave me a damn headache. People are way too comfortable about the things they talk about and how loud they talk about them on public transportation. I remember thinking, *got damn, you too old for the bullshit.*

Thursday, April 9, 2020

It was still raining today. I forgot to mention that my mom was in the hospital for a stomach issue. I was stressed out from that because when she called, she left me a voicemail saying she was in the hospital but didn't mention exactly why. I'm thinking it was COVID-related or something much more serious, but it wasn't. I started to call off from work today just from the stress the news alone produced.

There were two accidents today—one on Adams Boulevard and 7th Ave involving a Ralphs grocery store shuttle and two other cars. One was possibly a Mini Cooper, and the other looked like a Hyundai Accent. The grocery shuttle was damn near folded in half in the middle. Praying that everyone involved is okay. I was also happy I didn't have to detour, but when I got further up Adams, I could see that Magnolia Avenue was blocked off as well. I detoured down Vermont Avenue southbound, left on Jefferson Boulevard, then back onto Hoover Street. When I got back to Adams, it looked like another accident, but I couldn't see to the other side because law enforcement and tow trucks were blocking the scene. People can't drive for shit in the rain out here. They don't reduce their speed or anything.

A few minutes later, we all got text messages on our ATMS radio system telling us that a woman in a wheelchair was trying to board at Washington Boulevard and Fairfax Avenue and that she had fecal matter and a urine smell coming from her. We were advised not to pick her up. When they provided the description, I realized I knew exactly who she was. A few weeks before COVID, she boarded my bus going into downtown L.A. while I was doing the 14/37.

I was on my second trip driving down Olive Street, and when it came time for her stop at 9th Street, she kept apologizing to me. I had no idea why until I saw that she urinated on the floor of the bus, and the fluid rolled down the aisle all the way to the front past the yellow line where passengers are advised to stay behind. I was *pissed*. She wanted me to accept her apology, which I did, but I told her to exit so I could get the bus cleaned. The passengers were frustrated that they had to get off as well. When someone releases vomit, urine, semen, or fecal matter, they call these bloodborne pathogens (bodily fluids with the possibility of having blood), and you have to get the bus cleaned immediately. The control center will advise you on the nearest division where you can pull in for a cleaning. I had to pull the bus into Division 1 off 6th Street and Central Avenue to get it taken care of. I remember exactly what she looked like, and I know if I pick her up again, I run the risk of the same thing happening and having to deal with frustrated passengers afterward.

The remainder of the day was cool. I got to La Cienega and Beverly Boulevard, and there's this man who always wears a tight bodysuit, a dark blonde wig, and heavy makeup while dragging a rollaway bag. I've seen him before—he rides other lines like the 2, 217, 4, and 16. When I pulled into the zone, he got on with his usual one bag. I was about to close the door, and he suddenly yelled out,

"Waaaaaaaaaaait!"

I looked, and he carried on three more big bags onto the bus. I'm thinking, *where in the hell did these bags come from?* I continued in service, and when he got off at Fairfax Avenue, it took forever with all the extra bags. It literally took this dude two minutes to get on and two minutes to get off. That time is very vital to us, especially if we need to use the restroom.

Sometimes, we have to use our best judgment. There are times when we pass up an individual for being an inconvenience, only to end up picking them up later because we didn't see them— either blending in with a crowd, hiding behind a bus depot, some bushes, or some other random shit, especially at a major intersection. I continued along the boulevard, driving through, and there were a handful of people at stops not paying attention, so I kept it pushin'.

The day ended well, but a lot of my coworkers weren't happy because MTA announced schedule changes, meaning fewer runs and cut hours. Me being a part-time operator, I'm fortunate that I always budgeted my money to the best of my ability and never lived above my financial means. We bid Tuesday—I'll see how things go from there.

Friday, April 10, 2020

Today there was a detour in downtown L.A. at 7th Street. It looked like they had a machine out repaving the roads, and they were going to be working on it for a few blocks. I guess the city figured it could catch up on well-needed construction with the lack of traffic and pedestrians throughout the city. Smooth day, but a few things got the best of me.

While detouring, I had to come back up 5th Street after going up Los Angeles Street. Right before I hit the right turn back onto my original route, there was a homeless man at Hill Street with no pants on—just a black leather jacket and some black leather tennis shoes. That was it, nothing else. I shit you not, what I saw next made me cringe. This dude bent over and wiped his ass with a blanket he was carrying. The motion of his wipe was equivalent to somebody doing an overhead tricep workout, his backside clinching the blanket as he pulled it over his shoulders. All I could do was shake my head. I damn near wanted to say a prayer for that blanket.

This is one of many reasons why I don't like picking up homeless-appearing passengers with a blanket. When I used to do Line 2 back in 2010, I remember picking up a ton of passengers in the AM during rush hour at Western Avenue heading westbound to UCLA. After picking up everyone, I noticed all the passengers had moved toward the rear door, leaving most of the front empty. When I looked in the mirror, there was a homeless man in the senior/disabled seats with a terrible odor, sitting with a blanket to the side. You could barely see his face because his dreadlocks were so long and disheveled. I didn't feel like going through the hassle of getting him kicked off—it was my last trip for the day—nor did I want to ruin the commute for others, so I kept it rollin'. When I got to UCLA and alighted the remaining passengers at Weyburn Avenue and Westwood Boulevard, he got off through the front door, and his blanket was full of dried fecal matter.

My last trip, there was a family with a kid popping gum, and that shit had my ears ringing. That was some bullshit! Then there's this woman who takes pictures of the buses on occasion, she's like a damn paparazzi. I remember seeing her outside our division about nine years back near the division exit. The only reason I remembered her was because she has a signature pair of boots that she always wear. She'll wait in areas where you'd least expect to see her. I've given the "mustache scratch" on occasion. She can be annoying at times to be honest, because she jumps out of nowhere when you least expect it just to get a picture of the bus, catchin' you off guard. I've seen her a few times on Beverly Boulevard on my first eastbound trip near New Hampshire Street.

There was also a lady who kept moving back and forth in the seats, giving me anxiety. I hate when passengers do that. That shit is very worrisome. Why is it so hard for you to sit and stay in one place? They move as if they're plotting an attack on either a passenger or the bus operator. Pick a seat and stay yo ass in it! Makes no sense for you to be switching seats five and six times a ride, you better of standing up near the rear door exit.

Monday, April 13, 2020

Today was okay, I'm happy as hell that this is the last day I work with the asshole behind me. I'm praying to God that I don't ever have to see that knucklehead along any of my future routes.

On my first trip, this dude left the layover before me. I'm scheduled to leave the layover before him, but he left at the time I was due to pull out. He saw me still inside the layover once he pulled around the block to the first stop at Washington Boulevard and Fairfax Avenue. I was on the phone with my wife still inside the layover just watching him to see what he was gone do. Shit, he wanted to be in a rush? Well, be my muthafuckin' guest.

He waited a few minutes, then left. We all have been leaving a little late due to the city being a ghost town and running early along the route. I rolled along Adams Boulevard with absolutely no one to pick up until I got past Crenshaw. Once I got to Normandie Avenue, all of the passengers got off his bus and waited on mine. I pulled into the bus zone on the far side of the intersection; he's about twenty feet up from my bus with his hazard lights on. Vermont Avenue is a timepoint and we can't pull into the zone no more than a minute early according to our rulebook. By this point, I'm on time. The passengers rush my bus. I stop one of the passengers getting on to ask him a question.

"Hey, what's going on with him?" I asked, giving a quick upward head nod in his direction.

"He said he's eight minutes early and that you were on time, so he recommended we get on your bus to get to our destinations," the passenger replied.

All I could think was, *this muthafucka right here...*

When I got past downtown to Hope Street, doing the second portion of the route (Line 14), here he comes flying like a bat out of hell in the number one lane. Now mind you, I'm two minutes early, and the next stop, Beaudry Avenue, is a timepoint on the route. So much for him running "eight minutes early." I'm sure the operator that was behind him was getting his/her ass beat having to pick up more than the usual crowd of folks because of him running ahead of schedule.

Anyways, the day went smooth outside of that. My last trip, I had a loudmouth woman yelling about kicking somebody out of her house for having money for what she called "bullshit" but not having money to help her pay rent. Passenger conversations on the bus are like listening to a daytime talk show from the 90s. If you wanted to start a YouTube channel, all you'd have to do is ride public transportation. There is a topic to discuss every day. It's a damn shame how I'm always earhustlin' someone's convo, but I can't help it with how loud people are.

Tuesday, April 14, 2020

Today we had a special shakeup. A shakeup is when the company makes adjustments to the schedules of the bus lines and trains. Along with those schedule changes, we (the operators) have to bid on new assignments. A handful of operators were happy, and a handful of them were not. Some of our coworkers expressed frustration about hours, while others were happy they'd have more time at home to spend with family or be more productive with other things.

During the bid, our division supervisor calls our name over the loudspeaker, and we have to give them the sequence number of the assignment we want. Me being a part-time operator, there weren't many lines to choose from, and most were ones I don't like. I hate Line 2 (Sunset) and Line 4 (Santa Monica) with a passion. With all the bullshit that happens on those lines, they're not for rookie operators and require extreme mental fortitude. I picked an assignment with Line 217 that goes down Fairfax Avenue on Mondays, Tuesdays, and Wednesdays, and the 705 that goes down Vernon Avenue on Thursdays and Fridays. The hours on Thursday and Friday are only three hours each, but I'm not tripping—the sooner I can get home, the better. My wife hates me doing the 705 because of the area it travels through.

Right after we bid for new assignments, we had to go see the division manager. He had a box sitting on the ground, and we had to sign off on a paper stating that we all received hand sanitizer. He gave us a tall bottle of it. Afterwards, I caught up with a few of my coworkers in the lobby before signing on.

Out on the route, there was a dude at Beverly Boulevard and Gardner Avenue with a bag of recyclables. I've been seeing way more people riding the bus with recyclables—no surprise, especially at this moment in time. He got on through the back door. I continued in service heading eastbound toward downtown. Shortly after passing Hobart Boulevard, he starts coughing. By this time, I'm watching him through the mirror anxiously. He then gets up and walks to the entrance of the rear door with his belongings. When I arrive at Normandie Avenue, he makes his exit. After I picked up a few passengers and closed the door, he comes running up to the front, banging on the door and pointing toward the back, indicating that he wanted to get back on.

"Aye man, don't pick him up! He's back here coughing and spitting on the floor!" a passenger in the back yells.

As soon as the light turns green, I take off. People like him are exactly who we're most concerned about.

Driving through downtown looked like an abandoned city with zombies. A grip of people talking to themselves, walking through oncoming traffic with no regard for their personal life. The usual heavy foot traffic throughout the downtown streets was gone. When I got to the end of the line, I caught up with a few of my coworkers, and we talked about what we got in the shakeup. Before leaving, I heard a man yelling and screaming, sounding like someone was getting tortured with a barbed object. The screams kept getting closer and closer, like he was walking toward the layover. I told myself, *Let me hurry up and get the fuck up out of here.*

He was under the 10 Freeway on Washington Boulevard, near a tent, rummaging through what looked like his personal belongings while yelling at the same time. I guess he lost something valuable? It's now gotten to the point that anytime I hear someone yelling near a homeless encampment close to a layover, my heart starts racing, and anxiety sets in.

Later, heading eastbound on Adams, I got to Western and saw a drunk woman walking down the street, barely able to keep her balance, holding a pack of Marlboro cigarettes. She was having a hard time even getting one out of the pack. At the corner, she looked down at three empty alcohol bottles—one was Hennessy, the other was VSOP, and the last was a shot bottle of some unknown liquor brand. She was making an attempt to pick up the bottles but was so drunk she didn't want to fall, so she left them alone. She didn't look homeless or out of her mind—she was well-groomed and dressed. Since this pandemic started, I've been seeing more of this.

Once I got past downtown, I was running two minutes early at Hope Street. There was a middle-aged couple walking westbound on Beverly Boulevard, and in the opposite direction, there was a younger man walking toward them. It looked like he was going to jaywalk across First Street, but instead, he walked all the way into the number one lane just to avoid walking past the couple. I was thinking to myself, *I know we're supposed to be practicing social distancing, but got damn, that was a bit much.* He got back onto the sidewalk just before passing me. Talk about being extra'd out.

After killing some time, I continued up Beverly and found myself early again at Vermont. A few feet up from the stop, there's a Filipino fried chicken joint called Jollibee. The drive-thru was so damn long that people were making it hard for me to get out of the bus stop. The line stretched into the number two lane, almost into the intersection. I had to flag a few of the customers in their cars waiting to pull up to let me out of the zone.

Further up the boulevard heading westbound, I had a family—a man, a woman, and two young boys—who wanted to get off at Rossmore. The son hit the stop request before Larchmont, but no one got off, so I continued in service. I was passing the light at Rossmore when the stop request went off again.

"Hey, I wanted that stop!" the father yelled out in an authoritative voice.

"You gotta hit the request sooner than that!" I replied loudly.

When I got to the far side of the light, I dropped them off. The only thing I hate about making a stop outside the zone is when somebody got a grip of shit—they take forever. They had a grocery cart and a few other belongings, but at least they were quick about it. It can be a bitch when a passenger yells for a stop after you already passed it up when they didn't request it. I'm not one to hold people hostage—I have no idea what people are going through or how they'll react. The sooner I can get them off the bus, the better.

The rest of the day was smooth. Going back toward Washington and Fairfax at Adams Boulevard and Grand Avenue, there was a woman with her whole ass out, sagging and talking to herself. She was standing about two feet from the curb, obstructing cars from turning. All I could do was shake my head and pray she didn't do anything crazy.

The night ended great otherwise. While deadheading back, there was an accident at La Cienega and Airdrome Street. A Mitsubishi Lancer was partially wrapped around a pole on the northwest corner. What the hell do these people be doing? The streets aren't as crowded with traffic, and yet people are driving like they're on the 405 Freeway at midnight.

Thursday, April 16, 2020

Yesterday at work along Beverly, it was quiet. I didn't deal with a lot of bullshit like I usually do. There seems to be more people out here talking to themselves, or maybe due to the pandemic and the slowdown of the city, it's just more visible? Either way, seeing this shit every day is depressing. I'm sure the numbers will rise with everything we're dealing with at this moment in time.

I also forgot to mention yesterday I saw a guy near a homeless encampment putting his penis into a sock under the 110 Freeway on 1st Street right after Beaudry while I was heading back to Washington and Fairfax. To some, this would seem crazy, but this is now considered "normal" on L.A. city streets. We've gotten to a point where people do this on city streets regularly with absolutely no care in the world, it is always chalked up to being a mental illness. What makes matters even worse is that individuals like him are near public schools, so kids walking to and from home unfortunately bear witness to this.

Today I picked up a young couple who looked like they were homeless—I wasn't too sure. There are a handful of couples in the area between Vermont Avenue and Benton Way who unfortunately look like life is getting the best of them. Doing Line 14, I've come across a few who had poor hygiene and a lackluster appearance. The couple I picked up today on my third trip both looked like they could be in their mid to late twenties. The woman had her hair in a combo of semi-pressed but gradually transitioning into an afro, a tank top, and some shiny black tights. The gentleman with her was about the same height as her, wearing a blue t-shirt, basketball shorts, unkempt hair, and some sandals. He had the universal fit of a man going out for a booty call past midnight.

As I continued in service after they got on, they both leaned on each other and started kissing at the pole near the rear door exit. On the New Flyer Xcelsior buses, the stop requests are on the poles, and due to their oval shape, the slightest touch will make them go off. As they were kissing, the stop request kept going off. I tilted my mirror down to get a look around the passenger area to see who was the culprit. The woman was very thick—she had hips and a huge backside. The top of her backside kept hitting the stop request. I didn't mean to disturb their rendezvous as they kissed like they had free time away from their children.

"Aye, y'all on the stop request!" I yelled.

The dude said, "My bad, sir," and pulled her toward him off the pole, cupping her backside, then got back to his business. When they got off at Reno Street, they said thank you and walked up the street northbound. All I could do was laugh. I continued up the boulevard eastbound on the same trip and picked up a man who appeared to be drunk, but I couldn't tell. As I was heading into downtown, he hit the stop request for Union, but he was too late on the button press, so I took him to Loma Street. In a slurred voice, he yelled, "I'm a stupid mutherfucker, I know, I know!" Dude was so hard on himself for missing that stop, I felt kinda bad, but hell, I didn't know he wanted the stop prior.

The day continued to go smooth. I linked up with the usual group of coworkers at Washington and Fairfax after my first trip. On my last trip coming from the Beverly Center, I was going through downtown when I saw a couple at 6th Street and Grand Avenue. The girl was sitting on her dude's lap, and they were both smoking a joint on the bench. They saw my bus and decided to jump up and aggressively flag me down at the last minute. I did a gesture indicating to them that they needed to stand up, but by then, the light changed green, and it was too late, so I kept driving. People need to learn to stop bullshittin' and be ready to catch these muthafuckin' buses.

Friday, April 17, 2020

My first trip heading toward Washington and Fairfax, there was a homeless man lying in the door space of The Glory Church of Jesus Christ right on the southwest corner of Grand and 18th. There was a bit of traffic in the right-turning lane leading up to the church. The homeless man had a grip of blood coming from his lower waist, possibly the midsection, and it looked like he was wiping it away. A few minutes before that, paramedics were driving down the street like they were looking for someone but couldn't find him. I wonder if it was for him? I hope dude is okay—that was a grip of blood.

On my last trip, there was a guy at Grand Avenue and Washington Boulevard with a granny cart who was barely paying attention. He flagged me down and got on through the back. He was mad and said the driver in front of me passed him up. He also expressed that he wanted to file a complaint. After boarding, he walked up to the front.

"Say man, the driver in front of me passed me up. I want to file a complaint. What's his bus number?" he asked.

"I wouldn't have any knowledge of that, sir," I replied. He gave me a look like he didn't believe me.

"You don't know his bus number?" he asked in a tone of disgust.

I was looking confused as hell—he was deadass serious. Dude pressed the fuck out of me like I had access to some sort of operator database or some shit. I started getting irritated with how aggressive he was questioning me. I gave a sarcastic laugh with the universal "what the fuck" hand gesture to go with it.

"How in the fuck am I supposed to know that, sir? I just answered your question, did I not?" I asked as I was simultaneously looking at him and the road.

"You can't call the dispatcher?" he asked.

"No, I'm not allowed to call them for that," I replied.

He paused for a moment. "Well, what's your number?" he asked.

I was still looking puzzled. "Why you want my number? I'm not the one you need to file a complaint against," I replied.

"I'm not gonna complain to the company about you, man," he said in a much lower, more reassuring tone.

"If that's not the case, then why the hell you want my bus number?" I asked.

"So they can know what bus was in front," he replied.

"All you gotta do is call customer service and give them the line and time you rode. I'm quite sure you don't need me for that," I advised.

All he had to do was look at the top of the bus to see the bus number. Hypothetically speaking, he gets my number and makes me the fall guy for this complaint, and now I got a blocked sign-on and have to fill out a dumb ass miscellaneous report for that shit? Nah, I'm good. I gave up arguing with him. He wasted so much time talking shit about that driver and filing a complaint that he missed his stop at Adams and Grand and had to walk back from Figueroa.

That's another downside to being a bus operator—when your coworker(s) in front do something to piss off the passengers, they take it out on you. I'm aware that all my coworkers aren't saints, but hell, there's a flipside to that coin. Some of these passengers be doing bullshit too when it comes to bus operators, and when it backfires on them, then they want to file a complaint with the company.

Monday, April 20, 2020

I started my new assignment today. I miss the 14/37 at this moment, but it's all good. I'm doing the 217 that goes along Fairfax Avenue and Hollywood Boulevard. Hollywood Boulevard is completely deserted and looking like a ghost town. There are no tour buses, no cosplay characters, no beer-belly Spider-Man actors with dingy and faded costumes specifically, no one breakdancing near the train station entrance at Highland Avenue, no bucket drummers, nothing that would attract foot traffic. Of course, you still have your usual crowd of homeless people and bums. Traffic was so light that I ended up running early in each direction, constantly having to pull the bus over.

On my last trip going up to Hollywood Boulevard and Vine Street, a construction worker working at the site for the Vox Apartments got into an argument with a younger man for not wearing a mask on the bus. I thought it would end up the same way it did with the Asian lady getting mad at the young Hispanic girl earlier this month, but thank God it didn't turn out that way. Lord knows I'm not trying to stay another hour after I get off just to fill out some punk-ass accident report. To my knowledge, the younger guy was digging in his nose, and the construction worker caught him and called him out for it, which led to an argument between the two. They both boarded at my first stop on La Cienega and Jefferson.

"MTA needs to refuse service to fuckers like this. He's over here digging all in his nose and has the audacity to ride the bus," he yells to me.

They argued at each other for about two minutes. My anxiety was a bit high because I thought a fight was going to break out, but it didn't. They got off at Highland Avenue and Hollywood Boulevard. I honestly thought dude was gone take matters into his own hands and try to enforce some shit. You got people out here that'll get mad over any inconvenience (whether minor or major) that is distributed on public transportation from an individual and will try to be the judge, jury, and executioner.

It's only so much I can do. Last time I checked, I'm a bus driver, not a police officer. I don't know what these people are capable of, and Metro will throw you under the bus if an altercation occurs between you and a passenger after trying to enforce rules. They'll state that you "provoked an attack." Fuck all that. As a passenger, you're dealing with so many walks of life. At some point, you're going to encounter an individual or individuals who are annoying or don't follow any rules. Always remember, the objective is for you to get from point A to point B in a safe manner. Pick and choose your battles, because lord forbid you come across an individual who has no regard for human life, and unfortunately, there are plenty of them on public transportation.

Wednesday, April 22, 2020

Today, I saw Los Angeles County Department of Health going through Hollywood Boulevard inspecting homeless people. I'm guessing that's the procedure for them during this whole COVID-19 pandemic.

I encountered some disrespect. This Lil Rob-looking ass muthafucka was waiting for the bus at Fountain Ave, heading northbound—this was my third trip. I pull into the bus zone to pick him up. He puts his bike on the rack and gets on through the back door. He comes halfway up to the front and asks,

"Aye, are you the bus going to Calabasas?"

"No sir, that's near the Valley," I replied.

"You have no idea? I need to get toward that way," he said.

"I'm sure if you head out toward the Valley or ask around at the train station, somebody can help you out. But as far as riding the bus, I don't have any clue," I replied.

He thinks for a moment, then comes to a personal consensus.

"Well, fuck it, imma ride," he replies, then walks back near the rear door.

I could see if he asked me *"How to get to Inglewood"* or *"How to get to downtown"* or the beach, but this dude asked me how to get to Calabasas. Some people think because you're a bus driver, you know how to get to every city and every neighborhood via public transportation within all of California. Well, I'm here to tell you—that's far from the truth.

This dude literally rode a block up to Sunset Boulevard. He gets off, takes his bike off, and doesn't put the rack back in its original position. Any of my coworkers will tell you, when you use the bike rack and don't lift it back up, it is DISRESPECTFUL as hell. He starts to walk away. I tap my horn, pointing down at the rack. He looks back confused, so I keep pointing down at the rack, and he throws his hand up in a "whatever" gesture with a frown and keeps walking. One of the passengers outside saw how frustrated I was and lifted up the rack for me—I gave him a huge thanks. In my mind, I said to myself, "fucker." Next time I see his ass out here at a bus stop by himself, I'm passing his ass up.

On my second-to-last trip heading southbound on Fairfax, I pick up a dude with no shoes before I made the left onto Fairfax. When I got to Washington and Fairfax, another dude got on, and the dude with no shoes threw what looked to be a punch toward him. I got scared and thought to myself, *oh shit, they 'bout to fight.* Come to find out, they knew each other and were joking around. All I could do was laugh. They started shooting the breeze and got off at the train station—thank God.

My last trip was smooth. Heading down Hollywood, passing Cherokee, I saw a girl driving a mid-2000s Honda Civic with a sign on the side that read:

"Eat pussy, not animals."

When I arrived at Hollywood and Argyle (my last stop), a man who appeared to be homeless was trying to get on the bus. I hurried up and closed the door after dropping off the remainder of my passengers as he was making his way to the rear door. He looked perplexed, and his movements were a bit delusional. I gave him the cut-throat gesture and pointed up at the head sign. I don't want to run the risk of that person getting on, then I have to call the police because they don't want to get off. That shit has happened to me plenty of times.

Thursday, April 23, 2020

Today is my first day back on the 705. It's the rapid version of Line 105. This line runs from West Hollywood all the way to the city of Vernon, which is about a two-hour drive. Coming from West Hollywood via Santa Monica Boulevard, it goes down La Cienega, then makes a left on Cadillac Avenue, turning left onto Venice Boulevard, right onto Fairfax going into La Cienega, left on Obama Boulevard (formerly Rodeo Road), right onto King Boulvevard, right onto Crenshaw, then left onto Vernon Avenue all the way to the city of Vernon past the BNSF tracks right after Santa Fe Avenue.

Last time I did this line was back in 2014. My wife hates the fact that I do this line because it's in the hood and it passes some of the most ratchet spots in South Central Los Angeles. In my personal opinion, Vernon Avenue has to be up there as one of the most grimy boulevards in all of Los Angeles. I'm most familiar with the intersection of Vernon and Western Avenue. I grew up on 41st Street between St. Andrews and Gramercy Place. For my South Central L.A. natives, they know how close I lived. Back when I was in high school, my father told me he got robbed at gunpoint and was forced to strip asshole naked in front of the liquor store on the northwest corner. A few years back at that same liquor store, an old friend of mine I used to walk home with from middle school, Marvin Bradley, was shot and killed in the store's doorway from a drive-by shooting. He was only in his mid twenties.

Also, across the street adjacent to Louisiana Fried Chicken and the old Magee's Donuts, there's a burger joint called Master Burger, or as some of us from the hood call it, "Murder Burger." Everybody who goes to this place knows to keep their head on a swivel, grab the food and keep it movin'. This place can get sketchy. When I was a kid, I would wait for my mom to go to work when she worked overnight at Vernon Convalescent home and ride my GT Dyno there. My father would be out and about doing God knows what. The Lord protected my brother and me on plenty of nights going there. When I was much younger I would walk with my mother to the Pacific Bell building on the corner of 11th Avenue and Vernon to pay her bill. I also forgot to mention I was a ninth-grade student at Crenshaw High School before transferring to Fairfax High. I was in the marching band playing clarinet under Al Tarver. After band practice, I would walk down 11th Avenue all the way to Vernon heading eastbound, then continue up Gramercy Avenue all the way to 41st Street. So with all that being said, I'm no stranger to Vernon Avenue and it's get down.

I caught up with a coworker of mine in front of me. She's heavily religious in her Christian faith and very pro-Black. I'm very thankful for co-workers at the job such as herself. When I first started working for the company, she showed me the ins and outs of company-related things. It didn't matter what I needed—I could ask her anything, and she took the time to stop and help me out. When it came time for me to inquire about things I lacked knowledge about, I would ask those who looked to be veterans. Some of these individuals we called "high seniority" or "old timers" were dicks, bragging about how much seniority they had. Some helped me out when needed, but there were a handful of them who were disrespectful to newcomers coming out of OCI (Operations for Central Instruction). They would say things like, "Oh, you gone learn like I learned, rookie," instead of just being helpful. She is my leader on the line. It's always a blessing to have bus operators you're real cool with. The chemistry is great, and it makes driving along the boulevards so much smoother.

Driving near Western, it amazes me that there are still individuals hanging out drinking and doing drugs. Some of these people my dad used to hang with back in the day, and they're still out here after twenty-five-plus years. The MTA took the bus bench on the southwest corner away, leaving only the pole and line sign. It didn't make a difference—they all have lawn chairs, folding chairs, and recreational chairs. Last time, they had the 105 stop on the west side of the intersection and the rapid stop on the far side near the gas station, but I guess too many people were risking their safety. People would see a rapid line and run across the street from the local stop and vice versa. So now, they have both the 105 and 705 stopping at one stop.

I forgot to mention the day was hot as hell, and there were more people riding than usual. Social distancing did not apply to public transportation. On my last trip, this dude got on the bus at Avalon and went to Crenshaw Boulevard. Mind you, it's a hot-ass day, and this muthafucka looked like the reaper guy from the Bone Thugs-N-Harmony "Crossroads" video, but with tighter clothing. I get anxiety picking up people dressed in winter clothing on very hot days. It always raises an eyebrow for me.

When I'm doing this line, I'm only driving for three and a half hours, so please forgive me if I don't have much to report on.

Monday, April 27, 2020

Today was not so bad on the bus side, but I dealt with some bullshit outside of driving. On my first trip, there was this African man walking up to the front real fast and aggressive. His facial expression looked frantic. I had to raise my hand to stop him in his tracks—I didn't know what to expect from this man. I don't remember the exact stop, but I do recall him getting on before Sunset Boulevard.

"Excuse me, sir, I lost my bag on the bus. How can I contact the company?" he asked with a heavy African accent.

"You gotta call customer service. How long ago was this?" I asked.

"It was the bus in front of you," he said.

"The one directly before mine?"

"Yes, the one in front of yours," he replied.

"Stay on. I'll take you further up the boulevard. If it was the bus in front, she's still at the layover."

"Okay, thank you, sir," he replied with relief.

I could tell this was important to him. I called the Bus Operations Control Center, and they called me back, telling me to drive the gentleman to the last stop so he could catch the bus going back. The dispatcher gave me the bus number and the run of the line. I dropped the gentleman off at the corner of Vine Street and advised him to cross the street going back in the opposite direction. I informed him what BOC told me, indicating that the bus was still at the layover. He was very appreciative and gave me a huge thanks before crossing to the north side of Hollywood Boulevard. When I got to the layover, I asked the operator in front of me if she found a bag on her bus. She said she found a lunch bag, but its contents were scattered on the floor when she discovered it. I gave her a heads-up that the gentleman would be waiting, going back in the other direction.

Here's the bullshit I'm talking about. While still waiting at the layover, I was hungry and decided to place a future order for some wings at the Burgerim on the corner of La Cienega and Jefferson near our layover. After my southbound trip, I walked over to pick up my order, and when I got there, it didn't look nothing like the shit I ordered. There were only two workers, one cook, and one cashier. I picked up my order, and something told me to check it before I walked out—the bag didn't feel right. I stopped at one of the tables, cracked the bag open, and saw five tenders and two wings, with fries that looked half-cooked and tiny. I thought to myself, *got dammit, this is not my order.* I walked back to the front, interrupting the conversation the cashier was having with a guy sitting at the bar.

"Excuse me, ma'am, this is not my order," I said.

"Yes, it is," she replied with an authoritative attitude.

"No, it's not, ma'am," I replied, still looking down in the bag confused.

"Yes, it is. This is all we could afford to give you as we have run out of a few of our items. We tried to call you, but you didn't answer the phone," she replied.

I checked my phone and saw that I had a missed call from an unknown number while I was driving.

"Well, this isn't what I want, ma'am. Is there anything you can do?" I asked.

The Ugly Betty-looking woman shrugged her shoulders like *"Oh well,"* leaving me with a fucked up order and continued talking to the guy at the bar like I didn't even exist. Now, I'll take some accountability for not being able to answer the phone. One, it was on silent, and two, it ain't like I can answer it while driving the bus. I was willing to exchange the order for some mini burgers and fries or at least get some form of store credit toward a future purchase.

Man, I've had my days of janky customer service, but this might be in my top five worst experiences. I picked up the bag and walked out, mad as shit. I didn't feel like arguing or causing a big fuss. My wild card will be a lengthy one-star review on Yelp. A lot of these jobs never paid people enough to give a fuck, and I'm sure nothing has changed since COVID. That's what the fuck I get for ordering wings from a lackluster ass food joint. She could have handled the situation much better, but it is what it is. Besides, I didn't have time to wait for another order since I had to go back into service. I ate the tenders and wings, but the fries? I threw them away. Them muthafuckas were soggy as shit and cold. With customer service like that, I wouldn't be surprised if this place closes down in the near future. People deal with shit like this and wonder why In-N-Out or Chick-fil-A stay packed.

Tuesday, April 28, 2020

Today was a day of reflection—well...every day is a day of reflection—but with limited bullshit happening today, it gave me some time to think. It's crazy how Hollywood Boulevard is structured on line 217. Coming northbound on Fairfax Avenue, we make a right turn and continue up to Hollywood and Argyle. Between Fairfax and La Brea, Hollywood is more structured and residential, you see a grip of people jogging and walking their dogs, having a normal day. Then when you get past La Brea Avenue, it's touristy, but now that all the tourists are at home due to COVID-19, you see more homeless people than anything. There's so much space on the boulevard now that you got homeless people sleeping on Hollywood stars in the middle of the sidewalk freely—there's hardly any foot traffic. Yesterday at Las Palmas, there was a homeless man just sleeping in the middle of the sidewalk, and people were just walking around him like he was roadkill in the street.

The boulevard has all walks of life—tourists catch the eyes of locals and vice versa—but for me, it's those who aren't tourists that always get my attention. Every now and then when I drive down Hollywood, the song *"Boulevard of Broken Dreams"* by Green Day plays in my head. The place has layers—one part nostalgia, one part desperation, and one part *"why am I even here?"* On the surface, there's glitz and glamour—the Walk of Fame, historic theaters—but the flip side to that is struggling artists, tourists getting hustled, homelessness, and a whole lot of forgotten history. Having talked to a few customers that came from other states to Los Angeles, it's very common for people to come out here and get caught up in some bullshit—whether it be drugs, the wrong crowd, crime, or all of the above.

Prior to my third trip going northbound, a young Hispanic girl, possibly in her late teens or early 20s, came up to my bus inside the layover. I thought she was trying to get on, but she just wanted to ask me a question. I had her come to the window because I'm not opening no door for anybody at the layover, *especially in Hollywood.* It's a ton of crazies nearby, and I don't know what these people got up their sleeve. Some of these individuals portray themselves as normal, then they'll attack yo ass once they have access to you. Her skin and clothes were real dirty.

"How do I get to Baldwin Park?" she asked.

"Shit, I don't know," I replied.

She paces a bit, maybe a few steps. "Is there any bus I can catch that would get me close to there?"

I put my right hand up to my chin, posted in a train of thought.

"Maybe you can take the train downtown and work your way from there?" I replied.

She shakes her head in agreement, taking heed to what I just told her. "Okay cool, thank you, sir."

She proceeded to walk out of the layover going toward Arygle. With everything that I've previously mentioned, is it possible she just got caught up in the same cycle as so many others previously mentioned?

Wednesday, April 29, 2020

Man, what was the deal with all the delirious movements today? On my first layover after making relief on the 217, there was this dude who looked like Daryl from Hall & Oates walking along the wall of the layover from the Argyle side. He walked to the corner, looked my way, then decided to walk back, grab his bags, and keep it rollin'. Did he want to shoot up some drugs or make a restroom stop? I don't know, but I know a handful of our layovers are safe havens for drug users that don't have a dwelling or a secluded area to do so.

A few minutes later, there was this Natalie Portman-looking ass woman who was very dirty and barefoot at the Selma side of the layover, talking to a guy. I was on my bus, so I didn't know what they were talking about. After she finished talking to dude, she ended up pacing back and forth in the layover for damn near fifteen minutes. I was like, *"what the fuck?"* She would walk between buses, peek out of the entrance and exit of the layover, then go back to pacing. The way she was pacing back and forth reminded me of that song from Rockwell "Somebody's Watchin' Me. Then she went and talked to an operator on the 180 for a moment before going on about her day. Quite evident she might have been under the influence of something or just mentally not there.

On the trip after, I picked up some bum-ass, low-budget Ludacris lookin' ass nigga on Fountain Avenue with a bike and his friend. He wanted to get off at La Brea. I continued up the boulevard to his stop. As he was getting off, a young Hispanic lady got on—her appearance reminded me of actress Sofía Vergara. She had on a tight long sleeve collared white shirt with a dark colored business skirt and her hair came down to the middle of her back. He started trying to holler at her in the rear doorway. I started tapping my horn at him to hurry up because he's wasting a grip of time, just standing on the sidewalk. The light was red for a while and eventually turned green while he was still conversing with the young woman. I closed the door, ready to leave, and suddenly this dude ran faster than Usain Bolt up to the front of the bus.

"Aye! Aye! My bike! My bike!" he yelled.

He started retrieving his bike, and I swear, I should've taken off with it. Him and his homeboy had the audacity to mean mug me like they wanted to beat my ass or something. I remember thinking *shit nigga at least I was courteous with the time that I allowed you to holler at ole girl, I can't wait for your ass forever.*

Passengers bullshittin' on the line and not taking other peoples commute into consideration, this is a regular occurrence in Hollywood. It happens all throughout public transportation but the sense of entitlement on this side of town with people who ride seems to be higher than other areas of L.A. I couldn't wait to get my ass off today—I am mentally exhausted. I'm ready for this week to be over with.

Monday, May 4, 2020

On Friday, I had heavier-than-usual passenger loads, and it dawned upon me that it was the first of the month—as the saying goes, "Everybody and they momma got paid." People were walking from the local stops to the rapid stops, so the rapid stops had way more people waiting. I pull into the zones, and people start bum-rushing the rear door, trying to make sure they get on first, all while disrespecting their fellow passengers. It's like survival of the fittest out there—people are so desperate to get on that, on occasion, it's hard for elderly people to board. When I would yell at folks telling them "No more!" and try to close the door, they still made it difficult by forcing themselves on anyway.

The ones that didn't make it would do some bullshit like stick their foot or hand in the door to keep me from closing it and leaving. It's like, "Bruh, there's no more fuckin' space on my bus!" I would even stop opposite sides of the street at the local stops to drop off passengers, and people would come running from the other side to try and get on. Light would be red and everything, they'd run against oncoming traffic! Man, I'm already over it.

These people don't give a damn about no COVID, especially when they've been waiting on a bus forever.

On my last trip heading to West Hollywood, I had a woman who was constantly coughing. It was so bad that I had to pull the bus over and look in the mirror. When I looked, you could still hear the muffled coughs—she had everyone nervous, including myself. It's sad that now we live in a world where coughing puts people on edge. You want to cause a riot at this moment in time? Cough in a crowded space.

When I got to work today, I didn't see a supervisor at the window, and plenty of operators were waiting for their sign-on. I was waiting for both sign-on and a key for a CEA unit to make relief on line 217 that goes down Fairfax and Hollywood Boulevard. CEA units are the cars the company uses for operators to drive to relief points. Relief points are stops or layovers where bus operators relieve another operator off of their shift and take over the bus run until they either get relieved or finish their shift, pulling the bus into the division yard. All bullshit aside, it took so long that we all started cracking restroom jokes amongst each other. Usually, there are multiple supervisors behind the window to tend to operator needs, but the past few days, it's only been one. I was so late to the relief point that I had to chase the driver down along the route.

I was a bit irritated with plenty of senior citizens along Fairfax today. It is very scary when elderly people start switching seats while the bus is moving—it's even worse when they lack the physical strength to hold onto a pole. I had a handful of elderly folks almost fall while the bus was moving. I always wait for them to sit when they get on, but you have those who try to move seats, then when you make an abrupt maneuver, begin coming to a complete stop, or hit a real hard pothole, it knocks them off balance—to where they lose grip and end up falling into some shit, or even worse, falling onto the floor. We understand the delicacy and do our best to avoid that with senior and disabled passengers. If I'm close to a stop, I'll pull the bus over and wait for them—last thing I need is for one of them to fall and I have to fill out a punk-ass accident report.

Pick a seat and sit yo old ass down, and don't get up until it's time for you to get off!

Tuesday, May 5, 2020

Straight to the point. Everybody is aware that due to COVID-19, ain't no one riding buses like that, and there is not a lot of traffic out here in these streets. So what does that mean? It means that buses will run early. But they're still disciplining us for running early, so what have a lot of us been doing? Running late by leaving the layovers later than usual. Every bus run has timepoints. Timepoints are what help to keep operators running the proper headway between multiple runs on the same line.

After getting off the phone with my wife, I look up and notice the radio says 10L. On our radio screen, it'll say a number and the letter L next to it anytime you're five minutes late or more. I got off the phone and got my bus started. As I'm sitting after starting the bus, here comes a road supervisor. He makes a left turn off Jefferson and pulls into the 217 layover under the Expo Line, driving around the half-circle looking into each bus window (two other buses were there), then he backs his unit into the corner near the porta-potties. I leave the layover and go into service. When I get to Olympic Boulevard and Fairfax Avenue, I receive a text message. I click the text message, and it's from the same damn supervisor. The text reads:

"Just a little late in departing. Watch your time, you are subject to a TRANS-19."

A TRANS-19 is a document that the company uses to write up operators. I ain't gonna front—yeah, I took that shit personal, and the reason being is because this supervisor, in particular, always sends annoying ass text messages. Some of these road supervisors' feelings would be hurt if we had a way to reply to these text messages that they send us. I get that they have a job to do as far as making sure we do ours, but he'd be the same muthafucka that will be waiting for me at a timepoint along the route, ready to write me up for running ahead of schedule.

It's hard to please everybody as a bus operator. When we run early on the route, we have to pull the bus over and kill time. That makes customers mad. At this moment in time, I do not feel like pulling a bus over to kill time. These passengers are ticking time bombs out here. They don't feel like waiting for you to kill time because you're running early. They want to be able to get on and get to where they have to go pronto. I don't feel like dealing with "Man, why we sittin' here!?" "I got somewhere I gotta be!" "Can you get a move on it!?" You know, the usual verbal harassment from passengers for running early.

Here's what trips me out about this company—you got dudes like him that bother people who are actually doing their job, but they're not cracking down on those who are out here lollygagging and playing games. When I used to do lines 35/38 a few years prior, I would see this same supervisor in particular talking to a female operator at the West L.A. Transit layover who was my leader on the same route. After they would finish conversing with each other, she would be more than ten minutes late, practically leaving at the same time as me. This was a regular occurrence, and I never said shit about it, but let my black ass leave late to avoid running early on the line, and I get threatened with a damn write-up. Also, another question I have—where in the fuck was this dude at when my follower was constantly leaving the layover at the same time as me on lines 14/37?

Later on my last trip, there was this dude who got on at Hollywood Boulevard and Ivar Street straight trippin'. He got on through the back door, pacing back and forth, yelling. The shit caught me off guard—he looked like the late actor and comedian Jim Varney. It's a grip of people that get on the bus who look "normal," then they start yelling at the top of their lungs about some shit going on in their personal life or whatever the case is.

"I am a fucking idiot! How in the fuck am I going to get to Lancaster from here with no motherfuckin' money!?"

"I'm a dumb motherfucker!"

"My ex-wife won't let me see my son!"

"My sister is being held for ransom!"

Dude was grabbing at the sides of his scalp like he wanted to rip his brains out. I was at a loss for words. My main concern was my safety and the safety of others. I began thinking to myself, *what I would do if he lost it and went to attacking me or other people?* You just never know with these people. This man was pacing back and forth, breathing all hard. I had to grab my pepper spray and put it in my front pocket because I didn't know what this dude was capable of. Shit, my heart was racing fast as hell with all the walking back and forth and yelling he was doing. A few times, he got as close as the yellow line near the front door. Luckily, he got off at the last stop going toward the Red Line station on Argyle near the W Hotel. I was so damn stressed out that I didn't even get out of my seat to check for remaining passengers before pulling into the yard. I just wanted to hurry up and get away from the area. I had to take a deep ass breath.

Dude had me all fucked up. It ain't normal to be seeing and dealing with these crazy ass people every day. Man, it's a lot of work...

Wednesday, May 6, 2020

Today on my way to work, I was running late. Yeah, I know—ain't no traffic, so I should've gotten there on time. I get it. On the 405, traffic was blocked off because there was a car on fire past the Manchester exit. I had to exit La Cienega going northbound. Soon as I got off, I hit bumper-to-bumper traffic. The fire department had La Cienega blocked too. I'm like, *what the fuck?* I bust a U-turn and make a left on Hyde Park, taking it all the way to La Brea Avenue. By now, I only have about thirty minutes to get to work. I'm working my way up La Brea, and there's only one lane right after Obama Boulevard (formerly Rodeo Road) due to road construction. I make a left onto Obama and take it all the way to La Cienega heading northbound.

By the time I get to Olympic Boulevard, I only have about eight minutes to spare. So, me being the courteous individual I am, I call the front window to let them know I'm going to be late. The supervisor at the window tells me I'll still get a miss-out if I don't get to the division on time. I'm already salty from all the traffic obstacles I had to deal with. At that moment, I didn't care. I took a deep breath and continued like I had all the time in the world. I figured, *hell I'll deal with whatever consequences come with being late.* Surprisingly, I had a minute to spare when I walked into the lobby. I was able to sign in on time, got my sign-on sheet with a relief key, and went on about my day.

While out on the route, there was this crazy woman walking across the street diagonally against oncoming traffic on my fourth trip heading back to Jefferson Boulevard and La Cienega. She was yelling at passing cars and started acting insane when she got to the middle of the intersection. It was a hot day, but she had on a blue windbreaker, a beanie, and some brown corduroy pants. These are one of many red flags bus drivers pick up on when it comes to passengers. *It's hot as shit out here, but you're wearing clothes like it's the middle of winter?* She appeared to be homeless.

I was at the light on Hollywood Boulevard and Gardner when she was trying to get on the bus. I waved her off and gave her the cut-throat "no" gesture. She stood at the doorway begging to get on. I pointed toward the curb, insinuating for her to get out of the street. When she did, the light turned green, and I took off. Fuck that. I've learned my lesson from previous encounters. I just witnessed her act belligerent while crossing an intersection catty-corner. Then let's say I let her ass on, and she fucks around and gets to cussin' and screaming at me and everybody else on the bus. Who will be blamed for that? I wasn't dealing with that today. Fuck that!

But on a brighter note, on that same trip, this elderly lady getting off at 3rd and Fairfax told me thank you for providing an essential service and said she appreciated it. People like her make you appreciate the job. It's a select few passengers like that. It brought a smile to my face—at least somebody appreciates it.

While deadheading back to the division heading down Vine Street, there is a homeless encampment on Vine Street and Lexington with people just chilling like they're at a beach. Passing by, you have to use the lanes closer to the turning lane because they have stuff protruding into the street. You also have to drive much slower because they're stepping into the street to get around multiple tents. They had lawn chairs, beach chairs, playing music from a radio, and cooking food. I haven't seen people look so happy in my life.

Friday, May 8, 2020

A smooth ass day, a day where nothing happened. Say what? Shocker, huh? Even on this Line 705, where everything goes down on Vernon Avenue, it was a smooth ass day. The weather was decent, the bus rolled perfect, and wasn't no one out here doing stupid shit. Thank God.

On the 705 today, my bus was overwhelmingly crowded, like original rush hour pre-pandemic traffic crowded at Santa Fe heading back westbound. I'm thinking to myself, *why is it so damn crowded?* A lot of operators don't allow that many people to ride, but it's hard to enforce social distancing out here on these lines. I always have the fear that one or more assholes who won't be able to ride the bus will do some shit like cough or sneeze and yell "Coronavirus!" in a Cardi B voice just because they couldn't get on. I remember back when the whole Ebola scare popped off a few years back, somebody on Line 33 going down Venice Boulevard took off their mask and dropped it on the ground, then stated that they had the Ebola virus. If I'm not mistaken, the driver and the bus had to be quarantined for a few days. People stay doing fucked up shit out here.

The load lightened at Central Avenue, the rest of the day was smooth. It was a hot ass day—it felt like the 90s. Anytime you see the vision of the ground or surfaces that look like they're vibrating, that's when you know it's hot as hell. Ain't no telling how many people are riding public transportation just for the air conditioner alone.

Later on, I saw on the news that they're making people wear masks starting Monday in order to ride the bus. My only problem is, how are they going to enforce this? Because it ain't like they got a heavy law enforcement presence riding these buses. Also to keep it real, anything we enforce can lead to what Metro considers a "provoked attack".

Monday May 11, 2020

I had a beautiful Mother's Day weekend. Love having a great weekend—sometimes it can help to start a good week.

Here's what happened today: When I was going to make relief, the CEA unit that was provided had the rear right wheel rattling so much, it felt like it was about to fall off. I didn't trust that at all. I called the window and told them I was coming back to get another unit. I know some coworkers who have the thought of "workers comp" from getting hurt trying to milk the system— I've never been that type of person. After obtaining the other CEA unit, I went to make relief. The operator I relieved was very thankful for that. Some of my coworkers don't care about the well-being of others when it comes to safety, but I do.

I arrived at the layover parking my bus along Selma Street. I went to the restroom and came out to a man wearing a blonde wig, brown crop top shirt, and a pink skirt, simultaneously staring into the window of the bus and doing glamour shot poses. On occasion, he would twirl like a ballerina. I didn't walk to the bus because I didn't want that individual knowing that was my bus. This person in particular seemed like a nut job—I didn't feel like entertaining the bullshit. Dude looked like a drag queen version of actor Adrien Brody.

On my second trip heading southbound, while waiting at the light on Fairfax and Wilshire, a black BMW ran the red light at 6th Street so fast it shook the bus as it drove by, the light luckily turned green before it crossed the intersection but whether the light was green or not I don't think this individual gave a fuck. Do you know how fast you have to be driving a sedan to shake a public transit bus? L.A. traffic is light due to this virus, so there are individuals out here thinking this is the "Daytona 500." On the same trip when I arrived at the Washington/Fairfax stop, there was a lady in a wheelchair who wanted to go to the train station. She had a diaper laid out in her seat and on top of her. I thought she was the same lady that urinated on my bus at 7th Street and Olive two months prior when I was doing Line 14. I almost refused service to her, but it turned out it wasn't the same lady. I hit the parking brake and deployed the ramp. She asked for help getting up, so I went ahead and gave her a hand. The lady began talking about her life and past problems she'd dealt with. I could barely hear anything she was saying, but I guess by me not responding, she asked:

"Are you okay, bus driver?"

"Yes ma'am, I'm good," I replied, looking in the mirror.

"Oh, I'm just making sure," she responded, continuing to talk.

"Are you going past Jefferson Boulevard on La Cienega?" she asked.

I shook my head no, my mouth and chin area looking like a pub-breeded dog.

"Not at all, ma'am," I answered.

When I got to the last stop, out of nowhere she started yelling obscenities at me. So many I couldn't even keep up with what she was saying or how she was saying it. I hit the parking brake and put the ramp out for her. As she was rolling down the ramp, she stopped halfway, pulled out a joint and a lighter.

"Oh, I'm gonna smoke a joint," she stated.

I gave her the cut-throat no gesture.

"Aye ma'am, you can't light that here," I blurted.

Boy, these people out here are just too much. She proceeded to light her doobie. She completely rolled off the ramp, yelling more obscenities at me—a couple of "fuck" words here, a few "muthafuckas" there. I just told her to have a good day, brought the ramp back up, and kept it pushin' to the layover.

At the layover after the 3rd trip at Selma and Argyle, I heard someone yelling at a road supervisor. From the bus, I'm thinking that the supervisor was arguing with a pedestrian who took a shortcut through the layover. People are too lazy to walk around the layover, so they shortcut through while buses are pulling in and out. But from the looks of it, he was arguing with an operator that was doing Line 180.

This supervisor in particular used to be an operator at my division many years back, but he has his moments where he "forgets" that he used to be an operator. I'm guessing he was sweating this operator about leaving on time. Hell, when I was doing the 14 a few months back, I had gotten to the layover five minutes late due to heavy traffic coming up Beverly Boulevard. I ran to the restroom at Cedars Sinai, and when I came back to the bus, I called my wife to let her know that I was okay (routine calls). I shit you not, it hadn't even been a full two minutes since getting back to the bus and placing a call. He pulled up, parking his vehicle in the parking lot adjacent to the layover. After he exited the unit, he walked up and peeked in the window like an elementary student after school seeing if his teacher was still in the class. He looked at me, knocked on the window, and tapped his watch.

"What time are you leaving?" he asked, with a demeaning tone.

His approach to me that day was very snobby. It's like, damn, I just got back to the bus after a restroom run and you're busting my balls about leaving on fuckin' time when I am already late? Him being a former operator, I figured he'd be more understanding, but unfortunately that wasn't the case. He pressed an operator doing Line 180 about the same thing but got a different response. I'm not surprised by this—it's actually joyous to see. I wish more of my coworkers would start verbally getting off in some of these road supervisors' asses. Some are cool, but you have those who abuse the shit out of their authority, and plenty of them used to be bus operators.

On my last trip heading northbound, there was a supervisor at the Beverly stop with about six other passengers. He's sitting on the stop bench—only thing he was missing was a burger, fries, and a soda. He came to the front door as I was servicing the stop.

"Operator, you can't stop here. The stop is abandoned," he announced.

I looked at him confused as I was still boarding and alighting passengers.

"Oh, it is? Is there a sign on the pole letting everyone know that? Why are copious amounts of people still waiting here daily? I've been picking up here since the shakeup started," I replied.

He began pointing in an upward direction.

"There is a sign here. The stop has been abandoned for two years. It's a construction zone. Do not pick up here," he commanded.

I gave him the Michael Jordan shoulder shrug—the same one he gave after hitting all those threes against the Blazers in the '92 NBA Finals.

"Aight sir, no problem," I replied.

I closed the door after the remainder of the passengers got on and continued in service. I was thinking to myself *muthafucka, why you sitting at the bus stop with the people and not telling them where to catch the bus at?* Metro has these bullshit ass paper signs that they put on the poles when there is a temporary stop adjustment, like the shit is supposed to stay there for a whole year. The sign he's talking about is higher than a giraffe's ass, and its front is facing the opposite direction towards the bank on the corner—the average person would not see it. The weather changes the sign in just a matter of weeks due to sunlight, morning fog, rain, and other weather elements. I also forgot to mention, people tend to tear the signs down just for the fuck of it.

I don't know why they can't make temporary signs equivalent to the ones that are already up—where you can put some form of weatherproof label that would inform people to catch the bus across the street. They need an alternative to those whack ass signs because they really don't last long or serve much of a purpose. The stop in particular used to have construction equipment and cones blocking the zone two years prior, and they made all the passengers cross the street to catch the bus on the nearside by the CBS studio, but all of it is gone and all the passengers felt safe that they could catch the bus in its original stop zone. If you were to ask any of my coworkers, they would tell you that they wouldn't pass up a stop with a supervisor at it. So if I passed up the stop with him and those passengers there, I for sure would have gotten written up for that. To be quite honest, dude was just being a dick.

Tuesday, May 12, 2020

My last day for the week on the 217 before I go do the 705 Thursday and Friday.

On my second trip heading southbound, when I got to Fairfax and Electric, there were three people waiting at the stop. The first person got on, but the other two dudes were originally waiting on the 105. As I'm about to close the door, here comes one of the dudes—he stands in the doorway of the bus and yells at the other guy.

"Come on!" he yells.

The guy is still standing there, and I'm about to close the door because, at this point, I don't have time to wait on indecisive muthafuckas. So he holds the rear door open, preventing me from closing it.

"C'mon man, let's go!" he barked.

I'm looking at him frustrated, with a body language of defeat.

"C'mon man, if y'all not on the same page, then y'all don't need this muthafucka," I said.

Dude finally gets on, and the guy that was initially holding the door tells him the same thing. They both sit down and ride to the end of the line. I hate that shit—when someone wants one bus, but because they see another one, they hop on just to be 'on a bus'. People are so damn impatient that they'll go around the city and back instead of waiting on the actual bus they need.

At the Selma and Argyle layover, I saw one of my co-workers I haven't seen since the new shakeup took place. He told me,

"Man, I can't wait to get back to the 602—this line got way too many crazy-ass people."

The 602 is a shuttle line that goes from Sunset and Pacific Coast Highway to Westwood near UCLA. Line 2 used to go all the way to PCH, but they cut the route short, ending it at Le Conte and Broxton. He wasn't lying about the people—Hollywood Boulevard is riddled with them.

Couple of other things that irritated me today—

On my last trip, some dude took forever to put his bike on the rack. Homie was struggling to lift that shit up like a strongman lifting boulders in competition. The shit took forever. I can't stand bike racks—most people that use them only go a short distance. This muthafucka got on at Jefferson and got off at Washington Boulevard. With the struggle he had lifting the shit, he could've just rode his fuckin' bike instead of wasting his time and mine to go two damn stops. I wish people would stop wasting bus operators time knowing full damn well they can either walk to the next stop or ride to the next stop.

Anyways... on the next one.

Thursday, May 14, 2020

Yesterday I forgot to do my entry—I was tired. I had a smooth day, but when I signed on for my assignment today, my sign-on was blocked. I'm thinking the supervisor from the day prior gave me a write-up. Hell, I didn't know what to expect. A blocked sign-on is a Pandora's box. It can be anything good or bad. Sometimes it's a drug test, sometimes it's something in relation to your paperwork like your license or credentials, sometimes it's a punk-ass customer complaint—it can be a range of things. Don't fuck around and do something you ain't got no business doing out here on these streets, then get a blocked sign-on—that shit will spook the fuck outta you.

Well, anyways, the reason my sign-on was blocked was because I got a customer service award.

"Whaaaaaat!?" I said to myself.

I feel like I haven't been my best self driving these past few years. Passengers been pressing my buttons and grinding my gears at an all-time high. A few passengers I've lost my patience with so much so that I gave them a piece of my mind. I've gotten to the point where I find myself not having a filter verbally with all the annoying shit that comes with our occupation. I try to stay as professional as possible, but that's long gone out the window depending on the individual(s). I must admit, I was quite amazed. I wish the company did way more to show appreciation to those who keep the city moving. I feel we are very underappreciated.

All fuckin' day today, people were asking me to let them off at local stops. Got dammit...

Since COVID-19 popped off, I don't feel safe with the way these people act. On my first trip heading eastbound on Vernon Avenue, a guy wanted to get off at Arlington. People think Arlington Avenue is a major stop for the 705, but unfortunately, it's not. Everytime I pass Arlington, passengers always get into a shouting frenzy.

"Hey, I wanted that stop!" he yelled as I passed the avenue.

I looked up at him in the mirror before stopping at the light at Gramercy.

"I don't stop there! The rapid does not stop there!" I blurted out.

"Oh my bad," he muttered.

People just get on buses and don't look at the signs—they're just happy that they're on a bus, period. I gained a sense of courtesy and cracked the rear door open for him. He hurried up and got off, giving me thanks. Then on my westbound trip afterwards, a lady that got on at La Brea wanted to get off at the Clemson Street stop on La Cienega. I was low key upset.

"Ma'am, I can't make it a habit of making local stops—that defeats the whole purpose of a rapid," I stated.

"It's okay, sir. If you're unable to do so, don't stress it," she responded.

She understood and was real polite about it. I began to have a change of heart.

"If the light turns red, I'll look out for you," I said.

As I'm approaching the intersection at Clemson, the light turns red. I hurry up and crack the door open.

"Right now is your time to shine, ma'am—be quick about it!" I shouted out.

She hurried up and got up with swiftness, exiting the bus.

"Thank you!" she loudly shouted out.

The rest of the day was smooth sailing.

Friday, May 15, 2020

I hate when I'm driving the bus and get the fuckin' misconception that someone's gonna let me over. Case in point—heading westbound on Vernon after picking up at Santa Fe Avenue, there's this truck moving slow as hell. I'm thinking, cool, maybe he's giving me space since the lane narrows after Alameda 'cause of parked cars. I've got my signal on, checking my mirrors, thinking it's all good. This dude in a GMC truck creeping like he's letting me in—then outta nowhere, he stomps on the gas like we're racing to the damn finish line. I had to swerve back into my lane before shit got real. He wasn't letting up, and I'll be damned if I'm doing paperwork for a bullshit accident because I thought someone on these streets actually had some decency. I laid on the horn out of pure frustration as he sped past, only to catch him at the next light on Compton Avenue, sitting there like a dumbass, texting.

That's the shit that gets under my skin. These clowns make you think they're being courteous, like they're following the rules, but really, they're just distracted. They're not slowing down for *you*, they're slowing down because they're on their phones, not paying the fuck attention. It's annoying as fuck. First thing they teach you when you learn to drive is share the road—but these L.A. drivers? Selfish as hell. I'm not even in their way for long, but it's like letting a bus over is some massive inconvenience to their life. There are zero consequences for texting and driving.

Sometimes I really wonder if these people even realize how fuckin' reckless they are. I'm not in a damn Corolla—I'm in a 30,000-pound bus with people onboard. One bad move from them, and I've got lives at risk and a whole ass situation on my hands. That GMC dickhead really had me fooled, then punched it like he was in a Fast & Furious movie, just to sit at a red light like a jackass. Shit like that wears on you.

I always try to start my shift calm and professional, but with every dumb-ass move I gotta deal with, it chips away at my patience. It's like I'm supposed to be the adult out here while everyone else is playing bumper cars and sending texts. The texting especially drives me fuckin' nuts. These people will drift across lanes, brake late, block intersections—all because they can't go five minutes without checking their phones. I'm out here watching *them* to keep *my* bus safe. That's insane. I'm the one with the commercial license and the training, but I'm the one driving like I've gotta compensate for every clueless idiot on the road. It's frustrating dealing with this shit every single day, excuse my rant.

Monday, May 18, 2020

On my first trip heading up on the 217, some dude looking like an extra from the TV show *Baywatch* was laid out at the corner of Hollywood and Argyle like he was on the beach. Only thing he was missing was a picnic basket and a shade umbrella. He had on swim trunks and had a towel laid out on the sidewalk near the new Amoeba location. All I could think of was how dirty that ground is. Hollywood sidewalks have been subjected to a grip of shit and piss. As much as they power spray these sidewalks I'm not too sure if that will ever be enough.

On my third trip going back to Jefferson boulevard, I called out the last stop to everybody that was still on the bus. There was one guy in the back still sitting until I called it again. He gets up and walks down the stairs halfway up the aisle toward me.

"Why!? Why is this the last fuckin' stop!? What the fuck!?" he shouts out.

He was a tall dude with dirt blonde long hair and dirty skin. He had a handful of belongings on him—he appeared to be homeless. Dude demanded that I answer his question, but I didn't even bother. I just let him be. I was ready to get to my layover—I had to take a piss. I constantly have to remind myself that it's not me, it's them and the things that they are dealing with. *Woosaaah.*

Further into the day, on my last trip heading northbound from Jefferson Boulevard, there were two people standing in the street waving traffic off to go into the number one lane just before 3rd Street near the Whole Foods exit. From down the street I seen something in the road near the curb, but I was too far away to tell exactly what it was. When I got closer, it was a man lying in the street with his head busted open. Shit was insane. I have no idea how it happened, but I know for a fact dude is going to need major surgery. He had so much blood coming from his head that it started to roll down the curb toward the storm drain. *What the fuck?* Shit was like a horror movie. Damn, that's not something I wish to see at all—but being in the city of L.A., I'm not surprised.

When I got to the 3rd/Fairfax stop, there was this older woman with tree trunk-looking legs, I'm guessing from lymphedema. She was getting on and grunting with every step. She had about five bags of things and could barely walk—she was morbidly obese. All bullshit aside, she flopped down in the handicapped seating area on the door side and the bus rocked real *hard*. It was like the wrestlers Yokozuna or Andre the Giant sitting on the bumper of a Mini Cooper. If it wasn't for my seat belt and the driver's barrier, I'm sure I would have probably fell out the seat.

Man, I'm not one to weight shame, but damn that shit scared me. I never experienced nothing like that before. I remember when I first started working for the company, plenty of my co-workers told me, *"Stay here long enough, you'll see and experience some unimaginable things."* Well, this was one of them.

Tuesday, May 19, 2020

My trips were relatively smooth for the whole day. The weather was nice and sunny, and everything was going cool. But that third trip? That one was something else. It was the trip going northbound—I'm headed up Argyle, and there's a dude in the back of the bus standing near the stairwell before the exit. I hear the sound of a lighter being flicked. My passenger mirror was angled a certain way, so I couldn't see him clearly. I re-adjusted the mirror, and what do you know—this muthafucka is lighting a joint on the damn bus.

"Aye man, what the fuck you doing?" I yell out.

"Wait a minute, driver," he said, still sparking his lighter.

I exhaled a deep breath of frustration.

"C'mon, dude. Why you couldn't wait until you got off the bus to do that shit?" I asked.

"Aw driver, it ain't that serious, man," he replied.

I'm upset as shit, shaking my head. I mean, what the fuck am I supposed to do? He finally gets his joint lit and blows smoke right in the doorway as he's getting off.

"Have a good day, man," he said out loud.

I gave him the whatever hand gesture as he walked out the rear door. All I could do was shake my head. People smoking on public transportation is nothing new to me. I chalked that one up to the universe and kept it pushin'.

Then, on my last trip, a girl started complaining about "too many people being out." Under my breath, I murmured, "Yeah, you're one of them."

Wednesday, May 20, 2020

I was at the Fairfax Avenue and Willoughby relief point waiting to make relief, the relief time is 1:29 p.m. In my rearview mirror, I happen to see a bus at the stop prior at Melrose Avenue. It's crazy, I look at my watch and it shows 1:19 p.m. I'm thinking to myself *nah this can't be my relief, they're early as hell.* Welp, I was wrong. It was a young female operator running ahead of schedule. She pulls into the bus zone and before I could walk up to the front bus door, she hops off ready to make a dash toward the CEA unit. Usually an operator will brief you on the day such as detours, any minor mechanical failures, if there are any knuckleheads you need to avoid picking up, etc. She didn't do any of that, she was ready to go.

"You ain't wasting no time today, huh?" I asked.

"Nope," she replied.

"Alright now, have a good day. I left the car keys in the unit for you," I told her.

"Alright, thank you," she expressed happily.

She didn't waste no time getting out of there. Maybe she had an emergency or had to run to the restroom, hell I don't know. But then I had to kill time and run the risk of being lectured from one of the passengers. Luckily, the whole time I waited, no one complained.

I logged on and continued northbound. I get to Las Palmas and there's no one at the stop so I keep it rollin'. Las Palmas is the stop after Highland Avenue heading eastbound on Hollywood Boulevard. I'm thinking it's for the next stop but no—it's this girl with an aggressive tone.

"You don't stop here!? I hit the stop!" she barked.

I cocked my head back with a frown like a parent looking at a verbally disrespectful child.

"I'll get you on the far side of the light, ma'am. You hit the button late," I said out loud.

"Oh okay, thank you so much," she gleefully responded.

I don't like holding people hostage, I do not have time for the bullshit and I don't know what these people are capable of. The faster I can get them off the bus the better. I could tell by the initial tone of her voice she was ready to go off, but because I was generous enough to let her off on the far side, her voice got polite. A lot of times people are on their phones, distracted and not paying attention, then before they know it, they look up at the last minute and the bus is passing their stop—or already leaving it. They'll make it seem like it's your fault when in actuality it's theirs. We're not fuckin' mind readers out here.

When I got to the layover on Selma there was this homeless caveman-looking dude running around the street and sidewalk near the layover barefooted. It's like damn—every time I get to this layover it's always some crazy ass person occupying the area doing some crazy shit. He would lurk around the layover talking to himself and pacing back and forth, but boy was I in for a surprise. Although I had to use the restroom, I didn't get off the bus immediately, and I'm sure you have an idea as to why. At the layover, there is a mural painted on the Argyle Bar and Lounge building with Kobe and his daughter Gigi, and it's a stucco-based wall. This man ran along the wall like Spider-Man—now mind you, he's barefooted. I'm sittin' on the bus like *look at this crazy ass muthafucka here.* This dude probably can walk across thumb tacks with ease, stucco is not feet-friendly. He finally hit the corner and headed northbound on Argyle, I hurried up to the restroom after.

The rest of the day was cool, but this one thing irritated the fuck outta me while deadheading back to the division. When I was about to make a left turn onto Vine from Selma heading westbound, here comes a dude who looks like a combo of rappers Murphy Lee of the St. Lunatics and Future flying on a fixie bike. The light had just hit yellow as I'm sitting in the intersection. He stopped halfway in the crosswalk and started riding in circles waiting for me to complete my turn.

I stopped in the middle of the intersection and waved him to continue. I get tired of these disrespectful ass bicyclists because they come outta no fuckin' where and expect you to stop on a dime for them after doing some bullshit. You can have your head on a swivel looking back and forth as you're driving and it still won't prevent you from damn near hitting these idiots. City of L.A. gave them all the power to be dicks on the road, that's why I don't feel sorry for them when they get they asses hit while doing dumb shit on the road. Negligent bicyclists are one of many bus drivers' worst nightmares.

ESSENTIAL: Diary of a Public Transit Bus Operator Volume 1

Friday, May 22, 2020

Yesterday was one of the short days, and the short days have been beautiful. I'm only at work for three and a half hours. What bothered me yesterday was the lack of communication from those above us. I'm speaking about the supervisors on the road and the control center regarding a detour that was issued earlier in the route. I received the text message for the detour when I was at Division 7 laying over. When we got to the streets the text message listed, everything was clear, and nothing was obstructing the route—it was near Santa Fe and Vernon Avenue. We never got a message telling us the detour was finished.

Metro has a habit of issuing a detour and not canceling it until people start calling the company, saying that a particular bus isn't "running" or "hasn't shown up." Some operators are strictly by the book and will do the detour until they get a message from BOC officially telling them to cancel it. The streets will be clear, and everything will be back to normal, but they'll still follow the detour. I hate doing detours. Depending on the line and what part of the city you're in, they can be very frustrating. One thing I can't stand about detours is when passengers start panicking and rushing up to the front, asking where you're going, as if you're taking them to San Diego or some shit.

Also, yesterday, I had another victim of the rapid. On my next trip, a kid was riding westbound, and he had a messed-up facial expression after I passed up Arlington Avenue. Looking in the mirror, I could tell he was pissed. He started walking up to the front, and I swore up and down that he was about to have some words for me. As I passed 4th Avenue, he kept walking but then stopped—I'm guessing he thought twice about it or finally realized he was on a rapid bus. He got off at Crenshaw and began walking eastbound. The rest of the trip went smoothly.

Now, my vent for today: I'm tired of all these old-ass dudes with these beach cruisers that they can barely lift. Some elderly guy took so long to put his beach cruiser on the rack at Vermont that I ended up hitting the parking brake and writing a grocery list for the store this week. By the time I finished, he finally started stepping onto the bus. It's a grip of people out here with these big-ass bikes that are heavy as shit knowing damn well they can't lift them. I'm not a fan of beach cruisers because the bike racks on the bumpers aren't compatible with them. You got these hard-headed muthafuckas who put their bike on with one of the wheels hanging off the tip of the rack, then tell you, "Oh, it's cool. I rode with it like that before." It's all fun and games until you hit a hard-ass pothole or a deep dip in the road, and that "sweet chariot" of theirs goes flying off.

Continuing up Vernon eastbound, when I got to the train station stop at Long Beach Boulevard, there was a homeless woman who had her pants pulled down past the cheeks of her backside, sitting on the concrete looking downward. I remember thinking *what happened in her life for her to arrive at that point?* Shit was terrible.

On my last trip heading westbound at Normandie, I had just dropped off a few passengers and was ready to continue in service. The light turned green, I hit the gas crossing the intersection, and someone yelled from the back—

"Backdoor! Backdoor!"

I looked back—it was an older Hispanic man yelling that he wanted to get off.

"Man, what happened to you when I was letting everyone off at the stop? I was there for like three minutes straight, man. God damn!" I shouted.

He started walking down the stairs, his body pinballing off the poles as he made his way to the rear door. I saw that he had a 25oz tall can of malt liqour on him—probably a 211, the wording was red, and the can was silver.

"Oh shit, you're drunk. Nevermind."

I pulled to the far side of the light and dropped him off. Half of the passengers on my bus started laughing. I was amazed at how he managed to hold onto his drink, considering how hard he was bumping into the poles—ole infinity gauntlet hand-having ass. There's never a week without a dull moment on these buses. The rest of the trip was a breeze.

Tuesday, May 26, 2020

Yesterday was a great day. One of the best parts was a special needs adult man who took the time to thank me and told me to have a great day just before getting off the bus. He rode all the way to the West L.A. transit center on my fourth trip. To some, this might not mean much, but to me, it meant everything—it brought back great memories. When I was younger, I drove special needs students for First Student as a school bus driver. What was so cool about special needs students was that they never let negativity get them down. They were always upbeat and always showed you the utmost respect. I was very thankful for that exchange—it brought a huge smile to my face and made the Monday that much better.

I had a regular day today, but the highlight was at my first layover involving a Dash driver. They don't layover at our layover zone, but they make relief at our layover parking along Argyle. At Selma and Argyle, there are two layovers—one at the hub under the apartment building on the northwest corner and another on Selma east of Argyle. I was parked at the layover outside the one under the building. I began crossing the street to use the restroom, and as I walked up, I heard someone yelling.

I'm thinking to myself, *oh shit, another one of these crazy-ass people in the layover* and on the low, my heart started beating heavy. You could hear the yelling from across the street. I hesitated, wondering if I even wanted to walk over there, but I bit the bullet and kept it pushin' to the restroom. To my surprise, it wasn't some random crazy—it was a Dash bus driver arguing with what sounded like a woman on the phone. His voice echoed through the layover and out into the street.

"What the hell are you talking about!? When have I ever said you was my girlfriend!? We ain't in no muthafuckin' relationship!"

As I walked back to my bus, I put my fist up to my mouth and thought to myself, *ouch!* I tried my best to mind my business, but he was so damn loud it was impossible. Well, whoever was on the other side of that phone, if they didn't get the message then, they damn sure do now.

On my second trip heading to La Cienega Boulevard and Jefferson Avenue, there was a dude at Fountain and Fairfax who was real dirty and appeared to be homeless. He was pretending to be a superhero—flying. He had a blanket that he was using as a cape and a Burger King paper crown on his head. He was in the number two lane but so close to traffic that I had to take up two lanes just to pass him up. Situations like this bring up a huge amount of anxiety—you just never know what these individuals are capable of. You gotta tread lightly, passing them by, hoping they don't jump in front of your bus.

Wednesday, May 27, 2020

One funny highlight of the day was when I was heading back eastbound on Hollywood Boulevard. There was a guy at Wilcox trying to catch Line 212 in the street. The bus was sitting at the light after servicing the stop. He was at the back door knocking to get on, but the operator wouldn't open it. The light turned green, and as the operator drove off, he started running alongside the bus across the intersection, still trying to catch it. As I'm approaching Wilcox, there's no one at the bus stop, so I kept driving. He sees my bus at the last minute and starts running toward the stop, but by then, it's too late. Out of sheer frustration, he eventually stops running and throws up the middle finger as I drive by. All I could do was laugh. If he was patient and stayed at the stop, he would have been good.

On the next trip, I had a woman get on at the Jefferson Boulevard and La Cienega train station, and she rode all the way to the end of the line at Hollywood and Argyle. She was tired and fell asleep at the back of the bus. She appeared to be homeless.

"Last stop! Last stop!" I shouted.

She was still sleeping. I was low key upset, *I'm ready to pull into the yard, and now I gotta take extra time to get this woman off* I thought. Homeless people using the bus as shelters is now the norm. It's even worse if you do a late-night service going into the early AM—they'll ride your bus all night, making it hard for people who get off work late. Some get off with ease, others will wake up and go right back to sleep.

I hit the parking brake, got out of my seat, and walked halfway up the aisle, putting my hands to the sides of my mouth to project my voice.

"Last stop, ma'am! Last stop!"

She finally woke up but fell back asleep again.

"Seems like you need medical help, let me call an ambulance for you," I said.

She immediately woke up and got off. All I could do was shake my head and laugh. I hit the "Not in Service" code on my head sign and pulled into the yard with ease.

ESSENTIAL: Diary of a Public Transit Bus Operator Volume 1

Thursday, May 28, 2020

Today on the 705, I drove past the Crenshaw Mall, reflecting on how affluent the area used to be when I was a kid. I remember taking Line 40 from St. Andrews Place and King Boulevard to Crenshaw, walking with my mom and brother to the mall. I used to be happy as hell going to the Baldwin Hills Crenshaw Plaza, or as we called it, "The Crenshaw Mall." Growing up in South Central, this was the main attraction for a lot of us that grew up in the hood but closer to the westside of L.A., I didn't start going to Fox Hills like that up until I got older.

Those memories feel distant now, with the mall closed off due to the coronavirus. As I'm driving the 705 eastbound, I witness the sidewalk that once had tons of foot traffic—people going to Magic Johnson Theaters, the mall, or the Santa Barbara Plaza— now taken over by a homeless encampment. People are sleeping like they're in their own bedrooms. I see beds, both regular and blow-up, dressers with pictures of children sitting on top of them, and clothing scattered from trash bags all over the sidewalk. Man, this shit is wild, and I'm extremely saddened to see it.

ESSENTIAL: Diary of a Public Transit Bus Operator Volume 1

On my second trip coming westbound, I picked up an Ed Helms-looking ass muthafucka at La Cienega and Jefferson. As soon as he got on, he randomly yelled, "Fuck!" real loud, almost shattering my eardrum. I'm thinking, *oh shit, here we go*. There's a middle-aged woman sitting near the front of the bus, talking on the phone in Spanish. He sits next to her and stares for a few seconds, listening to her convo. Then, out of nowhere, he snaps.

"Excuse me, can you shut the fuck up!?" he yelled.

The way he barked at her was equivalent to the Gunnery Sergeant from *Full Metal Jacket* yelling at Private Pyle. I immediately got mad as fuck. The woman put her phone down on her lap briefly.

"Excuse me, sir, he's harassing me," she expressed.

I was already aware of what was happening and was in motion to rectify the situation.

"I got you, ma'am, it's okay," I replied.

I was flooring the gas, passing up Adams, when I hit the red light at Washington Boulevard. I looked directly in the mirror at the knucklehead harassing her.

"Aye man, imma need you to leave the passengers alone," I demanded.

"What are you gonna do about it? Call the police?" he shot back.

I quickly put my hand under my chin in a pondering gesture.

"You know what, that's not a bad idea," I replied.

"Go ahead and call them!" he blurted out, chest puffed up.

I hit the police button on the radio. The light turned green, and I crossed the intersection, pulling into the West L.A. Transit Center. As I came to a complete stop in the bus zone, he started spewing obscenities at me. I hit the parking brake and turned toward him.

"Say, man, you don't got the luxury to ride my bus fuckin' with me or the passengers. You gon' get yo ass off this bus, I guarantee you that."

He started walking to the front. Now, mind you, we were using caution tape to seal off the front and double-crossing the wheelchair seat belts to keep people from coming up due to COVID-19. But our manager stated the company didn't want us doing that anymore and that if we continued, we would be subjected to a TRANS-19. There's also a rule in our rulebook that prohibits us from "tampering" with Metro equipment.

He came right up to the barrier and started ranting.

"Why are you fucking treating me like this when I just got my ass attacked, when I just suffered an assault before getting on?"

I looked at him with a straight face, not phased.

"Muthafucka, you probably suffered an assault 'cause you fuckin' with people. You hopped your ass on my bus fuckin' with folks, so I'm not surprised that happened to you. But I don't give a fuck about all that—I need you to get off this bus. Thank you very much."

Before he could continue running his mouth, the radio phone rang. I picked up the receiver and held it up, facing him.

"You hear that? That's the control center. If I hit this button to talk back to them, it's over, bro. If the sheriffs roll up, it's a Pandora's box. So, what's it gonna be?"

He had a minor bitch fit and threw a quick tantrum.

"Fuck it! Let me off at the front door right here. LET ME OFF!!!" he shouted.

All bullshit aside, I could see the vein popping out of his neck. I cracked open the front door, and he stormed out. These muthafuckas always act tough and think you ain't gonna call the police. You got some people that will wait until they hear a siren, then act like a bitch and run off the bus into a neighborhood to get away just in case the cops are looking for them.

Some of these people will use mental illness as an excuse to commit heinous acts, but they know exactly what they're doing. Because of people like him, I started carrying pepper spray and a taser. I always do my best to expect the unexpected. The way he walked to the front was aggressive, like he wanted to throw hands. Truth be told, I thought he was gonna spit on me and run off the bus, like a lot of other cowards have done to other operators. I remember thinking, *if this muthafucka spits on me, I'm hopping out this seat and knockin' his ass out.* I will gladly lose my job for one of these punk-ass low-lives doing something vile like that. Luckily, that didn't happen.

The rest of the trip went smooth. As I was pulling up to the stop at Venice Boulevard and Cadillac Avenue, the woman he had been harassing stopped before getting off to give me a huge thanks.

Monday, June 1, 2020

Today I went to the Dunkin' Donuts on Hollywood Boulevard and Argyle, which is down the street from the layover at Selma. I tried to open the door, but it was locked. There was an employee inside, and he was giving me the cut-throat gesture. He walks up to the window of the door.

"Y'all closed?" I ask.

"Yea, we're closed," he shouts through the closed door.

I look down at my watch.

"It's early doe," I stated.

"It's due to the George Floyd protests," he replied loudly.

It dawned on me at that moment that on the way up, I did see people boarding up their businesses.

"Oh okay, understandable. Thank you!" I shouted back as he's still looking through the door.

I walked back to the layover. I just needed something to satisfy my hunger at that moment, but wasn't nothing open. People who owned businesses closed up shop early and boarded up their windows as if a hurricane was about to hit the area. All along Hollywood Boulevard and Fairfax Avenue, businesses were closed up. There were protests the whole weekend, and as protests happened, businesses got hit afterwards. While watching Fox 11 News, some protestors vandalized a 45-foot NABI bus near 3rd Street and Fairfax Avenue. The operator of that bus was doing Line 16. To my understanding, they were unharmed—thank God.

On the trips afterwards, I seen the National Guard arrive along both Hollywood Boulevard and Fairfax Avenue. Truth be told, they were a tourist attraction—they were taking pictures with people and their kids. Some portions of the boulevards you didn't see them, but anywhere there was a bank nearby, there was a larger presence of them.

There are tons of people out, and with the frustrations of another Black man killed by law enforcement and people having lost their sources of income and their everyday routine life due to COVID, it seems as if all of those things combined has brewed up the reactions we're seeing now.

Despite what the news was reporting, me being on the street, I didn't encounter too much. I can't front, I was pondering what to do if I encountered the same situation as the operator on Line 16. I'm willing to do whatever it takes to get back home safely—I'll deal with the consequences later.

My day went okay, and I made it home safe.

Tuesday, June 2, 2020

Today there were more protests in the Hollywood area. I was making relief on Line 217 going northbound but had to drive to Melrose because Fairfax was blocked off at Santa Monica Boulevard. MTA had us detouring, but the detour would only last for so long. They had us making a right on Melrose Avenue, left on La Brea, then a left on Santa Monica. After I relieved the previous operator, I followed the detour. Sure enough, when I got to Santa Monica Boulevard, L.A. County Sheriffs had it blocked off and there was a crowd of protestors on the west side of the intersection. The crowd was peaceful, but very loud. The sheriffs were suited up in full riot gear.

I crossed the light at Santa Monica to the far side of the intersection and threw on my hazards—hell, I didn't know where to go from there. We were advised via text not to go to Hollywood Boulevard due to protests and to wait for further instruction. My follower on the same line pulled up behind me and did the same thing. Passengers started coming at me all at once, frantic with questions: "Where can I catch this line?" "Where can I catch that line?" "How do I get to the train station?"

"How do I get to Hollywood from here?" Man, it was a headache answering those questions.

I got off the bus and began conversing with the other operator. He had gotten out the seat and was standing on the sidewalk too. While we're talking, a road supervisor pulls up and walks over to us.

"I'll see how we can get you guys around here. Streets are blocked in different parts of the city," he said.

He pulls out his walkie and calls the control center to explain his plan for getting us through. With the protest crowd yelling in the background, it was hard to hear the convo, but he came back to us a minute later.

"Well, there's no way we can continue on regular route. I'm going to have to have you guys go back the way you came. There's no way any of the buses can get onto Hollywood Boulevard. Go back up Beverly to Fairfax. Lay your bus over at 1st and Fairfax, and when the time comes, continue in service southbound. Follow me—I'll guide you guys back onto La Brea."

Me and the other operator agreed to the instructions. We got in our buses and followed him. He made a right on Lexington, right on Sycamore Avenue, right on Santa Monica, then a left on La Brea and let us go our way. When I got to Fairfax, I was about forty minutes early going in the opposite direction. Hell, we couldn't go to Hollywood so it knocked off nearly half the trip. While I was waiting at the layover, my wife texted me: "No call?" I jokingly replied, "I was getting a blowjob from one of the female passengers." But seriously, I called her to let her know I was okay and that I'd call again on the other end. With everything going on, I get why she panics if I don't check in.

For the rest of the day, we did not go to Hollywood Boulevard. They had us detouring down Beverly Boulevard to the Cedars-Sinai Hospital layover where the 14 and 16 layover at behind The Beverly Center. Fine with me—it gave us an even longer break. I love long layovers, especially when there's somewhere nearby to get food, but I was too lazy to walk anywhere. I just snacked on my container of cashews.

On my last trip going northbound at the West L.A. Transit Center stop, there was this lady that's always talking to herself like she's arguing with an angel on one shoulder and the devil on the other. She sounds like Jennifer Lewis with schizophrenia and looks like a homeless woman dressed for winter with layers of clothes on—I'm not bullshittin'. She usually rides the 217 between the Red Line station and 3rd Street, and sometimes the 16. There was also a guy at the stop, sitting behind the depot in a wheelchair. He wasn't paying attention but saw my bus at the last second and decided he wanted to get on.

"Waaaait!" the bag lady yelled after I picked up everyone.

I looked in the mirror, already frowning because I knew she was on some bullshit.

"Ma'am, what's going on?" I asked.

"The gentleman in the wheelchair wants to get on your bus," she shouted.

"Where at?" I asked. "I don't see anyone."

"Just wait a minute, driver!" she yelled.

The gentleman in the wheelchair was "stutter rolling." He could barely roll because the rubber on his wheels had worn down. I had a red light at Electric Avenue.

"Wait, driver! Wait, driver!" he yelled as he struggled to roll forward.

It looked like someone was sticking a stick between his spokes every time he tried to roll. I can't lie—he wasn't at the stop, and I didn't feel like waiting. So I didn't want to take any chances. A guy at the stop saw him struggling and ran up to help, rolling his chair to the front door. I deployed the ramp so he could roll on.

"Thank you!" I told the gentleman who helped him.

"Just keep doing the good work that you're doing, my man," he said before heading back to the bench.

While people were still boarding, I got a detour notice from the company telling all operators we were to drive down 3rd Street because Fairfax was blocked off by the National Guard and LAPD. I informed every one of the detour as they got on. Between Pico Boulevard and Wilshire, I only picked up a handful of people. When I got to 3rd Street, I let everyone know that it was the last stop unless they were going to La Cienega Boulevard. I let the man in the wheelchair off and there was this woman who appeared to be Eastern European with a heavy accent. She struggled to speak English and seemed upset.

"I don't know English, please help! Please help!" she said.

"Okay ma'am, what do you need?" I asked.

"I need to get to Hollywood Boulevard," she replied, gesturing her hand like a chef's kiss.

"Ma'am, Hollywood is closed off. There are various protests going on, you won't be able to get there."

"How can I get to the Red train station? I just need to get to a Red train station."

I thought for a moment to help her best I could.

"You can take the 780 to Hollywood and exit at Western," I advised.

She was struggling to understand what I was saying, so I wrote down the directions on a piece of paper. I had her follow me outside the bus so that I could point to her where to catch the bus she needed. Once she read it, it all made sense to her.

"I love you like son. Thank you so much," she said.

I smiled. "You're welcome, ma'am. Thank you I truly appreciate that."

She crossed to the southeast corner of 3rd and Fairfax near the Citibank to wait for the 780. After that, more people swarmed me with questions about bus service and I answered them the best I could. People didn't know where to go or what to do—everyone was out here moving like chickens with their heads cut off. I felt like I was in the middle of a disaster with how everyone was acting. I got back on the bus and headed to the Cedars-Sinai layover.

I was hyped because I thought I was getting off work early, but that wasn't the case. When I arrived at the layover, we all got a group voice message from the control center telling us we had to wait before pulling into the division due to protests nearby. There's a sheriff station next to the division off Santa Monica Boulevard, and buses were lined up along San Vicente waiting to pull in. It took an hour before dispatch said we were clear to go. The National Guard was surrounding the division—inside the yard and even on the rooftop of the parking structure. There was a rumor that looters thought our parking lot was the sheriff's lot and planned to vandalize our vehicles, but that never happened.

When I got to the lobby, I filled out my overtime slip, rushed to my car, and headed home. I was a little stressed because the city had a 6 p.m. curfew due to all the protests and looting. They claimed if you weren't getting off work or handling business what they considered to be "essential," you were subject to being stopped by the law enforcement.

Wednesday, June 3, 2020

When I got to the division today, the National Guard still had the division surrounded. They were at the exit and the entrance, as well as the parking lot. There were more protests going on in regards to the death of George Floyd.

Today on Line 217, there were still protests in various areas of Hollywood and parts of downtown L.A. What's so crazy about these protests is that people would break up and form sub-protests. We were issued detours, but it seemed like every time we followed one, we got held up somewhere else along the line by other protestors. My main concern was coming across some individuals like the ones who tore that bus up on 3rd Street and Fairfax. Thankfully, that didn't happen.

On my fourth trip heading southbound, I saw NBA player JR Smith walking northbound on Fairfax, crossing the street at Melrose with two other dudes. I gave a honk at him and threw up a chest pound. He waved back. He had just made the news recently because someone who was "protesting" tried to break into his vehicle. This happened somewhere in the Miracle

Mile/Hancock Park neighborhood of Los Angeles. He caught the guy in the act and put paws on him.

The rest if the day went smoothly. When I got home, I was scrolling through Facebook and saw something a friend had posted on his page. I'm keeping his name private because he still operates buses for another transit agency. He wrote:

"If there's one word I NEVER want to hear again, it's the word 'essential.'"

He went on about how we've always been essential, but before the pandemic, people treated our work like it was menial, like we were replaceable. Now, all of a sudden, we're called heroes—but instead of hazard pay or real support, we just get "thank you" ads and memes.

He ended it saying he never wanted to hear the word *essential* again.

Reading that was a straight-up mic drop. I felt every word of it.

Thursday, June 4, 2020

Back on the 705 today, really smooth day.

On my first trip westbound there was a homeless man laying at the bench on La Cienega and Obama. When I rolled up, he jumped up with the quickness and jumped on my bus. He was very dirty, his hair wasn't groomed and his clothes were hella dirty. He was running up and down the aisles like a kid on a preschool playground. Some people were startled by it, I wasn't. Hell, I drove a school bus for over a year before working for Metro and the majority of that time was with children with special needs so I'm not as startled by it like others. He would simultaneously lay on the seats and play down the aisle like a little kid. I was praying that no one would come to the front and ask if he could get off, it's always that one passenger that wants you to be the fuckin' police or worse take matters into their own hands because of a temporary "inconvenience".

Everything went smooth, my last stop was at Beverly Boulevard and La Cienega due to Beverly being closed off from possible protests and looters. He got off with no problem.

Deadheading to the division there were roll off construction dumpster bins blocking Beverly Boulevard and San Vicente. It was open to one lane with a road supervisor guiding people through because the lane was very narrow. As I'm pulling into the division, Melrose was blocked off with more bins similar to the ones I seen at Beverly—looters been hitting rich White neighborhoods heavy especially businesses off of Melrose Avenue. Santa Monica Boulevard was blocked off, so all the buses had to pull into the exit of the division adjacent to the Pacific Design Center's red building. The driveway was full of National Guard troops. When I pulled in and walked to my car, the National Guard was still on the roof of the parking structure—this time, they were smoking cigarettes and leaning over the balcony of the parking lot, just straight chillin'.

Friday, June 5, 2020

Today was a great day but funny.

On my first trip on the 705 heading to Santa Fe, there was a young woman closing all the windows on the bus. She got on at King Boulevard and Crenshaw. I hate when I have windows open and people start closing them because the shut sound is so loud you end up thinking that you hit something along the boulevard. After closing all the windows, there was one that was still open with a construction worker sitting under. She walked to it, reached over to close it and the gentleman that was sitting under it gave her the cut-throat gesture.

"Nope! Nope! Noooooo!" he said real loud.

"Can I close it?" she asked.

"Nope," he replied.

She still tried to close the window, totally disrespecting what the construction worker just told her, so he went off. An argument broke out between the two. I could barely hear what she was saying because they both were in the back of the bus arguing and she had on a mask.

"Go sit cho ass down, funny shaped ass bitch! I needs my air up in this muthafucka and you're not shutting my window closed with yo funny shaped ass. Go sit cho ass down please thank you," he blurted out loud.

I couldn't do nothing but laugh my ass off, shit had me dying. I've never heard somebody call someone on public transportation "funny shaped." She was being mad disrespectful just reaching over people and closing windows and the whole time no one was saying anything. Hell, at least ask if you can close them as opposed to taking matters into your own hands. He was the only one to say something to her. It irritates me when people ride MTA buses and just start doing things with no regards for the others that ride.

On my second trip there was a dude doing unnecessary humming, sitting in the front all loud with a granny cart. Irritating as hell. He got on at the train station, but he didn't ride for long thank God. People fail to realize that we not only need to see but we need to hear as well. He sounded like he was humming the song played on the ending credits of *The Jeffersons*. I wanted to turn around and tell him, *"QUIT ALL THAT GOT DAMN HUMMIN!"*

On that same trip I had a passenger giving me props for being a bus operator, especially during this COVID-19 pandemic. I told him that I would add him to the 1% of passengers that actually appreciate what we do. When I said that, another lady said,

"Hey I appreciate you guys too. As a matter of fact, I feel that y'all should be making way more money than what y'all make, especially during this pandemic."

A few other passengers were in agreement and were giving me props too. Bus was full of positivity. I pray that I can get more of that. I don't plan to make driving a bus a career, but hey, while I'm here I'll always be thankful for those who are appreciative.

Monday June 8, 2020

Today was a hot ass day. It was 88 degrees—jeez! I'm thankful for the newer buses that we have because the older ones run the risk of the A/C not working all that great. Although I haven't seen them in a while, the NABI 40-foot buses have a shitty A/C on a hot day. The sun beams through the windows of those things something serious, and the inside ends up feeling like an oven. I don't pull a bus out the yard when doing the 217—I make relief. Out of my whole time driving for MTA out of Division 7, that's one line where they give you top-notch buses. Very seldom do I have to worry about the A/C not working.

After my third trip, when I got to the layover on Argyle, there was a homeless man yelling at the top of his lungs at two young women walking down the street. As aggressive as he was yelling, I thought they were going to get attacked. He left them be, and they continued north on Argyle. I kept my door closed until he vacated the area—I was at the Selma layover next to the Kobe and Gigi mural. You just don't know what you'll encounter with as many of these individuals are walking on city streets and I'm damn sure not trying to find out. Once he cleared out, I hurried up and made my run to the restroom.

Gradually, it seems like things are "opening up." The bars along Hollywood Boulevard have opened back up after being deemed non-essential. People couldn't wait.

Tuesday, June 9, 2020

Today we placed bids for other assignments. Metro cut back on plenty of the assignments and hours we had since COVID hit. Kids are doing virtual learning and the majority of people are working from home virtually. I mean damn, we just placed bids for assignments a month ago. I hear we're supposed to bid again sometime near the fall. Well anyway, I'll be back on the 705 going down Vernon for the next go-around, but this time it's five days a week. There was an assignment where the 705 is done Monday through Thursday, then the 217 is done for three hours on Friday and you get off in the early afternoon. This was right up my alley. I work to live—I don't live to work. I had my eyes set on that assignment like a bird hunting prey, but one of my co-workers who had more seniority got it. It's all good though.

Today on the 217, my second trip at the Jefferson/La Cienega layover, there was a road supervisor there. This is the supervisor that likes to send you threatening text messages on the ATMS. These dudes get their jollies off fuckin' with operators on those messages, and luckily there's no way for me to sarcastically respond—and they know that. Every time I see one of his messages I think to myself, *man, get this bullshit off the radio,* it's a damn shame. Anything that bothers this man, he's gonna text you about it. All you gotta do is blink a certain way and he'll send a message expressing his disgust.

At the Hollywood layover after my third trip, there was a homeless man wandering around. This dude was barefoot and eating food out the trash bin that was sitting on the parking divider for the operators. He also drank the rest of a 7UP that was in the same bin. It shouldn't take visuals like that for me to be thankful for the blessings that I have in my life, but truth be told, I'm reminded of it every day with the homelessness I see on the city streets.

The day was smooth, but I was low-key irritated by a female passenger who was trying to hold a conversation with me. Sometimes you just want to drive. Every now and then, you'll get questions about how to get around the city, but sometimes it's a bit irritating when someone tries to talk to you while you're trying to focus on driving. And it's hard to hear passengers because on a hot day like this, you got the A/C on full blast, the driver's fan blowing near your ear, you're hitting potholes throughout the route, and on top of that, the farebox components and the driver barrier doing a ton of rattling from the tires hitting the uneven pavement. Some conversations I don't mind—but there are plenty I can do without. And with all that going on today, this was one of them. You get to a point where you just got one-word replies like:

"mmhmm."
"yeah."
"okay."

...until that individual gets off the bus.

Wednesday June 10, 2020

I was just tired today, mentally and physically. It got the best of me so much so that when I got home I had a meltdown. I mean, I didn't swing at the air or anything, I just was steaming pissed. The real reason was for a write-up I got from that one supervisor on the 217 back on the 11th of May, for picking up those passengers on the far side of the light at Beverly going northbound.

I get tired of some of these folks. Some of them pick on the operators that actually go above and beyond to provide amazing customer service. I got my ass to work today and when I signed on, there was a red box on the computer screen with the words inside: "YOUR SIGN ON HAS BEEN BLOCKED."

When I informed the window supervisor that my sign-on was blocked, I was issued some paperwork that was a write-up. The write-up was bogus as fuck. The road supervisor in particular stated that it was for me not reading the bulletin board notice in regards to that bus stop being a construction zone. By rule, bus operators are responsible for reading all the division bulletin boards and staying up to date on anything that involves operating MTA transit buses. I'll mention it again—ALL the construction equipment at the northeast corner where the bus stop is located was GONE. Cones, vehicles, and all. The building next to the Chase Bank that the equipment was for was no longer under construction or showing any signs of it. That's why the passengers who were catching the 217 northbound at Beverly felt safe to catch it at its original stop. He knew full damn well if I passed him up while he was there with those passengers, he would've gave me a write-up for that too.

When bus operators receive write-ups, we're supposed to sign off on them. Well for this one, you know full damn well I didn't sign that shit. I grabbed it from the window supervisor and stormed straight to the manager's office. When I got inside, the division manager and one of the assistant managers were conversing with each other. One of them could tell how heated I was and did their best to calm me down before I explained what happened.

I told one of the managers,

"This write-up is some bullshit."

I told them the road supervisor who wrote me up was sitting right there at the stop with the passengers. I explained that the building looked completely finished and that the zone no longer had any construction equipment blocking it. Then I asked them,

"What would've happened if I passed the stop up with him and those passengers sitting right there?"

They both agreed with me. The division manager said they would remove the write-up off my record.

Little shit like that—we shouldn't have to go through. I don't mind being held accountable for a legit mistake, but this one doesn't apply. To be honest, it was a double-edged sword. I legitimately thought he was just doing one of those "check downs" or whatever the hell they do when they stand at the stop with their clipboard. What's so cold about some of these road supervisors is they'll act all friendly, give you a "verbal warning," ask you how your day is going with a big ass smile showing all thirty-two teeth smiling like the muthafuckin' cat from Alice In Wonderland—then two weeks later, BAM, you sign on and got a write-up waiting.

I always hear the saying, *"Be the change you want to see."* I've thought about being a supervisor one day, but at the same time, I don't want to sacrifice any portion of my dignity. I also don't want bad blood with any of my coworkers by abusing a position of authority or having to "obey orders" from management over some minuscule shit.

The division I operate out of in West Hollywood got a few former operators turned road supervisors, and I can feel the bad energy from some of them by the way they act which wasn't a thing before getting promoted. I know a few operators that would make great supervisors, but for whatever reason, the company won't promote them. I'm talking about folks with spotless records, who give great customer service.

I don't plan to be here forever, I already had my feelings but this pandemic has elevated the feelings that I already have.

You'd think we'd get treated like royalty, right?

Nah... that's not the case.

Friday June 12, 2020

I was so frustrated from Wednesday that I ended up taking a sick day yesterday. I just couldn't do it, especially after that bullshit write-up I received.

I'm doing the 705 today. I usually pull out the yard late, because by the time I get to Wilshire and La Cienega I'm about three minutes early. It's bad enough that I have to deal with that anus of a road supervisor on the 217—last thing I need is to pull up to that stop and he's waiting there with a clipboard, ready to shoot his load because he "caught" me committing a rule violation.

Today at various stops, people were standing in the doorway holding the door open for folks that were running to catch the bus. I hate that shit. If you are not at the stop, you are not priority. It slowed me down so much that when I got to the end of the line, I barely had layover time. I don't mind people being good Samaritans, but man, I don't have the time—nor do I feel like waiting on someone's granny that's a block away, moving slower than a sloth to get on the bus. I be wanting to tell the people, *"Hey, how 'bout you and that individual you waitin' on wait for the next bus, 'cause you holdin' me up!"*

Also, I forgot to mention, you gotta use extreme caution when picking up someone running for the bus. People be doing stupid shit out here, then try to run and get on the bus to get away from the person or persons they done did some bullshit to.

Also today, some crackhead dude at Broadway going eastbound got on asking me if I could drop him off at Main Street.

"Aye driver, you think you can stop at Main?"

"Nah bruh, that's what the 105 is for," I replied.

"It's only up the block," he said, pointing in the eastbound direction.

I got angry and replied with a pissed off tone.

"Dawg, the 105 is coming—I just passed it up at Crenshaw Boulevard."

He finally gave up.

"Nevermind," he said as he got back off and went on about his business.

Main Street is literally the next block up from Broadway eastbound. They're so close to each other that you're better off walking to the bus stop as opposed to waiting. A lot of these passengers are spoiled as fuck.

The remainder of the day went cool. Can't wait for this weekend.

Tuesday June 16, 2020

Not much to mention for today, it was a decent day nonetheless. While downstairs walking to my assigned CEA unit, I greeted one of my co-workers who usually pulls a bus out the yard.

"What's going on man? Don't you usually pull a bus out the yard?" I asked.

"Yea I do, but I got a random drug test today—but honestly, I don't feel it's random."

I was confused for a moment.

"What chu mean?" I asked.

"Well, I confronted management and the steno yesterday about hours of vacation time that they were supposed to pay out. Shit, that was over more than a month ago and they still haven't paid it out. Now all of a sudden I got a drug test," he replied.

"Well you know what to do when you get to that clinic," I said as I'm looking at my watch with a big ass smile.

"Yup, imma milk the shit outta the time," he stated.

We went on about our day afterwards.

Plenty of my co-workers have been drug tested from the company after the following:

- An accident they feel was your fault
- Always close to or being late to work
- Poor appearance or bad hygiene
- Convos that management feels are inappropriate
- Sheer retaliation from a wrongdoing with no accountability coming from those above

I'm sure there's more, but those are the unspoken main reasons why. I remember when I first started working for the company they said that drug tests were "random" and only issued under suspicious behavior. But since being with the company eleven years, that's not the case. You can get drug tested for any reason they deem appropriate. If you confront management or a supervisor about something—and depending on the individual—don't be surprised if that paperwork to go to the clinic is already waiting on you.

Thursday, June 18, 2020

Yesterday the bus that my relief driver had didn't have any air conditioning. That is a nightmare! It can be very uncomfortable, and if the driver is not comfortable then the passengers are not comfortable. I did a battery shutdown on the bus at the layover and started the bus back up. The A/C ended up working again but it didn't work shortly after. I hate when I make relief on a bus and the operator you're relieving isn't honest with all the mechanical failures on the bus. Some of them have this *well I'm off now so it don't matter* attitude. Throughout the day the A/C was on and off, the climate ended up getting cool enough for me to keep the bus. The A/C didn't hit like it normally does but it was cool enough for me and I was pulling the bus in.

Today I was doing Line 705. On my second trip heading to Vernon and Santa Fe I had a standing load of people, gang of people riding damn near all the way to Central. One dude had a bike that he put on the rack. When it came time for his stop he was trying to get off at the front door. I told him that it's only rear boarding and exiting. He copped an attitude. I was going to cut him some slack but then he got mad and started cussing at me.

"I gotta get my bike, muthafucka! It's not even that damn serious, man. Fuck you!" he yelled.

With a frowning face looking in the passenger mirror, I cocked my head back like an ostrich. *Oh the disrespect!*

"I pray that you're never at any of these bus stops by yourself homeboy, I'm going to pass your ass up next time!" I shouted at him.

He got off the bus and mean mugged me the whole time while he was getting his bike off the rack. Whatever... The nerve of this dude—his clothing was filthy and he was sagging with dirty ass underwear like he dragged his ass across a high school baseball diamond. I wanted to verbally assassinate this man after dishing out that disrespect, but I had to sit back and remember what my wife said: *what a lot of people yell at you about it's not your fault, it's them projecting their personal lives onto you.*

The rest of my day went great. I had requested the next day off about a week prior and I got it. Looking forward to my three day weekend.

Monday, June 22, 2020

I had a three-day weekend, but it wasn't all that great. On Friday, I got the news from my wife that a coworker of mine by the name of Jason Ross died in a car accident at the intersection of San Vicente Boulevard and Cabrillo early in the morning. My wife and I were at my mother and stepfather's house just enjoying an afternoon together, then all of a sudden she gasps for air and starts shedding tears as she's reading a text from her phone. When she did that, it was as if she wanted to drop her phone. That whole day we had been trying to figure out who the individual was because all on social media people were giving their condolences but we didn't know exactly who. She told us she'd just gotten a text from Jason's wife, Albina—LAPD had shown up at her house to tell her he died from his injuries.

We left my parents' house in utter disbelief. When we got home, we sat on our living room couch and we were absolutely speechless. Jason was real cool. We met each other at Division 7—we would always greet each other in passing. From the time I first spoke to him, a few years passed before he told me that he and his wife were expecting a baby. He even invited my wife and

I to their baby shower at Kenneth Hahn Park. A few years after, my wife and I invited him and his wife with their son Tyler to our wedding reception. The death of a coworker always gets the best of me, but this one here is hitting different. I'm going to miss my brother. May he rest in peace. I am at a loss for words—my heart hurts for his wife and child. My condolences go out to his family, especially his wife and son.

I now do the 705 five days a week. The new assignments for our shakeup took place this past weekend. I now have to pull out of the yard from Division 7 all the way to Santa Fe and Vernon using the 10 Freeway. That shit takes FOREVER! Then on Alameda Boulevard at Vernon, the left turn took twenty minutes. After sitting in all that traffic on the 10 East and then sitting in traffic to turn, my bladder was about to bust. When I got to Santa Fe I had to run to the restroom. I got out and looked up at the radio and saw that I was twenty five minutes late going into service westbound. There was another Rapid 705 in front of me—we rode each other's coat tails on Vernon Avenue all the way to the Westside.

On the same trip, I picked up a passenger at 3rd Street and La Cienega. Homie looked like Wesley Snipes character in the movie *Demolition Man*. I get to the end of the line, and he's the only person still on the bus.

"This the last stop!" I yell out.

"This ain't the last stop man, you got one more stop!" he shouts back.

I take a deep breath and just sit there. Of course I wanted to go full metal jacket verbally on this dude, but you know what—it's a waste of time. So I tilted my sunglasses down and looked at him in the mirror sternly.

"Sir, this is my last stop. I have to go inside of my division, and you're not allowed to go inside the division. You can get off here and catch the 4 continuing up, but this here is my last stop," I advised.

He gets loud with me.

"Man no! No! How you gone tell me!? I need to go to La Cienega and I'm not getting off of this bus until you take me there!"

This dude is dead-ass serious. I yelled back at him.

"C'mon man, cut the bullshit. This is the last stop for this line—let's go bro! What the fuck!?"

He continues sitting down on the bus, not moving a muscle.

"Well I'm not getting off!" he blurts out.

I hit the button to call the control center afterward. This Simon Phoenix looking muthafucka had me heated. I had a sandwich and chips I wanted to eat and he's interrupting me from getting to my food. *This is that bullshit man.* I felt like smackin' fire out that negro for holding me up. He was staring at me the whole time and didn't move. I had no choice but to call the control center. At that moment in time, I was hungry as shit and I had to use the restroom. I sat in the seat taking deep breaths and giving myself the Buddha hands to keep calm—I was real frustrated with this bozo. I'm really not trying to be calling the police on anyone, especially at this time.

After about two minutes a call comes through the radio.

"This is run 54 on the 705, badge #76454, bus number 6053. I have an individual on the bus who refuses to get off at the last stop here at San Vicente," I said.

"Can you provide a description please?" the controller requested.

"Male Black, orange hair, black t-shirt, black shorts, and black boots with a black backpack," I replied.

"Okay operator, hold your position. If he gets off, please call back," the controller advised.

As I'm sitting up, the unexpected occurs. The radio all of a sudden goes blank. *What the fuck!? Now the damn radio doesn't work!?* When the radios on the bus go out or experience a malfunction, sometimes it looks equivalent to a destroyed screen from the original Nintendo Gameboy—or an Etch A Sketch. *Ahhhh fuck, what's the worst that can happen!? Why now!?* I did my damnedest to play it cool, but my anxiety was through the roof. I didn't know what this knucklehead was capable of with as demanding as he was.

After eight minutes of sitting at the Santa Monica and San Vicente stop, his ass finally gets off the bus, talking shit the whole time. I hurry up and close my door and pull into the yard. *Punk ass idiot* was all I thought when he made his exit. Afterwards, I get inside the yard and head to the phone near the mechanics' desk hanging on the wall. All calls go straight to the control center, and you don't have to wait like you would on the bus radio. I was able to get in touch with the original controller of the call.

"How's it going, controller? I was able to pull into the yard safely. The knucklehead got off at the last stop on Santa Monica Boulevard."

The controller sounded relieved.

"Okay operator, glad you're safe. Whatever you do, please don't pick him up on your next trip."

"No worries in regards to that—but my radio went out," I said.

"If anything, please pull your bus over in a safe location and call from your phone," he recommended.

"That's a 10-4, controller. Thank you."

I walked back to my bus. I didn't have much time to spare, but I took the time to make me a bomb-ass sandwich for lunch earlier in the day, and I damn sure made the time to eat it. I didn't care about being late or getting rolled up on by a road supervisor—my hunger needs to be satisfied to be dealing with folks like him.

The work day went good but I went the rest of the day thinking about what happened with my coworker Jason. Damn I'm fucked up over that.

Wednesday, June 23, 2020

I forgot to mention that yesterday I ended up getting cussed out by an elderly G.I. Jane, Hispanic-looking woman. While heading westbound from Santa Fe Avenue, I picked her up at Avalon Boulevard with a handful of other passengers. I had just passed up a Line 105 bus right after the train station at Long Beach Boulevard. As I'm driving, I hear someone yelling, but I can't quite pinpoint who or where it's coming from. Sitting in that driver area with all the noise outside, combined with the components of a rattling farebox and driver barrier and the windows being open—it's very loud. You can't hear shit really inside the bus, especially coming from the back of the bus.

I close the window to better hear what's being said from the back, and it's the older woman I just mentioned. I finally understand what she's yelling.

"Hey fool I want to get off at Main!" she said.

I'm lookin' in the mirror as I'm crossing the intersection.

"I don't have a stop at Main, ma'am," I replied.

"You're supposed to stop!" she shouted.

All I could do was shake my head in frustration.

"Are you aware of the bus that you're on?" I asked.

"It doesn't matter what bus I'm on, let me off the fuckin' bus," she expressed.

I kept it rollin' as the next stop is Broadway.

"You should have got on the Local 105 that's behind me. It stops at Main Street. I'll get you off at Broadway, ma'am."

She proceeds to give me the middle finger with some choice words afterward.

"Eat my pussy, you mutherfucker!" she shouted.

All I could do was shake my head and laugh. When I was approaching the stop, I told the lady something she probably would have never expected.

"Ma'am, God bless you. I pray from this day forward the Lord opens up the floodgates of blessings for you. Thank you for riding my bus."

She threw her hands up and walked off. I'm sure she wasn't expecting that. Any other time I would have said something foul, but y'know—I didn't feel like entertaining the bullshit. Fuck all that. I'm trying to have my days as smooth as possible. I'm tired of entertaining bullshit out here on these buses. Being an MTA operator here in L.A., it's really not something you can avoid. The rest of the day was cool, but that was the highlight of the day.

Fast forward to today, my sign-on was blocked, and the reason being is because I had to sign a roster that has part-time operators that do not wish to be promoted to full-time. I stayed a part-time operator with the company. When you first get hired, you're part-time until you accept the offer to go full-time. When I first started working with the company, it took me almost two years to even get asked the question. Manpower is an issue at the moment, and the company is trying to promote as fast as possible due to a lack thereof. You got part-time operators getting promoted as soon as they get off probation, which is five months.

I've always signed the paper. I never desired to go full-time, and I have my reasons as to why. The main reason is being able to keep my assignment. According to our union contract, part-time operators can't be bumped off of assignments. Low seniority full-time operators run the risk of getting bumped according to the same contract. I've heard a few full-time operators say, "You only get bumped if someone comes off the sick list." Well hell, look at how many people are on the sick list at each division—it's damn near half of its operators per bus division, and people usually come back before the new shakeups. I am not a fan of getting bumped. When I drove school buses, I got bumped twice because of someone with more seniority than me—I was never a fan of that shit. Every shakeup, operators go through the hassle of doing homework on the assignments and picking the one that best suits their personal lives. All that gets thrown out the window when an operator who has more seniority than them comes and bumps them off that same assignment.

I feel that the rules need to be changed. If you come off the sick list or any type of leave, you should return to the assignment that you had before going. If you don't want your assignment, you either grab one that is available for bidding or go onto the extraboard until you can grab one you like. If you don't want your original assignment, that's your choice—but it shouldn't come at the expense of someone else's.

The extraboard is for operators who report to work and cover assignments of other operators who call off work or if there are bus runs that aren't assigned but need to be done for the day. Bus operators who hate getting bumped off of their assignments tend to go on the extraboard. They are given a time to report and they wait inside the division until the window supervisor calls for them to work. They can bid for the days off based on seniority. One of the perks to being an extraboard operator is being able to "shine" (operators that are on report for a whole shift without having to go out on the road), but with low manpower, it is a rarity that it happens.

People have a life outside of driving a bus, and bumping is something that contributes to a lack of manpower due to frustrated operators—not only at the division, but it trickles down system wide. There are a few other things that full-time operators get that part-timers don't as far as benefits and other things go, but I'm keeping my status as a part-time operator. It has allowed me to have structure in my personal life away from driving a bus. I'd probably pull out my hair if I was a full-time operator. The only full-time operators who are comfortable and have little to no worry of being bumped are those who have at least twenty years of seniority.

I always felt it made no sense to study and research the assignments you want before a shake-up. Someone with more seniority can swoop in and snatch your shit like a hawk grabbing prey.

To save myself that headache, I stayed part time. Our contract protects us from being bumped off assignments once we claim them. The amount of mental gymnastics I'd be doing if I get bumped off of an assignment that I structured my personal life around. Fuck all that!

My full-time coworkers always tell me how much money I'm missing out on and how dumb a decision I'm making, but truth be told, I've got my mind on other endeavors.

Thursday, June 25, 2020

On my trip going back to Santa Fe leaving Division 7, I seen a coworker running down Santa Monica Boulevard. When I made the right turn on La Cienega Boulevard to my first stop, he got on with a handful of other passengers. He was breathing hard and sat in the front.

"Whew! I made it thank God!" he exhaled.

As I continue up La Cienega southbound, we witnessed the aftermath of an accident by the Norms restaurant—somebody ran into the back of a Mini Cooper. So we struck up a convo based off of that accident. I didn't expect my coworker to go off on a tangent about a grip of other shit. He stated that he got equalized (when the company sends low seniority operators to another division to make up a lack of manpower) to Division 18 in Carson with fifteen other operators from ours starting the upcoming Sunday. Usually if you are a low seniority operator, you have a high chance of being shipped to another division. Looking at his badge number, he was fairly new—about seven months.

While having a convo with him, it dawned upon me that I actually was happy he was going to 18. This dude ran his mouth more than diarrhea. He was one of those operators that knew everyone's business—he just seemed very messy, and I am not a fan of operators such as him.

He was like a know-it-all, somebody who feels they know everything about the company and its business. Also, I didn't appreciate his tone of voice—he was talking to me like I was fresh on the job. Last time I felt energy of this kind was when I first got to the division and a few high seniority operators were acting like their shit didn't stink. I wonder if his mouth got him fired from his last job—he damn sure didn't know how to shut the fuck up. He stated that his last job had fired him. Well, truth be told, judging by this conversation we're having and his character, I'm not surprised.

He was one of those individuals that talked so much that it was impossible to get anything out of your mouth. Listening to him talk about his time being with the company and the things that he's been through—he took no accountability for anything. I ended up zoning him out, then after all of his mouth running I all of a sudden heard a sentence that provided relief.

"I need to get off at La Brea!" he shouted.

Boy, I never floored the gas so fast in my life. By the time I hit La Brea on Obama Boulevard I was running three minutes early—but whatever it took to get this annoying ass coworker off my bus, I was willing to do. I'll say a prayer for the operators out of the division that he's going to. They're in for a world of headaches.

Monday, June 29, 2020

I had a decent weekend. I was able to catch up on some rest. I was so tired Friday that I didn't take the time to write my entry, but hell, I'll do it here.

Is it bad that normal human reactions such as coughs and sneezes put us into a frenzy mentally? Friday I had a woman coughing so damn much on my first trip I thought about calling some medical help for her ass. I would be surprised if she still has her organs intact after doing that damn coughing. She rode from the train station at Long Beach to Vermont Avenue. With every cough, my heart was beating hard. This is one of many risks that us as operators are dealing with driving these buses during COVID.

Having talked to some of my coworkers, a handful of them have went as far as kickin' passengers off their bus for doing so, but I'm not doing all that. I feel like that's a set-up for disciplinary action and/or termination. Also, what if someone has a legitimate medical issue or disability that you aren't aware of? Metro trained us that not all disabilities are visible. Despite the risks that are involved, we are still showing up and getting the public to and from. I can't lie, at a few stops I gave her the same look that the actress Sara Garcia poses on the Nestlé Abuelita Chocolate drink mix.

Today on my first trip heading westbound going down Vernon, the traffic lights from Ascot to Hoover were out. I ended up being over twenty minutes late. The flow of traffic on Vernon didn't start to pick up until after Western Avenue. I got to the layover at my division with five minutes to spare. I went to the restroom, texted my wife, and continued in service afterward.

On the way back to Santa Fe going down Santa Monica Boulevard, there were two homeless men fighting each other across the street from the Shake Shack. I didn't know why traffic initially started to slow down in both directions, but I started seeing people stick their phones out the window to record something. When I looked across the street, that's when I seen the altercation. One of the men's shorts fell down to the ground as he was tangled up with the other guy. The altercation led to the man's backside mooning the whole boulevard as his manhood swung back and forth. Boy, it's something every day out here on these streets. What's even crazier is how people stop and hold up traffic just to record something for the internet.

The rest of the day went smooth. Only thing I had a problem with is people with these got damn bikes. The same trip where I saw the two homeless dudes fighting, there was a couple at Wilshire and La Cienega bullshittin'. They were sitting at the bus stop smooching, then right before I was about to leave they decided they were going to get on. The girl stood in the doorway to keep me from closing it after I picked up passengers. Her boyfriend got his bike and put it on the rack, but the shit took a total of three minutes. Then he ran back to the rack to lock it down. I was looking at my watch sarcastically.

"Any day now," I said out loud.

Then on my last trip, there was this woman that got on at Crenshaw that took FOREVER to get on. She was a voluptuous woman. I remember thinking *damn that seat is too small for all that.* She was real slow putting her bike on the rack. When she got to Western, she sped up the process of taking her bike off. Sometimes I wish Metro never got these damn bike racks—but hey, what say so do I have in that?

Tuesday, June 30, 2020

On my last trip going westbound, I got caught by the BNSF train at the Santa Fe layover. What tripped me out was that you had people honking their horns on Vernon Avenue at the train operator. Like what the fuck? Why are you honking the horn as if it's going to make the train conductor go faster? I didn't understand that at all. It took a total of fifteen minutes for the train to load up its cars and go on its way. Right across from our layover, there is a base for the train operators and there are a few tracks in the front.

I finally got into service. I picked up this girl at the Washington Boulevard and Fairfax Avenue transit hub, and she rode all the way to Beverly Boulevard. I'm heading north on La Cienega and get into the left turning lane at Beverly Boulevard and serviced the stop by the Sofitel Hotel afterward. I continue in service, and as soon as I made a right turn onto San Vicente Boulevard, she started yelling.

"Hey! Hey! Whoaaa! Whoaaa! Whoaaa! Stop here! Stop here! Un unh! Un unh!" she shouted.

At this moment, I thought I was solo driving the bus. Any bus operator will tell you—when you drop off all your passengers close to the end of the line, you drop your guard a little bit. When she yelled, it startled me. I'm thinking she got off the bus somewhere along La Cienega. I begin looking at her in the mirror like a deer in the headlights. She resembles the actress from the TV show *Insecure*, Natasha Rothwell, and she has on clothing like she lived in Antarctica. I guess from the clothing alone that should have let me know—it's a pretty warm day today.

Usually when I get to Beverly Boulevard, the majority of my passengers get off before the next two stops going into West Hollywood. Now mind you, I'm the rapid—I can't just stop anywhere and drop people off. Right after Beverly, the next stop is at Melrose Avenue, which is about half a mile up the road.

"Ma'am, why you wait 'til I left that stop to say you needed to get off? You are aware this is a rapid, right?" I asked.

"Let me off here, man. You going down there—I don't do down there, sorry. I don't want to have anything to do with down there," she replied.

While she's saying that, she's shaking her head like a baby that just tasted some bad food and is frowning. She had a heavy emphasis on "down there." Like—what the fuck is *down there*? What the fuck was she even talking about? I was just sitting there, confused as hell. She made it seem as if she went any further northbound that she would be going into an abyss or a black hole of the unknown.

I didn't argue with her. Last thing I'm trying to do is deal with a nutcase who's yelling because she wants to get off—fuck all that. The faster I can get them off the bus, the better. I'm almost convinced that people act as if they are mentally deranged for the sole purpose of getting off somewhere that's not a designated stop. I didn't argue with this woman at all. I pulled the bus over shortly after making a right turn onto San Vicente Boulevard and I let her ass off.

All I could do was shake my head. There are a ton of passengers such as herself out here.

Now that I'm writing this and thinking about it, I'm guessing that she didn't want to go to West Hollywood. Go figure...

Thursday, July 2, 2020

Not much went on yesterday on the street side of things, but a few things went down on social media. On Facebook, there are a couple of pages I follow with my coworkers. One page (I will not say) had plenty of my coworkers frustrated and mad for two reasons:

1. Some of their union dues went up
2. Metro stated that they do not want to give hazard pay to bus operators

A few of my coworkers were showing their check stubs on the page. One person showed her check stub previously and then showed the current one highlighting the increase in dues.

Another thing that was being talked about was allegedly the union and Metro haven't been able to come to an agreement as far as giving bus operators hazard pay. I'm not surprised by this at all. A few of my coworkers were talking about choosing a day to take off and "show" the company what they're about. In all honesty, that shit won't happen. A lot of my coworkers have too many financial responsibilities—from multiple kids, "infidelity bills," to multiple depreciating assets, living outside of their means, etc. A lot of them are not properly set up financially to collectively get together with other operators and fight for what's right, and the company knows that. Even if they did, plenty of them still wouldn't do anything because they don't want to fuck up their bag. If my coworkers develop the fortitude to do so then I'll be extremely shocked, but until then—all bark and no bite.

I wish we could be more about action and less talk when it comes to our future with the company. But hey, why am I so concerned? I plan on leaving at some point.

What fucked me up today was when I was on my way to work, pulling into the division driveway, there was a handful of L.A. County Sheriffs surrounding a bus operator who rode his electric bike to work—and they had a cameraman recording the interaction that was going on. I didn't know if it was a TV show or what. There were a few pedestrians walking by and looking as they all occupied the sidewalk next to the crosswalk that leads to L.A. Buns. A few of my coworkers were standing outside the front of division looking on. It was real confusing.

I parked my car, went downstairs into the lobby to sign on, and seen the same operator inside talking to a few others. He stated that he got pulled over for not wearing a mask. The city of West Hollywood instituted a mandate for people to wear a mask, and he got pressed for it heavily. I know we're not invincible from rules of any kind, but damn—they needed that many sheriffs to inform an MTA bus operator to wear a mask? Seemed a bit over the top, but I digress.

When I left the division on Line 705, I seen L.A. County Sheriffs all along Santa Monica Boulevard making sure people wore their masks. I haven't seen so many L.A. County Sheriffs along this stretch of the boulevard—on foot and in their units. Shit was new to me. If COVID wasn't in effect, you would have sworn they were conducting a manhunt for a mass shooter. After seeing that, I made sure to keep two on me at all times. I already do not like being bothered by law enforcement for anything—I damn sure do not feel like getting pressed about that.

Friday, July 3, 2020

This is the Friday before the 4th of July. With the first of the month that just passed and this upcoming holiday, my bus had a heavier passenger load than usual. On my first trip, I had a guy get on at Central Avenue with his girlfriend that was in dire need to get to a grocery store. We conversed with each other after they boarded.

"Aye driver, where the nearest grocery store?" he asked.

I put my hand on my chin to think of where.

"On this side of town I'm not too sure. I know there is one off of Vermont," I replied.

"Cool, I'll get off there, man. I need to get some groceries and I need to eat something. I'm feeling weak and my blood sugar is low—hopefully I can make it."

I started thinking to myself, *like damn bro why you didn't get you something to regulate your sugar before getting on the bus?* My anxiety went up a bit. At the time, I'm thinking *if he passes out I gotta stop service and call help for this man.* I also have to fill out an accident report at the end of the day if medical personnel comes out. I am not trying to fill out no damn accident report. I just kept thinking to myself *let this man be okay until his stop, Lord please.* I kept looking in the mirror to gauge his body language. His facial expression was equivalent to a frustrated Commissioner Burrell from the TV show *The Wire.*

I'm continuing up Vernon westbound, passing Hoover. He hits the stop for Vermont. The woman with him keeps him from standing up to get off.

"We got food at home, you don't have to go to the store. We'll eat when we get to the house," she said to him.

They bicker back and forth with each other. They didn't get off at Vermont but rode to Normandie. I was thankful that he was able to get to the stop safely, last thing I need is a muthafucka falling out because they didn't take care of their medical needs.

On my second trip going towards Santa Fe, right after Alameda, as I'm driving I heard a siren go off. It was the quick siren hits that law enforcement do when they don't want to fully use their siren. My heart started racing and I began looking in the mirrors vigorously, but at that moment it dawned upon me that I am at work driving a bus. I look over to my left and LAPD was approaching a lady driving a mid-90s Toyota 4Runner. Some might feel like I'm over exaggerating mentioning that but that's cool, as a Black man who grew up in South Central Los Angeles it is anxiety inducing hearing cops roll up on you. My day had been going so smooth driving the bus that I forgot I wasn't in my personal vehicle.

The trips afterward were beautiful. Seemed as if everyone handled their business for the day, and as time furthered I had fewer passengers. My very last trip I was able to count on four hands how many people rode my bus. It was a breeze. The sunset was beautiful and added the perfect ending to the day as I pulled into Division 7 with a smile on my face.

Monday, July 6, 2020

Today while deadheading on the 10 Freeway eastbound to Santa Fe, once I passed Grand Avenue, the bus started to obtain a rough transmission. What it started doing was rocking real hard back and forth. On occasion, buses have a mechanical failure where when the bus tries to switch gears, it'll get stuck—and in comes the rocking of the bus. The check engine light and stop engine light came on, and once I got off the freeway before turning right at Alameda, the bus shut off. It required all the arm strength in the world to make that turn. I was able to get the bus started back up, but it shut off again when I got past 41st Street and Alameda. I got it started again and continued to Santa Fe, placing a request to talk to the control center.

When I got to Santa Fe, I pulled into the bus zone where the 60 and 760 stop at after making a left turn on Vernon. I got a call back and gave them the info, but I was a bit long-winded with what I was saying. Surprisingly, it was a friend of mine who has been promoted to a supervisor working the control center.

"That was a lot, but can you see if you can pull the bus into the Maple lot?" she asked.

The Maple lot is a layover in downtown L.A. where the 16, 20, and 33 layover.

"Maple lot or Vernon yard?" I asked.

"Boy, you know what I mean—pull into the Vernon yard," she replied.

I began laughing. "Okay, let me do that now while the bus is still running," I replied back.

I get off the phone. As I'm pulling into the yard, she sends a text message. It reads: *"Imma kick you!"* I started dying with laughter even harder. There's never a dull moment with her.

When I pulled into the layover parking lot in the yard, there was a road supervisor there ready to provide me with assistance. He informed me that the control center contacted him with everything that was going on. He advised me to wait for Division 2 to bring me a bus. About thirty minutes later, mechanics from Division 2 showed up. I gave it a pre-trip and the road supervisor on-site advised me to deadhead to West Hollywood due to how much time had went by. I didn't have to do my first trip—it helped to make the day go by faster.

On my second trip leaving West Hollywood, I picked up a young homeless man at Crenshaw Boulevard. He had two travel bags and a blanket on top. His clothes were real dirty. He was yelling on the phone loud as hell. He was so loud that I thought I was going to have to pull the bus over and ask him to get off, but due to whatever he was talking on the phone about, I decided to leave it alone. The anger in his voice—I could only imagine what dude was going through.

"You took the kids from me! You'll see how hard things will be now that I'm gone!" he said out loud.

I'm guessing that he was arguing with the mother of his children. Dude was extremely loud, and I literally thought he was going to be a problem. After he got off the phone, all you could see was anguish on his face. He had the look as if he lost it all and was ready to give up on life. The expression on his face was so strong, the shit took all my energy. This is the one of many walks of life we encounter driving public transit.

Wednesday, July 8, 2020

Yesterday was a chill day, but damn—I got pummeled by customers using the damn bike rack like crazy. On the first trip heading toward West Hollywood, I picked up seven bikes one way up. Seven fuckin' bikes? Yoooo! What the fuck? What made matters even worse is that the majority of them rode along Vernon Avenue. Like damn, man—y'all can't ride down the damn boulevard? That made no damn sense at all! Had me all fucked up, and I ended up being late to my layover because of these bikes alone. Sometimes I just want to turn into the Hulk and rip the fuckin' bike rack off the bumper.

There have been times where I've gotten a bus with no bike rack and that shit was magnificent. My co-workers won't admit it, but I am—I can't stand them damn bike racks for this reason alone. Most people that use them don't go far! Six of the passengers rode down Vernon. Only one rode past that going toward Rodeo Road. Don't waste a bus operator's time. I'll cut some slack if you got a messed up rim or a flat tire going a short distance, but I take it personal if your ass only going a distance that you can easily ride.

Today on my first trip, a passenger was asking me a question and I initially couldn't hear him. He asked me the question two times, then walked to the front.

"Did you hear me, driver?"

I'm looking at him in the mirror, confused.

"Huh? What's going on man, what you need?" I asked.

"Is this the rapid?"

"Yea this the rapid, sir."

"Oh okay, thank you," he replied.

It trips me out how many people just get on buses and don't read the head sign. I mean, my bus is red and my head sign is functional. One of the things that irritate me is when people get on the bus and start talking as if you're supposed to automatically know they're talking to you. I have to always remind people to address me by my job title. Not trying to be on some asshole type shit but there is like twenty-plus people on the bus and people using their phones. If you are not standing in the front of the bus where I can see you, how in the fuck am I supposed to know you're talking to me?

Muthafuckas will literally get on the bus and start talking, expecting you to know they're asking you a question. I would have never known dude was talking to me until he came all the way to the front. He damn near standing by the rear door asking a question like I'm supposed to know he talking to me.

On my second trip going back to Santa Fe, I picked up an older woman—she appeared to be Russian. She had a heavy Eastern European accent. She got on at the Beverly Center stop on Beverly Boulevard and La Cienega. She walked up to the front to ask me a question.

"Excuse me driver, do you go to Wilshire?"

I look over my shoulder to respond as I'm still picking up passengers.

"Yes ma'am, I go to Wilshire," I replied.

"Okay, can you call it out for me?"

"Yes ma'am, no problem. Don't go too far, it'll be coming up soon," I advised.

She said "Okay, thank you" and proceeded back to a seat near the rear door.

I continue in service southbound, and when I approached Wilshire Boulevard, I'm looking dead at her ass in the passenger mirror, calling out the stop as I'm boarding passengers.

"Wilshire! Wilshire! Wiiiiiiiiiiilshire!"

She's still sitting in the seat, not taking heed to me calling out the stop. I put my hands next to the sides of my mouth to travel the sound.

"Wilshire! Wiiiiiiiiilshiiiiire!"

I took a deep breath and shook my head. I eventually gave up and continued in service going southbound on La Cienega. I even looked over my shoulder to grab her attention. She's sitting in the back just looking with a straight face. I'm calling the stop the whole damn time while looking at her, but she didn't get off. Why—I have no idea. But what happened next just got the best of me.

When I got to Olympic, she ran to the front abruptly.

"Excuse me sir, did you pass Wilshire?"

I envisioned myself as a cartoon character turning red with smoke coming out of its nose and ears.

ESSENTIAL: Diary of a Public Transit Bus Operator Volume 1

"Woman, is you serious!? Ma'am, I was calling the stop and you didn't get off!" I shouted.

"No, I no hear anything," she said.

I was fuming, shaking my head with the tip of my fingers from my right hand touching my forehead with my hand partially closed.

"Ma'am, I was dead ass looking at you the whole time while calling the stop and you didn't get off. You can ask anybody on this bus—I called the stop out," I informed.

She begins pointing to the front door.

"I need off here. Open the door, please! Please!" she requested.

I open the door for her and let her get off on the near side of Olympic Boulevard. I was irritated as fuck. Like damn—you can't win for losing out here. I wanted to pull the hair out of my beard fuckin' with that woman.

On the same trip going to Santa Fe, this real big dude in a security guard uniform got on at Crenshaw Boulevard. Dude rode past Main Street, and when I got to the light at San Pedro, he walks to the front.

"Hey, can you let me out here?" he asked.

I begin shaking my head and giving him the cut-throat gesture.

"C'mon man, you're on a rapid bus," I barked.

"C'mon man, I live right here," he replied as he's pointing toward the corner.

I threw my hands up in frustration. I was angry as fuck.

"Next time, can you please ride a local bus? Do not ride a rapid!"

I open the door right at the corner and he gets off. I start to see him walking down the street, and I wasn't mad for letting him off anymore. Dude could barely walk down the street—it was equivalent to Patrick from *SpongeBob SquarePants* trying to walk in the sand.

It's getting to the point where I'm coming across passengers who frequent rapid buses but beg me to let them off at a local stop. I'm at the point where, when I start to see these people in the future, I give them a disclaimer that I'm not letting them off at a local stop. Yeah—it's gotten that bad.

Friday, July 10, 2020

Something to get off my chest before I talk about the rest of the day. I was a bit irritated with motorists not letting me over into traffic. I don't understand L.A. motorists. The road is meant to be shared. All day today I had to bogart my way into traffic much more aggressively than usual. People get upset when we aggressively get into traffic, but when we turn on our signals, people will purposely speed up. I try to wait for traffic to clear up, but depending on how heavy traffic is, I have to be aggressive and get into traffic. How hard is it to let us over? We're not going to be in your way for long. I wish people would stop treating buses like they're a burden to their everyday commute. It can be exhausting having to fight motorists just to get to the next damn stop.

Today on my first trip going to West Hollywood, some Treach from Naughty-By-Nature looking ass dude at Venice and Cadillac runs to the back door and blocks me from closing it. He came running to the stop from Cadillac and stuck his hand in the door, preventing me from closing it. These model buses have a slow ass rear door. An old ass person running from two blocks away can catch the bus fuckin' around with that rear door.

He begins talking to a middle-aged lady that just recently got on the bus from the same stop. He's standing in the rear door as he's talking to her.

"Ma'am, give me my phone back. I left it here at the stop," he said.

With her heavy accent, she could barely speak English, but I understood what she was saying.

"I don't have a phone. What are you talking about?"

I'm still looking in the mirror, confused as hell.

"I know you have my phone. I haven't even been gone from the stop all that long, and you and that other lady the only ones that were at this bus stop," he said.

I interject as I am getting frustrated with the shenanigans going on—besides, dude is holding up service.

"Hey!? What's going on, man? You can't be holding up service, bro. I gotta go!" I shouted.

"She got my phone, man!" he replied loudly.

Lady is throwing her hands up in confusion and shaking her head no at the same time, speaking in a heavy Hispanic accent.

"Ma'am, do you have his phone?" I ask.

"No, I don't have his phone. I don't know what he's talking about," she yelled, waving him off.

He's aggressively pointing toward the bus stop newspaper stand.

"Oh, so you for certain saw her pick up your phone with your own two eyes?" I ask.

"Yes," he replies.

"C'mon y'all, what the fuck? Hold that thought while I place this call. Ma'am, if you have his phone, please give it to him."

"I have no idea what he's talking about!" she yelled out with her arms and hands held up in confusion.

"I left my phone on top of the newspaper stand. I ain't been gone all that long—not even a minute—and I come back, my shit is gone!" he snapped.

I'm thinkin' *got dammit I ain't got time for this shit, man!* I proceed to call the control center. After a couple of minutes, dude gets off the bus and walks back in the direction he came from.

I started wondering, *did that woman really take this dude's phone?* At this moment in time I'm kinda like *what use does one have with someone else's phone especially if it's locked?* Hell, I wouldn't put it past her. People be having poker faces riding public transportation after having done some bullshit.

Anyways, I was able to close the door and keep it moving. Glad that didn't result in anything worse.

The rest of the day went smooth. On my last trip, I had to wait at Venice and Fairfax for eight minutes because of bicyclists. They were heading westbound, with about thirteen bicyclists blocking traffic at the intersection. I knew I was going to be there for a long period of time—hell, I started writing down errands I had to run for the week. It had to be at least three hundred bicyclist. I'm just glad I didn't have to do Line 33 that day.

Monday, July 13, 2020

On my second trip heading southbound on La Cienega Boulevard, an old elderly woman looking like George Washington was waiting at 3rd Street at the stop near Fatburger. She had a cane and got on through the front door, occupying the seats for seniors and disabled people.

"Do you go to the train station?" she asks.

"I go to two train stations, which one?" I asked.

"The one on Jefferson. Aren't you going to Vernon?"

"Yea, I'm going to Vernon. You have to get off at Jefferson for the Expo Line," I replied.

She low-key cops an attitude, waving her hand in an aggressive "whatever" manner. Her voice was sounding like the Wicked Witch of the West from *The Wizard of Oz*.

"How are you getting to Vernon?" she asks.

"Vernon and where?" I ask in return.

Her voice gets a little louder and she asks me again.

"How are you getting to Vernon!?"

I looked at her with frown in the mirror. I'm trying to process what this woman means by her question. But since she was pissing me off, I figured I'd try and do the same in return—so I sarcastically gave her the whole 705 route going eastbound. My voice was a little louder than usual while doing so.

"I'm continuing up La Cienega, left on Cadillac, left on Venice, right on Fairfax continuing onto La Cienega, left on Obama, right on King Boulevard, right on Crenshaw, and left on Vernon all the way to Santa Fe Ave."

I guess I gave her what she needed—she left me the fuck alone after that. Part of me wanted to say, "Bitch, how you gon' jump off the $1 bill just to be on some bullshit?"

"Okay, thank you," she said and went on about the ride. She didn't ask me shit after that. I am a bus operator, not a got damn Google Map.

On that same trip, a young lady was upset because she wanted to get off right after Pico Boulevard, but the Rapid 705 does not stop until Cadillac Avenue and Venice Boulevard. Right before I approached La Cienega, she yells at me:

"Hey, where's the next stop!?" she yelled as I approached La Cienega.

"Cadillac," I replied.

She's real upset that she's unable to get off, and her tone was very unpleasant afterward.

"What the fuck, you don't stop anywhere along La Cienega after Pico!?" she asks.

"No I don't. You have the wrong bus, ma'am."

"Well, go figure!" she shot back.

She's looking at her phone and aggressively tapping the screen.

Welp—in the words of the late great Notorious B.I.G.:

"And if you don't know, now you know, nigga."

These are the types of interactions that make you wanna throw on some sunglasses and drive in complete silence like you're in the damn Secret Service. It's always the ones who don't know where the hell they're going that got the most attitude. Like ma'am, *you* chose this bus—I didn't snatch you off the sidewalk. And that "dead president"? As I sit here at my computer desk typing this, I'm still tryna wrap my head around how she hit me with a full-blown Wicked Witch interrogation n' shit, voice and all, then followed it up with a sweet little "thank you." Man, that's that BULLSHIT.

Monday, July 20, 2020

A relatively smooth day. I didn't have any problems whatsoever.

Last week I only worked three days and took the rest off. On Tuesday I had a blocked sign-on. That big ass red box with the letters inside that say "Your sign-on has been blocked"—man, that shit always causes anxiety. You walk in thinking you're about to knock out a regular shift, and boom—screen hits you with that red-lettered stress. Just standing there like, *damn, what now?* It was for a uniform voucher.

I'm back from a four-day weekend. Friday I paid my respects to my coworker Jason and took a day to rejuvenate mentally. Damn, I'm still fucked up by what happened to him. It's been sitting heavy on me. Jason wasn't just some random coworker—you see the same people day in and day out on this job, share laughs, vent about passengers, life, all that... and then one day they're just gone. It puts things in perspective real quick. I forgot to mention that I saw his car accident on the Citizen app a few days after. Seeing his red Camaro wrecked the way it was just added onto how I was already feeling—like, *damn bro, what happened?* I've heard various things in regards to the accident, but out of respect for his loved ones, I didn't entertain any of it. Some stuff just doesn't need to be speculated on. Let folks grieve in peace.

Imma keep it a buck—working this job, it's had its ups and downs, and part of that is the people you work with. I can't say the same for everyone else, but you know how you have those coworkers that you're actually happy to see when you go to work? Like it's an abundance of love and respect? The ones that treat you like they haven't seen you in forever every time you talk to them? That was Jason whenever I seen him at Division 7. Nothing but good energy. He always showed me the utmost respect, and I gave it right back. That kind of vibe sticks with you.

Only thing that was a headache today was a guy who missed his stop at La Cienega and Jefferson on my last trip heading northbound. He was mad that he missed his stop, so now he had to wait until Fairfax and Washington to get off. All I could do was throw my hands up and keep it moving. Like what do you want me to do—reverse the bus? Teleport you? It's not my fault that your ass wasn't paying attention.

Some people get on the bus and immediately zone out. Lost in their phones, headphones with music blasting, texting, scrolling, talking to someone about bullshit—next thing they know, the bus is ten blocks past where they meant to get off. No matter what happens, it'll always be your fault as a bus operator. People riding public transit need to stay alert. Even if you are distracted, at least keep your head on a swivel. Glance up once in a while. Be aware of your surroundings. It's public transit, not Uber—I'm not coming to knock on your seat and say, "Hey, your stop's next." What really gets me is the attitude. Like they act personally betrayed when they miss their stop. Nah, bruh. I can't read your damn mind. You're responsible for you. Pay the fuck attention please.

Tuesday, July 21, 2020

First trip headed toward West Hollywood, and already folks on some bullshit. I got passengers pressing the rear door at red lights like they forgot where they at. Like—*what the fuck are y'all doing?!* This ain't a local line, and it damn sure ain't no Uber. Just because you feel like getting off don't mean imma stop traffic and roll out the red carpet.

Every time somebody pushes that door, my dashboard lights up like it's dry snitching—flashing and beeping, loud as hell, like I ain't tryna focus. And what kills me is the way they just sit there, mean-muggin' me through the rearview like I'm supposed to crack the door open all of a sudden. First of all—pressing the rear door like that is dangerous as fuck. Y'all out here treating it like it's a damn elevator button. I'm still in the middle of the street, cars flying by, and you tryna get out?

The bus has an interlock system—doors ain't supposed to open unless I'm fully stopped. Lord forbid that shit malfunctions and you fuck around and fall out. These are newer model buses, but unfortunately they still can encounter some mechanical failures.

Imma start calling the rapid a "build-a-stop" because that's what the fuck it be feeling like with people riding these muthafuckas trying to get off any and everywhere.

Don't even get me started on the last-minute screamers. All shift long I had folks waitin' till the exact moment I close the door and tap the gas before they decide to speak up like we in a damn emergency.

"Aye! Aye! Aye! My stop! My stop!"

Bruh... I had the door open for a solid two minutes. I waited. I looked in the mirror. You had all the time in the world. *Man, what's new...*

Thursday, July 23, 2020

On my first trip heading westbound, I picked up a guy at Santa Fe and he gave me a compliment on my sunglasses. It was funny because he looked like the rapper Kool Moe Dee but sounded like Danny Glover. I wear Locs sunglasses—if you ever seen a picture of the rapper Eazy-E then you'll know exactly what I'm talking about. He boarded at Santa Fe and Vernon. He got on through the backdoor and walked halfway up the aisle.

"Say man, can you spit a verse for me? Can you spit a Biggie verse?"

"You gotta catch me on my off day," I replied.

We both start laughing and I told him good looking out. I appreciate passengers such as him—those who help bring good vibes on the bus.

I continued in service and picked up a lady at Avalon Boulevard. She got on the bus and walked to a woman who was a little younger and demanded that she give up her seat because the seat was for "senior/disabled." The way this woman was asking, it was quite evident she had some form of mental issues. Hell, she got on the bus looking like an advertisement for a minstrel show with her eyes all bucked n' shit. She's pointing aggressively at the wheelchair logo on the window. The lady looks puzzled—she didn't understand a lick of English. The gentleman that complimented me on my sunglasses suggested to the woman another senior/disabled seat for her that was available near him, and she copped an attitude.

"Ma'am, it's other seats on this bus. Hell, it's a seat right here," he said as he's pointing diagonally across from his seat at an empty one.

"No, I want this seat here. I'm asking for this seat! Stay yo ass out of it," she advised.

He threw his hands up in frustration, letting them hit his lap.

"Look ma'am, I was just suggesting another seat. All the extras ain't serious—it's other seats over here."

"You need to stay your ass out of my business and mind your own. Shut you muthafuckin' ass up," she fired back.

He was not pleased with what was said and had some words in return.

"Nah, you shut yo ass up!" he suggested.

A lady sitting near the Hispanic woman begins translating to her what's going on. She gets up and moves to a seat near the rear door exit of the bus. The older, deranged lady finally sits down in the once-occupied seat, still arguing at the gentleman that complimented my glasses.

"Y'all know these seats are for seniors and disabled people. And I don't know why yo ass got involved," she said as she's staring at the man.

"Just shut yo ass up, woman. Please."

"No, you shut the fuck up!" she snapped.

I pull into the stop at Figueroa Street. I started getting a damn headache with all the arguing that was going on. I'm looking at the annoying woman through the passenger mirror as I'm servicing the stop.

"Can I get you to be cool until you get off, ma'am? Please?"

She had the same energy for me with her reply.

"Just do yo muthafuckin' job, driver. Just do yo muthafuckin' job!" she barked.

"Okay ma'am, my bus was fine before you got on. You got on the bus being all demanding and shit. You got on the bus being disrespectful as fuck. The gentleman recommended another seat for you and you got mad at him. I don't know what the fuck you got going on in your personal life—but hey, it ain't our faults," I said.

She begins giving me the whatever hand gesture.

"Whatever driver, just do you damn job and drive this bus."

I really didn't feel like entertaining the bullshit, but she was getting on my damn nerves.

"You know what, ma'am, have a good day and God bless you," I said.

I continued driving the bus eastbound. It's quite evident that arguing with this woman wasn't going to get me anywhere. I continue to drive. She's still babbling at the mouth. Me and the gentleman stayed quiet for the remainder of the trip. We arrived at Vermont, and as she's walking out the rear door, she has some final words for me.

"Yeah driver, make sure you do yo muthafuckin' job!"

As she was saying it, her head was moving the same way you would see on the WWE wrestler D'Lo Brown. After she exits, me and the gentleman share a laugh with each other. We converse with each other about how many insane people are riding the bus and how it seems as if it's increased since the beginning of the pandemic. He rode all the way to Crenshaw Boulevard. As far as that mean ass woman goes—I hope she doesn't ride in the future.

Monday, July 27, 2020

After having two beautiful days off of rest and relaxation, it's actually hard to get back into the groove of things dealing with the public. On the way to work I just felt drained—no other way to explain it. It requires a high level of mental fortitude to continue to do this job after so many years. It's been eleven years for me.

Today on the way up to West Hollywood, going down Obama (formerly Rodeo Road), it was down to one lane at the intersection of La Cienega. I can't stand road construction; as a matter of fact, anything that takes time away from my layover gets the best of me. A lot of times shit just be blocked off with no utility workers in sight, nor do the streets have any signs of a repair in progress—but today they were actually finishing the repavement between Obama and Jefferson Boulevard. Road construction can be draining at times, especially at the top of rush hour. It took a total of fifteen minutes for me to get across the intersection. Due to the northbound side of La Cienega being blocked off, I had to work my way to Jefferson Boulevard, then make a left onto La Cienega to continue my regular route. Since everybody was going the same way, I ended up being twenty-five minutes down. *Damn, there goes my layover.*

The second going eastbound was fine, but my last trip had a few things irritating me. Heading to West Hollywood, I got to Vermont Avenue and there's this crazy-looking woman running full speed at the bus from across the street. As fast as she was moving, it caught my peripheral vision in the rearview mirror. She probably ran a 4.5 in a 40-yard dash. She had no bra on and everything moved accordingly. She had on a black beanie cap with a green bomber jacket and a dirty striped dress that had black and white colors. Her facial appearance was equivalent to the character Sophia from *The Color Purple.* As she's running from the other side of the street, she's yelling toward a passenger.

"What you say, cuzz!? What you say, cuzz!?"

I'm looking in the mirror the whole time confused as hell. She gets in the face of a younger male passenger that's attempting to board through the rear door. She's pounding the palm of her left hand with her right fist at the same time.

"What was that shit you said, cuzz!? What was that shit you said, cuzz!?" she yelled at him.

He walks around her and gets on the bus. My main concern was that she was going to get on the bus and start doing some stupid shit or start physically harming other passengers. I hurried up and closed the door after the last passenger got on. She's facing the rear door, still yelling. I started driving off and she ended up kicking the back of the bus like a field goal kicker trying to hit a 55-yard game winner. I'm not gon' lie—the kick was hard as hell. Sounded like she kicked the light off the back. Come to think of it—hell, the NFL should give her a contract.

Continuing in service on the same trip, when I got to La Cienega and Jefferson, a dude got on through the backdoor with a question.

"Aye man, you go to Barnes & Noble!?" he yelled.

"Naw, you need the 217, sir," I yelled while looking in the mirror.

"Where are you going?" he asked.

"I'm going down La Cienega," I replied.

"I know that, but where you making a left turn at? Because you're not going to where I gotta go."

In the back of my mind I'm thinkin' *no shit, Sherlock*, but I answer his question.

"I'm making a left on Venice," I replied.

"Oh okay, man. Let me off, dawg!"

I open the door and let him off while I'm at the red light facing Electric Ave. I hate that shit when people get impatient to the point where they just start hoppin' on any and every bus, then want to bombard you with a grip of questions. Just be patient and wait on the bus you need. Also, everyone got a damn smartphone and Google everything else—hell, Google what bus you need and how to get there.

Tuesday, July 28, 2020

Driving down Vernon Avenue, cars can get reckless. People see a big ass bus and make illegal maneuvers all because they think we're going slow along the avenue. A knucklehead in a late 90s/early 2000s Lexus drove the turning lane coming all the way from Figueroa at a high rate of speed, cutting in front of me right before approaching the light at Hoover. Once he got in front of me, he encountered more bumper-to-bumper traffic and did the same thing—using the middle turning lane to pass cars after the intersection.

Vernon is a two-way street, but the majority of the boulevard is one lane due to parked cars. And when rush hour traffic occurs, people become real impatient and start doing dumb shit like that. I'm thankful to be a commercial driver because when I was a class C driver, I didn't have the defensive driving skills that class B and A drivers have. If I was going any faster than what I was driving, I'm sure I would have slammed into the back of him.

On my second trip going to Santa Fe, a text message popped up on our radio:

"Hey operator, when you get to your next stop can you check the seats for a red phone? If found please call back."

I didn't check until I got to the end of the line—unfortunately, I didn't see any phone. I hate to sound negative, but Vernon Avenue is full of people looking for a "come up," and depending on what kind of phone it is, it's equivalent to hittin' the lotto. If I lose a phone along Vernon Avenue, first thing I'm going to do is call the provider—because I know for sure I'm not getting that shit back.

On my last trip, I picked up a guy who boarded through the backdoor with a beverage in a Styrofoam cup with no lid on it at Cadillac Ave. Usually when I see that, more than likely there's an alcoholic beverage being consumed. Also, his judgment was a bit impaired.

On Line 705 going northbound after Cadillac, there isn't a stop until Pico Boulevard. I hear the stop request, and as I'm driving, there's another passenger calling for my attention. I can barely hear at first because I have the window open and the air from the outside is interfering with my ability to hear. I look in the mirror at the passenger.

"Is everything okay, ma'am?" I asked.

"He's trying to get off of your bus," the passenger replied. She's pointing at him as he's standing near the rear door.

"Yea man, I hit the stop all the way back there—what the fuck, man!?" the impaired patron stated.

"Dawg, this is a rapid bus. After Cadillac, I don't stop all the way up until Pico Boulevard," I replied.

At this moment, I thought he was going to lash out at me, but I was surprised by his response—his tone was much different.

"Ooooh my bad. Well, can I please get off here?" he asked.

"I'll look out for you today. For future reference, you need the 105."

I pull into the bus zone at Cashio Street, opening the rear door after coming to a stop. He begins making his exit.

"Okay, thanks operator!" he shouted as he was exiting. He damn near stumbled getting off but was able to recover, that's the last thing I need.

Some people purposely do that because they don't feel like waiting on a local bus. I didn't question this dude's antics because he appeared to be under the influence of alcohol. After driving for eleven years, I am highly aware that people ride Rapids with the hopes of getting off at a local stop. I won't be surprised if they get rid of this service altogether in the future. At times it just seems useless.

ESSENTIAL: Diary of a Public Transit Bus Operator Volume 1

Wednesday, July 29, 2020

On my first trip, there was a dude wearing nothing but basketball shorts and tennis shoes walking northbound on Crenshaw Boulevard, yelling as he was walking. There was a lady walking by, and he started yelling in her face—she damn near ran into the street to get by him. As I was approaching to make the left turn on King Boulevard, he was looking in the direction of the bus and started yelling at the same time. All I could think was *man please don't run for my bus, please don't run for my bus.* He begins running in the direction of the bus, but by the time I got to the intersection, I got the green arrow to make the left turn. I'm sure if I hit the red light, he would've caught up to me at the stop—thank God he didn't.

There have been countless times where I'd be driving and some mentally deranged individual would turn into a *Terminator 2* T-1000—dodging full-speed traffic and all to catch my bus—then go crazy disrupting my ability to operate the bus safely and interfering with people's commute.

It's wild how often moments like that blur the line between fear and frustration. I get it—people are struggling out here, and mental illness is a real, serious thing. But when I'm sitting up there in that driver's seat, in a giant fishbowl on wheels, it's hard not to feel like I'm just waiting to be the next episode of *When Keeping It Safe Goes Wrong.*

Even after I made the turn and put a few blocks between us, my hands were still locked on the wheel like I was in a NASCAR final. I kept checking my mirrors like he might suddenly appear running alongside the bus—arms pumping, face screaming—trying to beat the light. It's messed up, but part of me was already imagining him doing a superhero maneuver onto the back bumper while screaming, *"You ain't going nowhere muthafucka!"*

And the sad thing? It's not even shocking anymore. It's damn near routine. I've seen people throw full-blown tantrums, strip down like they're bout to shower at home, bang on the doors like they're auditioning for *The Walking Dead*, and threaten everyone from little old ladies to full-grown men trying to mind their business.

It's like every shift comes with a side of unpredictability—spin the wheel, and who knows? Could be a quiet ride, or it could be *Survivor: Metro Edition.*

Thursday, July 30, 2020

Today leaving the yard, the DVR compartment flew open when I pulled out. *What the fuck, man?*

The DVR compartment is located in the panel right behind the operator. It sits on two metal rods where wheels can roll on them—to my understanding usually they're pulled to get footage or provide some type of IT maintenance. Most of the time it's pulled after a traffic collision, an accident involving a passenger, bus operator, or both—usually some type of crime as well. The key design on the compartment is not your average key design and requires a mechanic or supervisor to lock it back. When the buses are sitting in the yard, the guys who fix the cameras on the buses will grab the video footage off the DVR, but a lot of the times they forget that they opened the compartment and don't close it back. There have been times where I've got to my bus and seen a laptop connected to it, downloading info from the bus.

I immediately pulled the bus over and started duct taping the compartment. I didn't feel like pulling back into the yard just for them to close it. I thought to myself *continue deadheading, then when I get to Santa Fe, I'll call for a supervisor to tighten the compartment.*

When I got to Vernon Yard, luckily there was a supervisor already there. I asked if she could lock the compartment for me while I headed to the restroom. When I got back, I gave her a big thanks. It's a good thing not too many people are waiting in that area in the front due to COVID. During regular service, people would stand right behind the yellow line in the front of the DVR compartment—right where the door would fly open. That DVR probably weighs about 50-60 lbs. If I had a passenger standing there and that thing flew open, somebody could get hurt—then it would be my fault because they'll say *you didn't thoroughly pretrip your bus.* Yeah, bullshit—I know, but that's how Metro get down. I got it closed—thank God.

On my first trip at Figueroa, there was a fragile woman who was staggering and looking like a zombie as she was crossing the street northbound. While crossing, she started walking toward the front of the bus just before getting on the curb. She was trying to get on the bus but I wasn't going to let her on. Anytime you see an individual of this nature, you don't pick them up because once they get on the bus, one of three things will happen:

1. She'll fall into a deep sleep and you won't be able to wake her up at the end of the line
2. She'll start to get on passengers' nerves so much the passengers will beg you to kick her off
3. Or she'll slip and fall causing herself serious injury—then you'll have to fill out one of those dumb ass accident reports

I flip the switch to the microphone and hit the switch for the speaker outside as she's banging on the glass of the front door. She's standing on the asphalt in the space between the curb and the bus.

"Step up on the curb, ma'am, so I can pick you up," I said through the mic.

She does so, and when the light turns green, I hit the gas. *Fuck that.* After almost getting a chargeable accident for an intoxicated passenger falling out the seat back in December of 2019, I'm not taking any chances with that. The operator doing the 105 behind me pulled up to the stop but went to the far side of the light and dropped off the passengers—avoiding having to pick her up altogether.

When I got to Vermont, I picked up a young woman who was talking to herself. She was pregnant, her clothes were dirty, and she appeared to be homeless. She talked to herself throughout the whole ride. On occasion, she would raise her voice talking real loud, then her voice would go back down to a normal tone. The times she shouted in between her normal dialogue would cause me to flinch.

I was praying that she wouldn't ride all the way to the end of the line, nor that she would go ape shit crazy. Luckily, she didn't do none of that, and she got off at Jefferson Boulevard. As she was getting off, she did a triple take. She would take a couple of steps and stare at me in the mirror, and did that three times before I flailed my hands and arms up in frustration—letting them hit my lap after they both reached apex. Then she finally got off the bus, walking toward the train station. I remember thinking to myself *who the fuck knocked her up?*

On the second trip heading to Santa Fe, when I got to Western Avenue, there was a man at the intersection pouring out a bag of clothes and setting up bottles in the turning lane to go northbound on Western Avenue. It's wild out here. Then there's this dude who usually wears nurse scrubs—I always see him at Normandie—but today he ended up walking to a local stop to wait for the 105. Whenever he doesn't make it to my bus, he gives me the middle finger. I don't know if he works for some type of medical office or a convalescent home but I always see his ass walking from Raymond avenue or Budlong. There have been times where he wasn't directly at the stop but he was close enough for me to wait a little bit. But the past few times he was taking his sweet ass time coming to the stop and I left. He threw his hands up as I was going by, and I gave him the gesture to run for the bus next time. Ever since then, he's been walking to

Budlong—but as I'm passing by, he gives me the middle finger like he's scratching his forehead. These people are funny.

Day went smooth. There were rumors that we're supposed to have a "blue flu" day tomorrow. I know that's some bullshit...

But but but, let's go back to December 19th of 2019 just for those wondering...

I picked up a dude at La Cienega and Beverly Boulevard heading eastbound that was extremely intoxicated. The sun had just set— I was doing Line 14/37. As I'm picking up passengers, there was a guy walking toward the front door but he was touching the sides of the bus. Truth be told, I thought he was a blind man. There are a handful of people who are visually impaired that don't have anything to help guide them but when they get near surfaces they'll use their hands. I thought this was one of those situations. After he got on, he sat in the front area where the senior/disabled patrons sit. I continued in service, and about a minute into driving I began smelling the scent of alcohol protruding from the human body. It's the guy that just got on. He began talking to a few passengers, and his words were slurred.

Further into the route, when I began driving around the curve after Vermont approaching Council Street, I heard a noise. But as I'm looking in the mirror, I didn't see anything. The way my mirror was adjusted, I couldn't see all of the front passenger area. Right after I look into the mirror, a few of the passengers began yelling.

"Hey driver, somebody just fell onto the floor!" a lady in nurse scrubs yelled from the rear seats.

I pulled into the bus zone at Council Street and see it's the same dude who got on intoxicated. *Aww shit* is all I could think. I hit the parking brake, getting out the driver seat to go help him.

"Just keep driving, operator. I'm just gonna stay here," he said.

I began shaking my head in disgust. I'm more so focused on an accident report as opposed to his drunkenness. I reach my hand under his arm so I can help him get back up on the seat, but he's so fucked up that it's a waste of time. I did my best to help him up. He tried to get up, but the abuse of alcohol prevented him from doing so.

"I gotta call the paramedics for you dawg—you can't stay on the floor, man," I said.

He was in a semi-fetal position, unable to move to full capacity. He didn't want me to call the paramedics, but shit—I had no choice. All of the passengers on the bus were upset but hey, what could I do? I couldn't leave him on the floor. I had to call the control center for him to get medical attention. About seven minutes went by, the paramedics came and rolled him off the bus on a stretcher. Dude was pissy drunk.

That night when I got to the division, I had to fill out an accident report. Approximately a month goes by from when this incident happened. I tap my badge for work one day and my sign-on is blocked. The supervisor at the window hands me an envelope and when I opened it, it shows that I have an Accident Review Board a little over a week from the current day.

I told the supervisor that it couldn't be for me because I haven't had an accident since 2009, but when she asked if anything happened on that date, that's when it dawned upon me about ole boy falling out the seat as I was going around the curve. Now mind you, I was going dead throttle—I didn't even have my foot on the gas. I had to have been going at least 15 miles per hour. That is nowhere near fast.

After reading the letter, I went straight to the instructions office and asked one of the supervisors there, "When the hell they start giving ARBs for drunk muthafuckas?" The supervisor I asked in particular was just as perplexed as I was. I didn't trip—I geared myself up for that day. But luckily, the ARB was dismissed when I arrived to the division, as those who were in the office came to the conclusion that I wasn't at fault.

I'm glad the ARB got cancelled because I had an arsenal of words assembled for whoever initiated that paperwork. I was willing to lose my job that day because that was some bullshit—there was no way I had control over that drunk ass man falling out of his seat.

But yeah—that's what happened on the 19th of December 2019.

Friday July 31, 2020

Today was relatively swell, I don't have much to report on. The guy at Normandie with the scrubs still out here giving middle fingers. I also picked up a mentally ill dude who resembled Crocodile Dundee who talked to himself from the time he got on at Wilshire boulevard to West Hollywood. I honestly thought he was gone do some bullshit on the bus, anytime someone gets on talking to themselves it's always raises an eyebrow. But anyhoo, he got off the bus and went on about his business with no problems, he also said "Thank you" prior to getting off.

Icing on the cake for a smooth day going into the weekend, I'm very thankful to get to the end of my shift with no problems.

It's crazy how something as simple as a thank you can shift the energy. He might've been in his own world the whole ride, but that small gesture at the end felt like a curveball—in a good way. Sometimes it's the quiet, weird riders who surprise you the most. Meanwhile, Mr. Middle Fingers at Normandie Avenue stays consistent like the sun rising in the east.

Honestly, days like this are rare enough that I don't take them for granted. Nobody argued about bullshit, no farebox worries just a smooth ass day. If this is the tone going into the weekend, I'll take it.

ESSENTIAL: Diary of a Public Transit Bus Operator Volume 1

Tuesday, August 4, 2020

Today is my first day back—I took me a three-day weekend. I needed a sick day. I didn't have the mental fortitude to come to work yesterday, especially with the way my body was feeling.

I don't really talk about it much, but I've been dealing with anxiety and depression. It came about since entering my 30s. I have my reasons as to why—but that's a story for another day. On occasion, I don't feel like coming to work, but back then when I was going through all of my mental anguish, I took so many sick days that I eventually got suspended over them.

Metro policy is that for every one sick day, you have to work sixty working days straight to clear it. If you don't, the cycle starts all over again for that new sick day. I don't like the policy because you have to work sixty *business* days, not sixty days in total—so you gotta work a total of three months straight to clear one damn sick day. Crazy shit. I know they're trying to keep people from milking the system, but so many operators are on the sick list at all of our divisions because a lot of them have become overwhelmed with the workload the job throws at them.

We're told *"Be happy that you have a job"* as a way to tell us to stop complaining—but we're still human beings at the end of the day. Plenty of us have a ton of things going on in our personal lives as well and still come to work despite that. Yeah, we're making money, but shit—some days the job demands more of you than others. And when you're not in the proper mindset, it can be detrimental to operating a commercial vehicle.

I advise anyone to take a day or two off—or however many days you need off—for your mental health. *I am not bullshittin'.*

Today I had a good laugh. On my last trip heading up to West Hollywood, I serviced the stop at Washington and Fairfax. There was a guy there that literally stared at the bus headsign for about twenty seconds. Then he looked up at the sign that shows all the buses that service the same stop, then stared at my headsign again—about the same time, if not longer. No lie, he did this about four times. He eventually gets on the bus afterward.

"Hey, is this the 705?" he asks.

"Yes, this is the 705," I replied.

I begin laughing, but he's unable to see me laugh due to me wearing my mask. Now mind you, my headsign works, and he didn't appear to be visually impaired. *Damn—you done stared at the bus headsign and the bus stop sign all that time, just to hop on and ask me if this is the 705?* I thought. Jokingly speaking, somebody is long overdue for an eye exam.

Wednesday, August 5, 2020

On my first trip heading westbound on Vernon, I was at the train station stop at Long Beach Boulevard and a Blue Line coming northbound had just dropped off. The light at the train station takes so long that it gives people enough time to run for the bus from the train—but it's very dangerous. They're running from the platform diagonally as the train is passing by, then they risk their lives running toward oncoming traffic going in all directions. Some people are running fast, then some people are running slow as I'm still sitting in the zone. I tell passengers all the time—these buses are not worth your life. Hell, half the people that are running for the bus don't even have nowhere important to go—that's the cold part about it. Those who *do* make sure they have enough time so that they don't rush or put themselves in a situation where they're risking their lives to catch public transportation.

On this same trip at Broadway, two young dudes had traffic stopped in the number two lane that I was sitting in—just to talk to each other. One was in front of me and the other was at the light in the number one lane. With no fucks given, they held up traffic for almost two light cycles. I was blowing my horn and everything, others were doing so as well, but they didn't give a fuck. With the way Vernon is set up, hell I had no choice but to wait.

The boldness of people's disrespect on the road trips me out at times. It's even worse when you're a public transit bus operator dealing with it all day, every day. It's bad enough you have to sit in traffic with green lights because someone is texting—but this here hit different.

ESSENTIAL: Diary of a Public Transit Bus Operator Volume 1

Friday, August 7, 2020

I forgot to mention yesterday—the day was smooth, but I was irritated as fuck at a passenger who used the bike rack to ride from Central to Avalon Boulevard. On Vernon that's literally three blocks away. He could have rode his damn bike instead of wasting my time. This the bullshit I be talking about when it comes to bike racks.

Back to today. On my second trip going down La Cienega southbound, I got to the light at Cadillac and Venice Boulevard. There was a bicyclist in the turning lane to go eastbound in front of me. The light changes and he's steady trying to plant his foot into the toe holder of the pedal—but it's taking a long ass time. *Lord knows I didn't feel like waiting through another light cycle, fuck all that,* I thought. I eventually became frustrated and change to the first turning lane, going around him. Ain't nobody got time to be waiting on his ass to get his foot on the pedal. If it ain't law enforcement or the paramedics crossing the intersection with their lights and sirens on, I do not feel like missing a cycle. Get cho ass out the way—thank you very much.

On the same trip, when I got to La Cienega and Obama, there was a crazy-looking dude that cut in front of a woman and her four kids—three sons and a young daughter to be exact. As I pull into the zone, the woman holds all her kids back.

"Wait a minute, let him get on," she said.

They board the bus after him, then the man sits in the back of the bus near the left window.

All of a sudden, I start hearing quick outbursts of shouts—equivalent to someone getting tortured with a taser or a stun gun. I look in the mirror and I see the guy snapping his head back like Fabo from the rap group D4L and screaming at the same time.

"Aaaaaaah! Aaaaah! Aaaaah!!!!"

The kids that got on with the lady begin to laugh simultaneously. *What in the Tourette's is going on here?*

"Hey y'all stop laughing—that's not funny," she tells the kids.

He starts up again. Thank God for us wearing masks, because everyone would see my facial expression. I was grinning from ear to ear and laughing in a light tone—I couldn't take it anymore.

As I'm approaching La Brea and Obama, he starts shouting again.

"Aaaaaaaah! Aaaaaaah! Aaaaaaah!"

The lady on the bus with her children is still laughing. The moms begin laughing with the children.

"Shut up y'all, shut up—it's not funny! Worry about y'allselves!" she said.

"He keep making all that noise scaring me, momma," one of her sons blurted out.

They are all now laughing amongst each other.

"Okay, we ain't gon' be on the bus for long—we getting off," the mom said.

The mother and her children got off at Coliseum and King Boulevard. I continue in service, and he does it a few more times before getting off at Crenshaw Boulevard and Vernon. He gets down to the rear door. As he's standing in the doorway, he has a stomp equivalent to a Black fraternity doing a step performance at an HBCU homecoming, and he's bobbing his head like a heavy metal rocker playing a guitar at a concert. When he gets off the bus, he begins jaywalking across Vernon Avenue toward Leimert Park—against oncoming traffic going westbound. I don't remember exactly what the guy looked like, but I do recall his facial expression—buck eyes, looking like Mr. Simms from the movie *Tales from the Hood*. I did my best to hold my laugh in, but I couldn't. Sometimes it's hard to keep a straight face with the shit people be doing out here.

On my last trip heading back to West Hollywood, I had to compete for a lane on La Cienega as somebody was riding one of those dumb ass Bird scooters all up in the street. It's hard to go around these individuals in a Metro bus when everyone is driving like they're at the Auto Club 400 in Fontana—being stingy and making it hard for you to switch lanes. It becomes so exhausting that you just say fuck it and ride behind them all the way up the boulevard.

Monday, August 10, 2020

It's Monday, and traffic seems as if it's back to normal—prior to COVID-19 normal. Like everywhere it's back to normal: on the way to work, at work, and on the way home. I loved it when there was no traffic. Do you know how long it used to take me to get to work? It would take an hour and thirty minutes. Pandemic hit—it only took me thirty five minutes. Huge difference, huh?

Also forgot to mention how clear the sky was all that time with less traffic on the road. Hell, you could see the Hollywood sign with ease coming south on La Brea passing Kenneth Hahn Park, and you could see the mountains looking east. Shit was beautiful.

I picked up a homeless woman with a grip of bags at Pico Boulevard. Shit—it took about damn near two minutes for her ass to get on. I remember thinking, *how in the fuck do these people get around with so much shit?* I was almost at the end of the line, so I didn't really trip. She got off at 3rd Street.

On my last trip heading to West Hollywood, there was a lady who got on at Vermont that wanted to get off at 4th Ave. She hit the stop around St. Andrews.

"Hey, you don't stop here!?" she yells as I'm driving past Arlington.

I take a deep ass breath out of frustration. *Here go the bullshit.*

"Naw ma'am, you are on the rapid!" I replied.

"Let me off here, I gotta use the restroom, please!" she said.

When some people ride rapid lines and want to get off at a local stop, they'll say some crazy shit or use the excuse that they either have to vomit or use the bathroom—just to gain a sense of sympathy so you hurry up and let them off.

"Damn ma'am, you see this big ass red bus—why you didn't wait on the local bus?" I asked.

"I didn't know, sir," she replied.

I didn't feel like arguing and giving her the rundown on the difference between local and rapid lines. She knows. I pulled over at 4th Ave, cracked the door open, and allowed her to exit.

On the same trip, when I got to La Brea and Obama, there was a lady there with one of those granny grocery carts filled up to the top. It took her a loooooooooong-ass time to get on the bus due to how heavy it was. Anxiety began setting in because I had to use the restroom. I don't know why we panic when that one person takes forever to get on and we have to make a restroom stop, I guess it feels like eternity. I ended up making a stop at the West L.A. Transit Center layover—I couldn't go any further because my bladder felt like it was about to explode. I came back and continued in service feeling like a brand-new person.

Wednesday, August 12, 2020

Today a dude rode my bus from Obama to Jefferson. There was only one problem—this muthafucka used the BIKE RACK. Obama Boulevard to Jefferson Boulevard is literally a ride away, like a five block ride. *Damn, these people are lazy as fuck!* When he got to his stop, I wanted to hop on the mic and yell, *"You muthafucka, stop wasting my damn time—you could have rode your bike here!"*

Now don't get me wrong—there have been times where people's tires have busted or rims got damaged in the process of riding their bike. I can cut some slack on that. But nothing was wrong with his bike! Shit was perfectly fine! He got off and rode toward the train station. Son of a bitch.

Also today—people bullshittin' with these dogs claiming that they're service animals. All day I been picking up people with unruly ass dogs. I've been driving a bus for eleven years, and you know the difference between a service dog and not. A service dog is much more disciplined than others. These dogs that people brought on the bus today were not disciplined—

barking and growlling at passengers. That shit is irritating to me. Sometimes I want to kick them off the bus, but I always think of the loopholes that these people find to sue the company and get you fired—so a lot of shit I let slide.

One that really got the best of me was this woman that got on at Washington and Fairfax on my last trip going northbound with an aggressive ass poodle. I mean this poodle was barking at everything in sight. The dog would bark at you if you blinked. I hit the parking brake at the same stop and turned to look at her. She picked her dog up and was able to calm it down. *Service animal my ass...*

Friday, August 14, 2020

Funny ass stretch these last two days—all the comedy landed on my second trips.

Yesterday, there's a lady that usually gets on at King Boulevard and Crenshaw with a ten speed bike and a grip of belongings. When she gets on, she takes a long ass time to load her bike and board. So far you know how upsetting it is when a bicyclist takes a long ass time to load their bike on the rack. This woman in particular has her bike and hella bags, and it can take her up to three minutes to thoroughly board—and to thoroughly get off.

I'm heading down King eastbound and I see her pedaling down the boulevard. She sees me and starts pedaling faster as I'm going by. I hit the pedal all the way to the floor. *Fuck that* is all I could think about as I'm going forty miles per hour passing the old Santa Barbara Plaza. I got to the red light at Marlton, heart beating, hoping she don't catch up to me. The light eventually turns green—she just passed KP Way (the light where the new Kaiser Permanente is inside the old Santa Barbara Plaza). There's one person at the Crenshaw stop,

I picked them up and keep rollin'. All I could think was *whew, dodged a bullet there.*

Same trip, I was heading down Vernon and got to Avalon Boulevard. A man in his early sixties starts yelling at me because he thought I was going to pass his stop. This cat looked like Captain Fuller from *21 Jump Street*. On the rapid line we stop on the far side of the light at Avalon. He spent the whole route trying to mack this Hispanic woman and thought he missed his stop. As I'm crossing the intersection he starts yelling in a panic.

"Hey! Hey! Hey! I need to get off here! I need to get off here! C'mon man, let me off!"

I frown at him in the mirror real quick before pulling into the bus zone.

"Dawg, you are aware that you are on the rapid, right?" I asked.

The panic coming out of his voice settles down.

"Oh okay—well, let me off, man," he requested.

"I got you, sir. The Rapids don't stop on the near side, we stop on the far side."

"Oh okay cool, okay cool—thank you, thank you," he expressed.

All I could think was, *you did all that damn talking—did you at least get the number?* That was too funny, man. It's always one of these middle-aged dudes trying to holler at the ladies on the bus.

Fast-forward to today...

On my first trip at Wilshire Boulevard, there was a man there who wanted to use the ramp to get on the bus. I forgot to mention—he was walking down the street fine and even ran for a bit. I'm not one to judge people's disabilities, but this dude? I'm judging for sure. He was walking normal at first, then when he got to the side of the bus he started using his umbrella as a cane—but still walking normal. Homeboy looked like he was auditioning to be the mascot for the Planters Peanut Company.

He gets to the front door but I pointed to the backdoor. He didn't want to get on the back, he wanted to use the ramp to get on, so he walks back to the front door.

"Hey man, can you deploy the ramp?" he asks.

I gave him a straight face look. He asks again.

"Hey man, can you deploy the ramp please?"

I hit the parking brake and exhale my breath in the same manner the parking brake does. Then I deployed the ramp. He walked up the ramp perfectly fine—no limp, no physical struggle of any kind. Now mind you, my bus was hella close to the curb and parallel. The space in between the curb and the bus is literally an inch, making it extremely convenient for passengers to board.

"The ramp is only for wheelchairs, walkers, seniors, visually impaired, and disabled patrons," I said as he boarded.

I may have been wrong for saying that, but man, I felt like he was taking advantage of the situation just for the fuck of it.

I continued in service and got to 3rd Street. I was going to keep going because I was running behind schedule and my follower was ahead of me, and there wasn't anyone waiting at the 3rd Street stop. Right when I passed the intersection, "handicap" hits the stop request. I hurry up and pull the bus over into the stop.

"I need 3rd Street! Right here, man, right here!"

"You getting off right here!?" I yelled out.

"Yes, I need 3rd Street," he replies. He's pointing at the rear door with his umbrella. I was already irritated from when he got on requesting the ramp.

"Got damn, man—you just being inconvenient today, huh?" I asked.

He walks to the front with ease and stands at the front door. I'm thinking he'll be fine getting off because the step on the bus is a few centimeters lower than the curb.

"I need the ramp, man," he requests.

I hit the parking brake and deploy the ramp for him to walk down.

"Thank you, sir. I appreciate it," he gratefully expressed.

I have a frown on my face and my head tilted down, not looking in his direction.

"You're welcome," I replied with a disgruntled voice.

I close the door and continue in service. People be out here bullshittin', man... He didn't show any signs of not being able to walk, and he didn't even have a cane—he had a muthafuckin' umbrella! Also just a reminder—dude was running for my bus with no physical ailments whatsoever. *An umbrella? Bruuuuh!!* Any weight put on that umbrella could've destroyed it.

This is the shit that be irritating us as bus operators. My coworkers don't have to admit it—I'm admitting it for them.

Tuesday, August 18, 2020

My usual Mondays—feeling like blah, because almost all my weekends are amazing and great. I wish I could continue them for all eternity. Well, until I get out of this seat, this is the reality that I have to deal with.

Deadheading on the 10 Freeway eastbound is still a hassle. People are out in full force now—they said "fuck a coronavirus." Traffic was so sweet when people were in the house.

Outside of that, I had a decent Monday. I met a guy at Washington and Fairfax who stated that he does art. When I pulled into the zone, four LAPD officers were talking to a homeless man. I was watching the interaction as the gentleman loaded his bike onto the rack and locked it. I was a bit irritated because—well, hey y'all know how I feel about bike racks. The gentleman was eager to get on the bus.

"Thank you operator—get me the fuck away from here, man. I don't fuck with police like that," he said.

"Damn, what happened? Is everything cool?" I asked.

He stated that someone waiting at the bus stop called the police on the homeless man for having a few "episodes." He mentioned that when law enforcement arrived, they began bombarding him with questions that made him feel uncomfortable. We talked the whole time he rode. He told me that he was an artist and provided me with his Instagram page.

His reasoning behind his frustration with law enforcement is because he claims that he had been harassed in the past for selling his art on the sidewalks throughout the city. As we furthered into our conversation, he told me that a wealthy man bought a few of his items near Beverly Hills and ever since then, he's been non-stop with his artwork. He felt that I didn't believe him, but I didn't have no doubts about it. I'm guessing the purchase of his art motivated him to keep at it.

After dropping him off, I finished my route and pulled up his Instagram page afterward when I arrived at the division. I'm not an artist, so I couldn't give a proper description on the type of art he does, but it looks like woven sketches of people and things—if that makes sense. Maybe I can buy some art from him in the future.

Now today—just another day of people straight trippin'.

On my first trip heading to West Hollywood, a dude got on at Broadway looking like Ray Charles. When he got to the back of the bus, he started going ape shit crazy. I'm not going to type the dialogue that he was spewing because it sounded like someone talking underwater—but amplified. He spoke his jibberish from there all the way to Crenshaw Boulevard. As he was getting off, he was holding a can of 211 malt liquor, so it's quite evident he was turned up. Yup—good ole 211. That'll do it.

On my second trip, while sitting at the light at Vernon Ave and Leimert Boulevard, some elderly skinny crackhead-looking woman came running for the bus. She got on and started trippin'. She was fussing and cussing at the people near her, and she started spewing unpleasant words toward all the passengers on the bus.

Being a public transit bus operator in L.A.—this is as normal as ketchup and mustard on a burger. I got to a point where I wanted to kick her off, but I kept it rollin'. She got off at Broadway. Prior to her getting off, she was standing in the doorway fussing and cussing at a few passengers. She finally got off and started to walk toward the front—and had the audacity to wave. *Bitch, you just made this ride a living hell and you want to say thank you afterwards?* Fuck outta here...

Today reminded me of a stand-up a comedian performed by the name of Frantz Casseus at the Laugh Factory about the Metro system in L.A. He stated that crazy people act normal until they get on—because they know if the driver sees that, he'll pass the stop up. If you get the chance, you can search the stand-up on YouTube. He performed it at the Laugh Factory on Sunset. The stand-up is spot on.

Thursday, August 20, 2020

A smooth ass day yesterday! I have nothing to report—it was just one of those smooth ass days. Weather was perfect, I had a good bus, A/C was working fine, everybody was respectful and chill. What more could I ask for? Didn't have to dodge no knuckleheads or anything. I'm very blessed and thankful for days like that.

Now fast-forward to today. When I got to the Santa Fe layover, there were two 105 buses and two 705 buses inside the layover, and the stop near the train tracks to go eastbound on Vernon had a TON of people waiting for the bus. At the Santa Fe layover there are only four spots for buses to park. I double park, run inside to use the restroom, and come back out to continue in service. One of my coworkers from Division 2 is double parked in the turning lane in the middle of the street—frustrated with all the buses in the layover. She gets out the bus, crosses the street, and starts to take pictures of the two 105s inside the layover. I'm guessing one should have left already. She crosses back to her bus. I'm sitting at the edge of the driveway ready to enter into traffic to go eastbound. One of the 105s ends up leaving right behind me, leaving an open spot for her to park.

I go into service and amongst the crowd of people, there are two older men frowning at me from outside. I know that frown when I see it—it's equivalent to a wife frowning at her husband after he done came home from "work" late. They get on with everyone else, but these two dudes in particular are talking mad shit.

"Man, I'm tired of these muthafuckin' drivas, man. I'm tired of this shit—it's like these muthafuckas be out here bullshittin' man," he barked.

"I feel you, dawg. Shit don't make no sense how long we gotta wait for a muthafuckin' bus," the second passenger complained.

They proceed to bad mouth me, but I don't give a fuck. I usually have a rebuttal—today I didn't. *Don't nobody give a fuck about you two niggas bitchin' and complaining,* I thought. And if it bothers them that much, they can catch an Uber or get a muthafuckin' car. It's that simple.

Then on my last trip, it took four minutes to leave the stop at Broadway. You wanna know why? Because of these punk ass BIKES.

An older man was putting his bike on the rack at Vermont, and another guy I usually pick up at Crenshaw was getting off. The one getting on had this big gold ass beach cruiser that was too heavy for him to lift. The dude that was getting his bike off had to help him put it on. He rode the bus to Broadway. *I mean, it's rush hour traffic—hop on yo bike and ride, dawg!* Broadway is literally a ride away and there was nothing wrong with his bike. When we got to Broadway, he was struggling like a five-year-old kid trying to pick up 200 lbs. Nigga knees was shaking and everything. I actually had to get off and help him. If I didn't, I would've been at that stop forever. These dudes stay riding bikes they can't pick up.

Tuesday, August 25, 2020

The traffic heading eastbound on the 10 Freeway lately? Atrocious. I can't stand it at all. It took me almost an hour to get from West Hollywood to Santa Fe and Vernon. When the pandemic hit, I was able to get around the city with ease—but not now. *Where in the fuck is everyone going?*

Friday was a smooth ass day overall. Only thing that made me laugh was a homeless mentally ill man at the corner of Stocker and Crenshaw Boulevard, at the southbound stop for lines 210, 105, and 40. As I was driving by, he kicked over a trash can and yelled, "Fuck you," toward my direction. When I looked, he was staring directly at me as I was heading northbound. There was an LAPD unit driving by too—I thought they were going to bother him, but luckily they let the man be. The rest of the day went smooth for me. Great way to start the weekend.

Monday—no complaints. It was a great day.

Deadheading to Santa Fe from the 10, when I was getting off at Alameda, there was a homeless man who had traffic backed up at the exit. He was begging for money, but he was standing in the middle of both lanes making it hard for cars to get by. He was doing a "scooping" gesture, and people were actually giving him money. At first, I thought it was a car that broke down or some police activity with as much traffic there was. Because of this alone, when I got to the start of my line at Santa Fe and Vernon, I was twenty-five minutes down.

On my last trip heading to West Hollywood, I found myself laying on my horn at Jefferson and La Cienega. A lady was texting and gave no fucks that I was honking. The light had been green for about fifteen seconds, but she didn't give a shit. One of many reasons I hate L.A.—it's a lot of entitled ass people out here, especially on the westside areas like West L.A., Beverly Hills, and Santa Monica.

And just when you think you've seen it all...

Today, I got to the stop at Washington and Fairfax on my first trip, and there's a dude sitting at the bus stop scraping dry skin from his foot—and hitting the residue off his shoe. It was so much that as I was going by, there was a mini pyramid of his dead skin. *Ugh...* And how much you wanna bet he turned around and hopped on one of my coworkers' buses? *Lord...*

Thursday, August 27, 2020

Another smooth day yesterday—gotta keep the momentum going.

I was irritated earlier by people not being ready to ride. There was a girl at Avalon and Vernon talking to a guy at the bus stop. I picked up a couple of people and was ready to leave. She comes yelling, "Wait, wait, wait, wait, wait!" *I fuckin' hate that shit.* Why is it so hard for people to be ready to ride the damn bus? A lot of people are either indecisive or playing see-saw with buses. They know they need a local, but if the local takes too long, they'll decide at the last minute to ride a rapid.

Then on my last trip, I had a kid that got on at Western and rode all the way to Beverly and La Cienega. The kid looked young as hell—he was a little Indian-looking boy, and he had a backpack, a hooded sweatshirt, cargo brown shorts, and some sandals.

As I was driving down La Cienega, I heard the voice of a young kid.

ESSENTIAL: Diary of a Public Transit Bus Operator Volume 1

"HEY! DO YOU STOP AT BEVERLY?"

I'm looking around, because with the way my mirror is angled I don't see anybody on the bus. I restructure my mirror so that I can better see who's in the back—and sure enough, it's a young man in the very back of the bus, opposite of the rear door.

I remember thinking to myself, *what the fuck is this kid doing out here?* He didn't look a day older than 7, but he carried himself like a grown ass man damn near. Who knows—might've been a grown man. I'm laughing as I write this. He was about 4 feet tall. Him being so young and riding public transportation—I had my questions, but I didn't bother the young man. The kid rode all the way to Beverly and got off. I told him to please be safe out here.

Now today—man, some dumb ass woman took it upon herself to smoke on the bus. As a matter of fact, it was the same woman who ran for the bus last week on Crenshaw and Vernon—the one that was harassing people and got off at Broadway. It was my last trip coming from Vernon and Santa Fe. I started to smell smoke when I got to Vernon and 8th Ave. I didn't think nothin' of it because someone at the light on Arlington was sitting in their car smoking a cigarette.

"Hey driver. This lady smoking cigarettes back here." a gentleman yelled out from the back.

I'm looking around in my mirror to see who, but don't see exactly who he's talking about.

"Who, sir?" I asked.

He points to the lady—she's getting off the bus at Crenshaw. I got a good look at her, and sure enough, it dawned upon me that it was that same woman. I'm glad she got off, because lord knows I don't feel like shutting down service for a disobedient ass passenger.

Driving a bus in the city of L.A., at some point in the year you're going to come across a jackass that smokes on the bus. It's inevitable to avoid. These people don't give a fuck. They know they can get away with bullshit, and they also know if you take the time to call law enforcement on them, it'll take forever for them to respond. Even if they do respond, they'll make a run for it and most likely get away.

The lady got off with no problem. I apologized to the passengers and informed them to open up any windows they could to get rid of the smell. I don't recall her getting on—because with everyone boarding through the backdoor, it's very hard to see who's who.

Friday, August 28, 2020

I ended up being real late at Santa Fe because—yup, you guessed it—the 10 Freeway eastbound. I was down about forty-five minutes by the time I got to the Vernon yard. I don't know why the fuck these people got me deadheading from Division 7 all the way to Vernon Yard. When I was doing the 705 a few years back, we always pulled the bus out and started service coming out of the division lot.

Today a dude complimented me on my hair. I've been cutting my own hair for the past eight years. It's not the best looking, but I've been able to save money doing it. I used to go to a barber, but after I added up how much money I was spending a year on haircuts and how much time I spent being at barbershops, I figured I could save some money on my own. He got on at the stop after the Vernon yard layover.

"Say man, who's a good barber?" he asks.

"I don't know, bro. I wish I could help—I haven't been to a barber in a while," I replied.

"Who cut your hair? It look pretty good," he said.

"I did it myself," I replied.

"Daaaaaamn, you did a good job. You look damn good, man," he complimented.

I was a bit shocked because I don't have professional barber skills like that—but it gets the job done, I guess.

"Oh, good looking out brother—I appreciate it," I said as I rubbed my hair in a brushing motion.

I'm not big on my own haircuts, but I guess I do well. We talked for a while. I explained to him that I bought all my equipment from Amazon, one by one, until I got everything and started cutting my own. It's not a professional cut, but it's enough to make the cover of a hair product box—maybe.

I don't know how we got on the subject of COVID, but we talked about it for a while. That's a convo for another day. On that same trip, when I got to the division, I kept rollin' but it dawned upon me that I didn't call my wife. She gets real worried when I don't call her. I was praying that she wouldn't panic. I called her when I got to the other end.

On my last trip, a guy got on at Washington and Fairfax playing a radio. He turned the volume up as soon as he got on, and I started to catch feelings in regards to the music. In a snap, we're quick to let passengers know to turn their music down. I was about to say something—until the radio started playing Nipsey Hussle's "Last Time That I Checc'd."

Once that came on, all my frustrations went away. The rest of the night went smooth.

Tuesday, September 1, 2020

On my first trip, a woman got on with a roller cart—you know, one of those carts that grannys use to go to the grocery store with. The problem was, when she got on, there was a very pungent smell coming from the back. The shit smelled like the crack of an athlete's toe. It smelled so bad, but I couldn't pinpoint where the smell was coming from. All I could think to myself was, *what the fuck does this lady have in this cart that got the whole bus funky?* I usually have an immune nose to a lot of bad smells after driving for eleven years, but every now and then a smell will catch me off guard. I can't recall the last time I smelled some shit that bad. I didn't feel like going through the hassle of trying to get her off the bus—I just let the "funk" ride.

On my second trip heading back to Santa Fe, a lady got on at Western Avenue and just started unloading all her frustrations onto me. She was one of those passengers that just get on to unload their personal life onto the bus driver. I can't go into thorough detail exactly what she was saying, but she complained about bus drivers and company supervisors treating her like shit out in public. She also mentioned that Donald Trump is going to make it tough for bus drivers because a lot of us are at work "under the influence of drugs and alcohol" and still come to work like everything is normal. She stated that he's going to make us take a drug test before and after work every day.

Every now and then, you come across a passenger like her. Ain't nothing you can do to avoid it. I started thinking to myself, *daaamn, I see why you had problems with supervisors and operators.* She stood in the doorway at Figueroa still talking shit. I just sat at the stop and looked at her in the mirror the same way a parent looks at a kid when they're doing nonsense. She finally got the picture and got off.

It sucks being multiple professions in one and not getting paid for it.

On this same trip when I got to Avalon Boulevard, there was a handful of passengers that ran from the local stop to the rapid stop. One of those passengers that ran to the stop wanted to get off at Hooper Avenue. Only thing is—I don't stop there.

"Aye man, I need Hooper!" he yelled.

Here we go with the bullshit again. My body language slumped and my face went flat with frustration.

"Dude, I don't stop here," I said. He's standing in the rear door exit area.

"Please man, I gotta get off!" he pleaded.

I was already upset, so I fired back with a question for him.

"Why didn't you wait for the 105!?" I asked loudly.

"I didn't see it," he replied.

I grew more angered with my response, throwing my hands outward like a concert band director with every few words.

"It was right behind me!" I yelled out.

He's not caring about anything I'm saying.

"Well can I get off here, sir?" he asks.

I pull the bus over in front of Taco Mama and let him off, he knew full damn well he seen that bus. It pulled into the zone at the same time as me—the shit was literally on my ass.

Then on my last trip, there's this dude that gets on at Long Beach Ave with a big ass cooler taking up all kinds of space on the bus. I usually don't like picking him up because he takes a long ass time to get off—because he's always coming across one of his "patnas" and talking to them when he knows full damn well he gotta get off the bus. Well on this trip, I saw him smoking a blunt nowhere near the curb nor ready to board the bus. No one hit the stop request to get off and he's the only one at the stop going westbound. I hurried up and kept driving. He yelled for me to stop—but by then it was too late. You need to be alert at all times when it comes time to catch a bus.

Fuck the bullshit. Bet you his ass was ready for the next one!

ESSENTIAL: Diary of a Public Transit Bus Operator Volume 1

Thursday, September 3, 2020

A beautiful day yesterday—what more can I say? One of the things I have to work on is seeing the bigger picture. All day up and down Vernon, I had a few near misses with people just running into the street to cross to the other side of the boulevard. Avalon Boulevard, Figueroa, Vermont, Western, and Arlington—I had to slam on my brakes a few times with muthafuckas just darting out into the street. Damn, people don't have no regard for their own personal life. I'm glad I drive at a safe speed, but sometimes I do get caught off guard.

Then today, right before my third trip on the 705, I was on the phone with my wife. I looked up and seen that it had been fifteen minutes past the time I was supposed to leave. I hurried up and got off the phone. As I was doing so, two supervisors rolled up and parked in the layover. I was thinking to myself, *damn, one of them is going to say something*—but fortunately they didn't. The supervisors on this side of town seem a little more relaxed than the ones on the Westside and Hollywood area. I'm not saying no names, but a few of my coworkers know which ones in particular I'm talking about.

People always ask me—from coworkers to passengers—"Have you ever thought about becoming a supervisor?" I've been told numerous times I'd make a great one.

Truth be told, I already have one foot out the door. I'm not gonna complain about it, I'm just going to handle my business until I can get something better or come up to where I don't have to have a boss anymore. That's the ultimate goal for me. I don't mind working a job or having a manager at any job, I'm just tired of all the politics and bullshit that comes with having a job. No matter what job I've worked, it always seemed as if there are those who get promoted that end up sacrificing a portion of their dignity in the name of "enforcing company rules and policies." Out of all the years I've been here, I've beared witness to this— especially involving a handful of those who've been promoted from bus operators to supervisors, or as Metro calls them, T.O.S. (Transit Operations Supervisor).

Also, as little as it's mentioned, those T.O.S. and those above them who create uneasy work environments in the name of "enforcing rules" also help contribute to a lack of manpower systemwide. That type of energy makes bus operators not come to work. It's already bad enough with the things that they have to deal with out on L.A. city streets.

Excuse my rant—just some random thoughts I felt the need to express in lieu of writing this entry for today.

Friday, September 4, 2020

I got to work late today and almost got a missout. I can't keep leaving my house at the same time anymore with traffic getting back to normal. It's okay—I haven't had a missout since January of 2010 and here it is 2020, so I'm not doing bad. It's all good though, no worries. Traffic was every damn where today. La Cienega heading southbound on my fourth trip—it took me twenty-five minutes to get from Jefferson to Obama. No bullshit—that's literally three blocks.

On the same trip when I got to Alameda, some dude was talking to another person while the light was GREEN. Everybody blowing their horns at them and everything, but they didn't give a fuck. The light at Alameda and Vernon takes FOREVER. Shit takes like six minutes damn near, because it's a four-way signal. I was mad as fuck—like *c'mon bruh!* I got to my layover about fifteen minutes down. I felt my phone vibrate with a few text messages, and when I got to the layover, sure enough it was my wife. Anytime she texts me, she's worried about my well-being.

I go outside the layover to place a phone call. As I'm talking to my wife, some *Ruth Langmore from Ozark*-looking-ass woman walks up and interrupts my convo. Her clothes are real dirty and she's barefoot—truth be told, she looked like she climbed out of a chimney. I'm standing on the sidewalk near the fence, just outside the layover. I tried to get her to wait a moment while I was on the phone, but apparently, whatever she had to say was more important. I mean, I wasn't gon' be on the phone that long. I tell my wife to hold on, frown on my face. I felt like Craig from *Friday* getting interrupted by Felicia while he was talking to his girlfriend. I hate when I'm on the phone and someone interrupts me—*especially* if it's not anything important.

"I'm on the phone with my wife, girl—what the fuck you want?" I asked.

"Do you know anybody that works in the back?"

I'm confused as to what the hell she's talking about and why.

"Huh? What are you talking about?" I asked.

"Do you know anyone that works in the back of the building here?" she asked, pointing to the back of the layover.

Behind the layover, it appears to be some form of a maintenance division for the Metro rail. I don't know what she would possibly want with anybody—or anything—out of there.

"No, I only layover here. I don't know any of the people that work there," I replied.

"Oh okay, sorry... sorry."

What the fuck this woman doing walking barefooted in the city of Vernon? I thought. She continued walking westbound toward Santa Fe. I continued my convo with my wife. I don't know what the fuck that was about, she didn't seem distraught or in danger. All I could hope for was that she's was safe.

On my last trip heading westbound, I was about to leave the stop at Santa Fe and some dude comes riding his bike toward me. I was going to wait, but then again I'm already late. I thought *Ehhh, he can catch the next one,* I thought. I closed my door and continued into the sunset. Besides, I seen a 105 in the rearview of my mirror, so I didn't feel too bad.

Looking forward to this three-day weekend.

ESSENTIAL: Diary of a Public Transit Bus Operator Volume 1

Wednesday, September 9, 2020

I don't have much to report today, but on a brighter note:

TODAY IS MY BIRTHDAY!!!!

I usually take a few days off and hit the L.A. County Fair on one of those days, but I wasn't too thrilled about going this year—especially since it got shut down due to the coronavirus. Still, I'm happy to have made it to my thirty-third year of life. That alone is a blessing. The day itself was relatively great. I'm thankful I woke up and got to see another year, but I honestly wish I had the day off. My wife was teasing me, saying, "You should've requested it off," and she's right—but hey, it is what it is.

On my last trip headed to West Hollywood, I got caught by the BNSF train. Son of a bitch—I had to sit there and wait while this dude loaded up all his damn rail cars. Ended up being fifteen minutes late. And in that moment, all I could think was, *man, I really should've taken today off—I wouldn't even be dealin' with this shit.*

But even with that delay, I was still in good spirits. I took some time to hop on social media and give thanks to everyone who wished me a happy birthday. That love hit different this year. I was smiling so hard I had to take a picture, cheesin' from ear to ear.

All in all, my birthday was great. Real simple, real solid. I'm blessed.

Showing some gratitude for my thirty-third year around the sun.

Thursday, September 10, 2020

A man at Broadway and Vernon was sitting at the bus bench on the gas station side, texting on his phone. Now mind you—it's about twelve people at the bus stop, standing and ready to get on. I pull into the zone and pick up those people. He's still at the stop, texting and not paying any attention whatsoever. As soon as the rear door is closing, here he comes—jumping up at the last minute with his hand in the air. He has a bike, hurries up and grabs it, and puts it on the rack. I've never seen a rotund man move so fast in my life. I got the straightest face known to man, but deep down inside I want to cuss his ass out. *Hurry yo muthafuckin' ass up man—shit* is all I was thinking. Only reason he was able to catch my bus is because the rear door interlock (unable to accelerate bus until rear door is thoroughly closed).

It trips me out how distracted people become using their phones. Smartphones can be a gift, but when it comes to passengers riding public transportation—they can be a curse.

Continuing on the same trip, there was police activity between Arlington and 6th Ave off of Vernon. I did a detour going up

Arlington Avenue and a few of the passengers started panicking. I hate when I detour, because everybody starts acting all frantic and shit. They act like you about to take them through a black hole or some shit. One of the passengers wanted to know if I was going to get back onto Crenshaw Boulevard.

"Hey, are you going to Crenshaw Boulevard?" one of the female passengers asked in a panic.

"Yea, I'm getting back to Crenshaw," I reassured her so she could calm down.

"Oh okay, because I need Crenshaw Boulevard," she replied.

I got bombarded with so many questions by so many passengers—it took all the professionalism in the world to answer them one by one without snappin'. When I got to 48th and Crenshaw, I let some of the passengers off. All the panicking and frantic behavior went away—thank God.

The rest of the day was smooth. On my last trip, there was a homeless man at the Washington/Fairfax terminal digging in his pants and flicking some type of debris away. I saw what he was pickin' at—I don't feel like going into detail though. After I serviced the zone, I hurried up and left because I didn't want him seeing my bus and making a last-minute decision to hop on. Last thing I need is the poles left with smegma debris from him touching them.

Tuesday, September 15, 2020

Yesterday heading westbound at Vermont, there was an elderly man that almost made contact with my bus. Before Vermont, Vernon has slow traffic (about fifteen miles per hour). As I'm going 15 mph crossing the intersection, an elderly man with a cane just stepped off the curb to cross the street. If it wasn't for bumper to bumper traffic—and if I was going any faster—I don't think I would've been able to stop in time. I didn't think he would step into the street like that. The light had been green for ten seconds before I even crossed.

Then when I got to Western Avenue, as I'm crossing the intersection, some young dude jets out of the front door of the liquor store on the corner and begins to run across the street heading southbound. He moved so fast I had no choice but to slam on my brakes. He stops in his tracks as he sees me coming and gets back on the curb. By me slamming on my brakes, I'm just thankful that no one fell on the bus. He bolted out that liquor store like he just got away with robbing a bank. Just imagine if I was in the process of crossing the intersection—I for sure would've hit him. The day wasn't too bad overall.

Now today on my second trip going eastbound approaching Vernon, I see a dude in the rearview jaywalking diagonally—running toward my bus against oncoming traffic. I thought he wanted the bus, but that wasn't the case. His facial expression was all fucked up, like somebody stole his car or something. He gets to my window breathing real hard.

"That punk ass driver going in the opposite direction left with my bike!" he said.

"Did you tell the driver that you were getting off prior to?" I asked.

He's still breathing hard, doing his best to get his words out in a proper fashion.

"Man, fuck all that! He knew that was my bike, homie!" the guy yelled out of frustration.

I had to explain to him from a bus operator point of view, taking into consideration how frustrated he was.

"Sometimes we don't remember whose bike is whose. You gotta communicate and let the driver know you need extra time to get your bike, my man. Hold up real quick," I said.

The man was real irate and extremely upset—and judging by his mannerisms, I wasn't too sure if he was going to take it out on me. Truth be told, the shit had my heart racing. You just never know with any of these passengers out here in L.A. As I'm talking to him, two LAPD officers on foot come running full speed to my bus. They were waiting on the Vermont side to ride the 204 going northbound. They heard him yelling at me from the northeast corner and quickly crossed the street. They get to the front door and I immediately begin talking to them. I could see it in their face—they were ready for an altercation to pop off. I hit the switch to open the door.

"Is everything okay?" one of the officers asks.

"All is well, officer. The operator going in the opposite direction left before the gentleman could get his bike off the rack," I said.

The second officer breathes a sigh of relief. "We seen him run across the boulevard diagonally toward your bus."

"Everything is okay. I'm going to give him the info needed to call customer service," I expressed.

Him and the other officer were both much more relieved.

"Okay, operator—we'll be going on our way. Thank you."

I gave both officers a thumbs up. "Thank you. You guys have a good one. Be safe," I said.

I continued talking to the guy, giving him the number to customer service and what info he needed to provide. With the way the guy ran across the street and toward my bus, it did look sketchy. I'm glad nothing worse came of that. I gave the guy all the info on a piece of paper with the customer service number on it.

"Here you go, bro. Make sure you give them as much info as you can. If you remember the bus number, provide them with that—the direction you were heading and the time. Hopefully this helps."

He was much more relieved with all the info I gave him.

"Thank you, driver. You been a big help," he said.

He runs back across the street and goes on about his day. I continue in service eastbound. Usually most people will wait back on the boulevard the whole day for a bus to come back with their bike, but you never know if it's that driver's last trip—so it's best to contact customer service and see how you can get your bike back. You'd be surprised how many people leave bikes on the racks. Some people also get off the bus thinking they have a world of time to grab their bike—then they realize they don't, as the bus is leaving the zone after picking up or dropping off a few people. Hopefully my man gets his bike back.

Wednesday, September 16, 2020

I got to the layover much earlier today. It usually takes a long ass time to get to Santa Fe, but today it was smooth sailing. I left the division earlier because my bus was parked separately in a different lane—so I wasn't blocked in like I usually am. I left about ten minutes earlier and got to the layover only three minutes late. Thank God!

Also, I gotta share an awesome last trip I had with a female passenger that rode from the train station.

"Do you go to Normandie, sir?" she asked.

"Yes ma'am, I do," I replied.

She boarded and sat in the seats in the front.

"I need to get to Denker, but I'll ride your bus," she said.

"I can catch up to the 105 for you if you'd like?" I asked. There was a 105 about half a mile up the road.

"No, that's okay—I can walk," she said.

I was shocked by her reply. That's not a response that's popular amongst a lot of passengers.

"Oooooh, that's a first. Usually people do not like walking," I said.

"I do not mind walking at all. I'm just thankful that you guys are still running during this pandemic," she giggled.

We continued talking to each other. She stated that she had two kids who drive buses—her daughter works for Riverside Transit Authority, and her son works for MTA out of Division 2. She said that since her kids had been working with the company, she's very understanding of what bus operators go through regularly. She thanked me for my service prior to exiting the bus—I truly appreciated that. That was the icing on the cake to a great day.

I forgot to mention, further into my last trip, a dude was running for the bus at Venice Boulevard and Cadillac. He's running and flagging the bus down. It's still a red light as I'm facing westbound after servicing the zone. I wanted to make a right turn, but because he was running across the street from the south side, I had to wait. He steps up and boards the bus—but as soon as I make the right turn, he starts yelling at the top of his lungs.

"Aye, this the wrong bus! Please driver, please! Let me off here! Let me off here, man!"

What the fuck, man!? What the fuuuuuuuck!?" I yelled back.

As hard as I yelled at dude, I'm surprised I didn't pop a blood vessel.

"I need the 733!" he yells out.

"No shit, Sherlock!" I responded.

I pull the bus over, blocking the emergency entrance at Kaiser, and let him off. I didn't care where I dropped him off—I just wanted his ass off my bus so he could leave me the fuck alone and go on about his day.

I'm fuckin' tired of that shit. That's why sometimes I don't like picking up people after servicing a stop. Some of them don't see the line they actually need—they only see "a bus"—then when you make a turn or don't go in the direction they actually need to go, that's when they start flippin' out. This is one of those irritating regular occurrences that comes with driving public transportation.

Friday, September 18, 2020

Today on Vernon going westbound during my first trip, there was a dude waiting in the parking lot at the shopping center on the northeast corner at Western with his bike. He seen my bus but initially didn't get on. I had about eleven seconds left on the light after I boarded and alighted a few passengers. As soon as I close the door and start proceeding from the zone—*here he come*—running full speed with his bike. He ran in front of the bus, preventing me from going any further, and I had to slam on my brakes.

I should've ran his ass over—man, what the fuck? This muthafucka seen me, made eye contact with the bus and everything. I don't know if he wanted the 105 and made a last-minute decision to ride mine or what. Even if it was a last-minute decision, you don't do no shit like that. Just wait for the next bus! Then he took a long ass time to load his bike on the rack. I was mad as hell at him. I was mean-muggin' him like a shoebill stork. He rode his bike to La Brea and Obama, and I still gave him the same look when he got off. *I wish people would stop doing dumb shit out here...*

Then on La Cienega Boulevard heading southbound, there was a woman driving a BMW M3 in front of me. It was bumper-to-bumper traffic, and every time traffic eased up—she was still in the same position. It was like she gave zero fucks about what she was doing. I kept having to blow my horn at this damn woman to move her car up. I stayed honking at her from Melrose Avenue all the way to Beverly Boulevard. For the life of me, why can't people pull their cars over and text? This shit gave me a headache. I do my best not to generalize, but that side of town is full of a certain folks who give absolutely no fucks about nobody but themselves in traffic.

Hurry up weekend—I need you!

Monday, September 21, 2020

Coronavirus? Where? On my first trip, I serviced the Blue Line stop at Long Beach going westbound. Along the route all the way to Vermont, my bus was crowded from the front to the back. Maybe there was a run in front of me missing—hell, I don't know—but man, I busted my ass picking up all those people. It was mentally draining. I kept telling people that I couldn't pick up any more, but they're not trying to hear that shit. They kept forcing themselves on, even stopping on the opposite sides of the street doesn't work. A handful of people still ran across the street, risking their lives to catch my bus.

Continuing in service, when I got to Crenshaw I picked up a guy who claimed he was a former RTD operator. We talked for a moment and he stated that he lost his job because he had a serious drug problem. He mentioned that when the crack era hit the hood of L.A., he developed a serious habit and couldn't maintain his job because of it. Not too many people talk about the things they've been through during that era—I was all ears listening to this gentleman. You see stories and documentaries on it, but to actually hear it from someone who had what most consider "the best job" was enlightening. A lot of people who've dealt with something similar are ashamed to speak on it—but he wasn't. I was shocked, but appreciative that he felt comfortable enough to talk to me about that.

On a brighter note, right after I passed Arlington Avenue, there was a young Hispanic girl sitting on the hood of her car in the middle of the street with two balloons—one was a two and the other was a zero. Two of her friends were in front taking pictures of her. I remember when I was twenty years old. Lord, I didn't know the curveballs that life would throw me upcoming. May the Lord bless her with plenty of good days to come.

At the Santa Fe layover, there was a girl who was originally waiting at the bus zone near the train tracks walking my way. I was standing outside the layover talking on the phone with my wife. When she got to me, she asked a question.

"What time is the bus leaving?" she asked as she looked at the time on her phone.

I put my phone down to the side.

"Just be patient, there will be a bus coming soon. You have to catch one of the two, right? Just be patient," I said.

She walked back to the area with the other customers. People come and ask like they're about to go find an alternative or call someone to come pick them up. You gotta wait either way—just be patient. Mean-muggin' bus drivers, questioning them, and all the other bullshit people be doing at bus stops near the layover isn't going to make them move any faster. What makes me even more mad is people who bug you about what time a bus comes or leaves are usually the ones who don't have anywhere important to go. Responsible customers give themselves plenty of time to get to their destinations.

Wednesday, September 23, 2020

A moment of self-reflection.

I think back to when I first started driving for the company and how friendly I was when it came to interacting with passengers. Now, a lot of that has deteriorated.

Today on my third trip, we had a detour going up Stocker from Crenshaw because the section from Stocker to King Boulevard was blocked off. People started panicking and asking the usual questions "Where you going?" "What you doing now?" and more thrown right behind. I found myself responding in an unpleasant tone.

It's gotten to a point where questions get the best of me. I just remember reflecting after work, sitting in my personal vehicle like, *daaamn, I'm a whole different person now.* I was feeling bad because my usual self is much more positive and outgoing—but it's gotten to a point where I'm like a ticking time bomb with all the negative elements I have to deal with driving a bus daily in the city.

I do my best to remain positive, but it's hard—*man*, I'm feeling the need to check myself before I wreck myself. Those very same bus operators I used to complain about with all my classmates in grade school... I'm now one of them. One of the most common sayings people throw around is, "Bus drivers always have an attitude." Well, it's safe to say—after eleven years—I know why now.

I think a portion of it is because I didn't plan to work here that long. I just wanted to pay bills and bust the next move. I took for granted the negatives that came with this job. Internally, I have things I gotta deal with. Every time I look in the mirror with this uniform on, I don't feel like the same person I did when I first started in June of 2009. I feel like I'm looking at someone who *settled*. I'm working on a change. I don't know exactly when or how—but it's coming. I can feel it.

One of the good things about driving is that you have plenty of time to think and reflect. I also started to ask myself: *What will I do if I lose my job today?* There are elements in the city that are huge contributors to that. With all the curveballs thrown at us every day, it's something I seriously have to consider—what would I do if it got to that point?

It's something I need to start working on now, because it's getting BAD out here. It's so bad that I bring weapons to work just to protect myself in case something goes down. Even if you encounter a situation that's nowhere near your fault, it seems like the company will still throw you under the bus to cover themselves. I am at full understanding that I'm just another number. Hell, they don't even call you by your name—they call you by your badge number.

I don't plan to be a badge number forever.

Thursday, September 24, 2020

Today on my first trip heading westbound, there was a man with a granny cart that got on at Central Ave. He had a ton of stuff in it and could barely roll it, let alone pick it up. He stood right in the exit way of the bus. As I'm continuing in service, people were struggling to get off at the rear door. A lady sitting next to the backdoor asked him if he could move his cart, and he took it personal.

An argument broke out between the two. I never get involved with passengers arguing with each other unless it interferes with my driving or it's life-threatening to the parties or surrounding passengers. I swore up and down something was gone pop off, but nothing happened—thank God. He got off at La Brea Avenue.

Then on my last trip heading westbound, a couple at Western was arguing with each other. The girlfriend got on the bus, and the boyfriend was standing in the rear door looking for the 105. I started to close the door and he made a last-minute decision to get on. The 105 is literally a few blocks behind me. They get on the bus arguing, back and forth. As I'm heading down Crenshaw

Boulevard, the boyfriend starts yelling for me to stop at 43rd, near the McDonald's.

"Aye man! Aye, this our stop, bro!" he shouts out.

I was mad because the bus he needed was in his view—but they both got on mine arguing, then his ass pull that bullshit.

"*Man, what the fuck!? This is a rapid—I don't stop there! I knew I shouldn't've picked you up, man. You know full damn well you needed the 105 for this stop. Don't play me for no fuckin' fool, man!*" I yelled at him.

He ended up lowering his voice, just talking in a low tone to his girlfriend. He gets off at King Boulevard.

This that shit I be talking about—people knowing they need a local bus but catching a rapid. Shit is gettin' old, man...

Thursday, October 1, 2020

On my first trip yesterday, a woman rode my bus who wanted to get off at Main Street. Main is not a stop for Line 705. She presses the stop request and as I'm passing Main, she starts talking shit.

"Hey! Hey! I did hit the damn button to get off the bus!" she yelled. She had some serious bass in her voice—shit was extremely disrespectful.

I immediately pulled over to the farside of the driveway for the AutoZone. What I really wanted to say was *"Bitch, who you fuckin' yelling at?!"* but instead I replied in a loud voice—more professional, but I had to let it be known.

"Do you know what bus you're on, ma'am!? HUH!?" I asked.

With a sure tone, she answered me back.

"I'm on the 105."

"No, you're on the 705, and the 705 does not stop at Main. Y'all are killing me out here! Next time ride the 105, please—thank you!" I expressed.

"My bad, sir. I'm sorry, I didn't know," she replied.

She did all that damn yelling and wasn't even on the right bus. *Damn, people don't read for shit out here.* Man, it's requiring a world of strength to keep driving these buses. Outside of that, the rest of my day went cool.

Today, though? Today was a hot ass day. Felt like it could've been in the mid-90s. Thank God for these New Flyer buses—the A/C works magnificent.

While heading down La Cienega, I saw Van Lathan at La Cienega and Wilshire. I gave him a honk and a black fist, and he gave the same in return. I'm not going to thoroughly explain who Van Lathan is—we got Google now. Then on my last trip, I got yelled at by an old man because he rode the rapid but wanted to get off at Main Street. The stop he got on at—the Local Line 105 picked up at the same time as me. Why he didn't get on that bus, I have no idea. But he decided to express his feelings to me.

"I press! I press! Estupido! Estupido! I press!"

I'm looking in the mirror because I don't know what's going on, but I see him giving the gesture of a button press. A woman sitting in the back speaks for him.

"He wants to get off right here at Main," she said.

I heard some unpleasant words from him in Spanish. I'm not the most fluent, but I know when someone's being disrespectful—and I definitely caught the word *puto* in the middle of all his yelling. Just for the shit he was talking, I had a few words of my own.

"¿Qué dices? Muthafucka, I do not stop here, man! Fuuuuuuuuck! ¡Necesitas uno-cero-cinco! *Uno-cero-cinco! Unooooo ceroooooo cincooooooooo!* You were at the stop when it picked up—what the fuck, man!?" I yelled.

He's yelling back at me in Spanish, throwing up his hands like Tony Soprano expressing his disgust to one of his goons. I dropped his ass off at Broadway. *Lord, get me off this damn line.*

Outside of that bullshit, my day was cool. After that madness, I couldn't wait to get off work...

Monday, October 5, 2020

On my second trip, I came across something that threw me off for a second. There was a homeless lady at Normandie, laid out near the gutter of the curb—half her body hanging off, dead asleep like the world had completely clocked out on her. At first glance, I'm thinking, *damn, is she even alive?* It was one of those positions where you don't know if you need to call for help or just keep it movin'. Because of where she was lying, I had to pull into the zone about 30 feet early—couldn't risk getting too close. I tapped the horn lightly to let the passengers know they needed to walk up to the bus. But as soon as I hit the horn—*BOOM*—this woman jumps up like somebody hit her with a damn defibrillator. No bullshit, the way her eyes popped open and her body flinched up, she looked like a dead person coming back to life.

Next thing I know, she's speed-walking straight toward the bus like nothing ever happened. I'm still picking up my last few passengers, and she just hops on without saying a word. I wasn't trying to be rude, but in the back of my mind I'm thinking, *damn, do I really wanna let her on?* Not because she's homeless, but because you never know—especially with folks who just woke up confused and probably dealing with something mentally. I wasn't in the mood for a scene, a meltdown, or anything close to it. She walked straight to the back, stretched out across the rear seats like a construction worker clocking out after a long-ass shift, and passed right back out. Out cold. I figured she'd be on there until the end of the line, but surprisingly, she woke herself up and got off at La Brea—no issues, no drama, not a single word. Honestly, I was relieved.

Since COVID hit, it appears as if the number of homeless and mentally ill folks riding the buses has gone way up. Some just need shelter—somewhere warm or dry for a couple hours. Others, though, bring chaos with them. And that's where it gets tricky. You wanna show compassion, but it's a gamble. You deny them, they might block the bus in the street. They might start bangin' on the windows or even damage the bus. You let them on, you risk having your entire ride thrown into chaos. It's a lose-lose sometimes.

You do your best to keep the peace for yourself and your passengers, but some rides just come with built-in stress. Today could've gone left real quick, but thankfully it didn't. I was also lucky that no one said anything about her taking up all the rear seats. In some neighborhoods, people would've been up front within two stops, complaining like a muthafucka.

I always gotta remind people: I'm a bus driver—not law enforcement, not social services, not mental health support. I'm just here to get everybody from point A to point B in one piece. That alone is a job.

The rest of my day went smooth, and I'm grateful for that.

Wednesday, October 7, 2020

On my last trip heading to West Hollywood, traffic was jammed up at Stocker Street and Crenshaw Boulevard as I rolled northbound. I saw two LAPD officers standing in the middle of the street over someone laid out while paramedics worked on the body. There was blood—a lot of it. It was clear whatever happened was serious. People were pulling over, getting out of their cars, walking up the street and recording like it was a damn show. Other LAPD officers had already set up a barricade on the sidewalk by Louisiana Fried Chicken, keeping the crowd from getting any closer. The whole energy was tense—chaotic but quiet at the same time. That eerie kind of silence that only hits when something real is going down.

By the time I made it closer to King Boulevard, it looked like the person had been involved in a hit-and-run. When I got to the end of the line, I checked the Citizen app on my phone, and sure enough—it said someone had tried to cross the street at the last minute and got hit. The driver didn't stop. Just kept going.

The turning lane was blocked off, so I had to continue north on Crenshaw Boulevard, detouring up 39th Street, cutting over to Marlton, and looping back onto King. A few minutes later, as I headed further down Obama Boulevard, the paramedics passed me. I could see them in the back of the ambulance, vigorously working on the individual they picked up. They were going hard, doing everything they could. But based on all that blood I saw back there in the street... man, I'd be shocked if that person survived.

You really can't trust motorists out here in Los Angeles. Especially if you're jaywalking or trying to cross at the last minute.

When I was in training with the company, one of the first things they drilled into our heads was, "Make sure they see you." Meaning don't just move. Make sure that driver makes eye contact or clearly sees you before you do anything. It could literally be the difference between life and death.

Pedestrians need to move with that same awareness. People out here give zero fucks. They're distracted, texting, driving like the road belongs to them. And then you've got those who are just complete assholes—no sense of caution, no accountability, no regard for human life.

It stuck with me. One second you're just trying to cross the street... and the next, your life's hanging by a thread.

Thursday, October 8, 2020

I had a great day today. Traffic wasn't too bad, passengers were on their best behavior, and for once, it felt like everything was flowing the way it should. As I drove, I caught myself thinking about how thankful I am to have been with this company for eleven years. Eleven years in a seat most people couldn't last one in.

This job is dangerous as fuck. That thought crosses my mind on the regular, but today—since things were calm—I actually had space to sit with it. Reflect on it. I've lost coworkers to strokes, heart attacks, all kinds of health issues tied directly to the stress of this job. And then there are those who didn't make it home because of incidents on duty. (R.I.P. Alan Thomas. That one still hits.)

I think about all that, and then I look at myself—still here, still pushing. I've done pretty damn well to have lasted this long behind the wheel. Trust and believe, I've had things go down on my bus that would make the average person fold on the spot. But somehow, I've been able to maintain. Keep it cool. Keep it moving. People really don't understand what we sacrifice just to keep this city moving. Getting Angelenos from one end of L.A. to the other ain't just about driving—it's about patience, survival, reading people, staying alert, and swallowing stress on the daily. It's not just physical—it's mental, emotional, spiritual. This job will drain you if you let it.

Every year it gets tougher. If things don't change soon, there'll be more operators going out than coming in. And if I were MTA, I'd be doing everything possible to retain the ones still holding it down—because the ones that are here? They're rare gems. They don't make them like that anymore.

I don't want to be here so long that I end up as a picture on the window with a five-gallon water jug underneath for funeral donations. That's a real fear of mine. Lord knows how many times I've walked into a division, seen a familiar badge photo taped to the glass, and a jug sitting next to it—operators signing on and dropping in cash out of love and respect.

That shit stays with you.

I remember when I first started back in 2009, working 12-hour shifts every Saturday and Sunday. Long-ass days behind the wheel. I'd get home and feel like my head was about to explode. It got so bad, I went to the doctor thinking I had some kind of illness. Told them to run every test they had. Everything came back clean. I was a healthy young man. No issues. Come to find out—it was just work-related stress. *Daaaaaaaamn...*

I had never felt anything like that in my life—until I started driving a public transit bus.

Friday, October 9, 2020

Some lady was trying to get on my bus at Hooper while I was heading eastbound on my second trip. I'm thinking to myself, *what the fuck is this bitch wearing?* She was dressed like it was winter, but it was warm as hell today. She stood out like a light pole spray-painted pink—rockin' a tan trench coat, a big-ass tan brimmed hat, and some blue jeans like it was December. As I'm sitting at the red light, she starts banging on the rear door and trying to pry it open with her fingers. I hit her with the cut-throat gesture to let her know that door ain't opening. But she keeps knocking on the window and yelling from outside.

"I need to get to Broadway! I need to get to Broadway!" she yelled, then hit her hips with both hands like she was fed up with the world.

I point westbound to show her where she needs to go. "You need the 105 across the street!" I shouted.

But she thought I was pointing to the rear door and just stood there like I was about to open it. Then she walks up to the front door.

"C'mon man, the store clerk told me this is the bus I need!"

I'm still at the red light, so I grab the mic, flip the switch, and speak through the external speaker.

"Don't listen to the store clerk, listen to me. You need the 105. This is the rapid, ma'am—I do not stop at this stop, and I'm going in the opposite direction. Broadway is back that way. Now who you gonna listen to? A store clerk or an eleven-year bus veteran who was born and raised in the city of L.A.?"

She's still trying to get on the bus like she didn't hear a word I said—just being hard-headed as hell. The light finally turns green, and I hit the gas with authority. She chased the bus for a few steps but gave up once I crossed the intersection. I remember thinking, *ma'am, you ain't catching my bus running—especially with all that bullshit you got on.*

I'm sure she figured it out eventually. I'm off the next two days and I'm looking forward to it.

Monday, October 12, 2020

Today an elderly Jamaican man rode my bus at Broadway. He was visually impaired and clearly frustrated with the service. He had a question for me soon as he boarded.

"Drivah? Drivah? Let me ask you question, mon. Why do 705 take so long, mon? It's like when I'm waiting on 705, I see nothing but 105. Then when I cross the street to catch 105, that's when the 705 comes, man. It's so frustrating and confusing, mon."

"Sir, that's why you pick one bus and stick to it," I replied, smiling from ear to ear.

I didn't have much to say after that—I just let him get it off his chest. Honestly, I felt him. Earlier today, I also found out they're getting rid of the 705 after this upcoming shakeup. Not surprised at all. Running a rapid line down a boulevard that's basically one lane defeats the whole purpose. And besides, I'm tired of people running game—getting on the 705 and asking for local stops like they didn't know damn well they needed the 105 in the first place.

Inside the division parking lot, lines 105, 30, and 705 all share the same layover lane. I always park along the wall near the Pacific Design Center because when it's time to leave, there's always a bus or two blocking me in. I also leave the layover a little late on purpose since I usually end up running early by the time I hit 3rd Street and La Cienega anyway.

While I was standing in the driveway of the Pacific Design Center on my phone, I noticed a road supervisor creeping through the lot, scoping each bus. I've got 20/20 vision, so I spotted him early. He looked down at his onboard computer, then started scanning the yard like he was looking for something specific. He circled once, came back around, cruised the wall—and boom, saw my bus. Dude stopped, reversed, and parked right behind it.

I remember thinking, *what this dude want?*

That's when I decided I couldn't leave the layover late like I usually do. I rolled out on time and ended up killing some time at the La Cienega and Santa Monica stop. Wilshire is a timepoint, and if a supervisor's nearby, I don't feel like getting written up for being early. The westside has its fair share of supervisors who live and die by the book—some of them take the job way too serious.

Then on my second trip, there was this girl who just wouldn't stop asking questions. In the short amount of time she was on the bus, I couldn't even keep up with how many damn things she wanted to know. Some questions were about the city, others got way too personal. Sometimes you just wanna drive your bus in peace. Some conversations you don't mind having, and others you just keep responding with "mmhmm," "yeah," "right," and "okay." I don't mind helping folks get to their destination, but it's irritating when I give you a full itinerary and you still keep asking like I'm a GPS. At one point she even asked me about a street I had never even heard of. I wanted to tell her, *girl, pull out that smartphone and Google your destination.* She got on at Beverly and got off at Wilshire. I was happy as hell when she stepped off. With all those questions, I was about two seconds from telling her to go apply for the FBI.

Tuesday, October 13, 2020

On my third trip coming from West Hollywood, I spotted a woman at the 105 stop moving and dancing like one of those inflatable air dummies at the tire shop. I could see her ass all the way up the block from the light before. Anytime I see a passenger dancing at the bus stop, that shit always raises antennas. That usually means, brace yourself. Me being on the rapid, my stop is across the street—far side of the intersection, near the gas station. But she's flagging me down, standing in the 105 zone like I'm just gonna make a detour. I start thinking, *if I cross this light now, she might have time to run across the street and catch my bus.*

But as I'm creeping closer, it becomes real clear—she's not all there. She's talking to herself, her clothes are filthy, and she's got random pieces of fabric and debris tangled in her hair. Delusional vibe all the way. Now the last thing I want is her darting through traffic to try and catch my bus. So I do what any operator would do—I coast. Real slow. Dead throttle, inching toward Pico Boulevard like I got nowhere to be. Soon as the light turned yellow, I floored it. Crossed that intersection thinking I made the clean getaway. I start servicing the far-side stop... then I check the rearview mirror.

Welp.

Guess who ran her ass across a red light of active traffic, damn near getting clipped from both directions—just to make it to the bus?

Her.

And to top it off, the rear door on my bus wanted to act brand new. Took so damn long to close that she managed to stick her arm in right before it shut. All that slick maneuvering I did? Wasted.

Soon as she got on, she started talking to herself loud as hell. Every now and then she'd burst out yelling random shit, just outta nowhere. I was praying to every bus-driving angel that she wouldn't ride all the way to the end of the line. But thankfully, she got off in the Jungles—Coliseum and King Boulevard. Praise be.

All I could do was laugh. Sometimes, you'll go out of your way, pull all the tricks, think you've done everything right to avoid picking up *that one* rider... and they still find a way to get on.

Friday, October 16, 2020

Another day, another person riding the rapid when they needed a local.

A dude gets on my bus at Crenshaw Boulevard with his girlfriend—knowing good and damn well he needs the 105. I pull into the zone and open the doors. She gets on first, no questions asked, and he's outside loading his bike onto the rack like it's just another normal day. They come in, sit near the rear door like they're getting cozy for the ride. Now anybody who rides regularly knows the 105 cuts through the Jungles, turning left at Marlton. Meanwhile, the 705? Straight down King—no detours, no local stops. That's just the route. It's been that way.

We keep rollin' and I approach Marlton, and the second I pass it, this dude hops up like he just realized the damn bus was heading to Vegas.

He speed-walks to the front, looking stressed out.

"Aye man, aye man, what the fuck!? You ain't the 105!?"

"Naw, homie. I'm the rapid," I tell him, straight-faced, already tired.

Now he's standing near the farebox, borderline panicking.

"Man, let me off dawg—I needed the local bus!"

I'm just shaking my head at this point. I've had enough. I'm exhausted with folks hopping on this bus and acting brand new—like they just woke up in another dimension.

"I don't stop again until Coliseum," I say, keeping my voice even.

He throws his hands up like I'm doing him dirty.

"C'mon man, I need to get off!" he keeps pushing.

As I'm approaching Buckingham Road, I figure I'll entertain a little curiosity.

"Say man... how you didn't know what bus you was getting on?"

And of course, the answer every operator hears at least ten times a week. "My bad, man. I just didn't know."

Bruh... bullshit.

I didn't even respond. At this point, I'm numb to the excuses. I've heard them all. Folks will hop on anything with wheels and a Metro logo and then blame the driver when they end up in the wrong place. But I don't like holding folks hostage—especially when they're already frustrated. I'll help if I can do it safe. I make a stop at the red light on Buckingham and let him and his girl off. I'm watching him walk away and thinking, *this could've been avoided if you just read the damn sign.*

People out here want full-time Uber service on a public transit schedule. They act like we're supposed to read minds, change routes on the fly, and drop them off wherever they feel like getting off. It don't work like that. And truth be told, I'm burnt out. I'm tired of the confusion, the entitlement, the unnecessary arguments that drain your spirit more than the traffic ever could. It's like we clock in not knowing what kind of energy we're about to deal with. Happy riders, angry riders, confused riders, dangerous riders. Spin the wheel and pray.

Sometimes I don't even trip on the nonsense itself—I trip on how normal it's become. That's the part that messes with your head. The fact that dealing with entitled or reckless behavior feels routine. Just another shift in L.A.

Man... I need this weekend to come through bad. I've been running on fumes all week—mentally and physically. Just wanna post up somewhere with no requests, no routes, no damn bus numbers. Just peace.

Monday, October 19, 2020

On my first trip coming from Santa Fe, some bullshit popped off at Pico Boulevard and La Cienega. There was this Michael Blackson-looking-ass nigga at the corner, trying to climb onto the top of the bus using the rear right tire. I'm approaching the light and see him pacing on the southeast corner like he's about to breakdance on a piece of cardboard. He for sure was off something.

I watch him walk up to the back side of the bus, then I see him plant his foot into the space between the top tire and the fender and reach his right arm up toward the top of the bus. I'm looking in my rearview like Steve Harvey after a dumbass answer on *Family Feud*.

Is this nigga trying to climb up on my bus? I thought.

Sure enough, he was. I laid on the horn and started waving him off. He still was trying to climb up. I begin moving the bus at dead throttle, just creeping forward, and he steps back down onto the sidewalk. But the second I came to a complete stop, he tries climbing back up again. Man, I kept that bus rollin' real slow—easing into the intersection on a red light just to keep him off. Once the light turned green, I floored it and serviced the stop on the far side. I was waiting on him to run across the street and try some more dumb shit, but luckily, he stayed put. Thank you, Lord.

Another thing that bothered me today—people not knowing light cycles. What do I mean by that? Right at Beverly Boulevard on the same trip heading to West Hollywood, I was making a left turn. This car in front of me just sat there the whole damn time *after* the green arrow had gone off. I was completely perplexed. *Why in the fuck didn't she turn?*

This intersection allows you to make a regular left turn after the green arrow—as long as you yield. But some people think if the arrow disappears, that means they have to sit and wait for it to come back. Naw. If there's no red arrow prohibiting you from turning, take your ass through the light! That kind of cluelessness grinds my gears—and I deal with it at least twice a day, depending on where I'm at in the city.

Then when I got to the layover at the division, I stepped onto the bus floor and saw Starburst wrappers *everywhere*—all over the front portion of the floor. I was mad as fuck. Come to think of it, it was from a guy who got on at La Brea Aveneu and Obama, Boulevard He ran for the bus earlier with his so-called "service dog." Boy, was I pissed. He had to go through at least three packs of Starburst, judging by how many damn wrappers were on the ground.

I remember thinking, *Next time I see that muthafucka, I'm passing him up.*

Damn, how hard is it to throw your trash away? If you're gonna eat on the bus, at least be decent enough to clean up after yourself. Almost every stop in this city got a trash can. Ain't no excuse for that. Most bus stops have a trash can near it.

Tuesday, October 20, 2020

Random thought today.

I often wonder if my job environment is playing a role in me not progressing to the next step in life—or at least the next step as far as success goes. What do I mean by this?

Driving in the city of L.A. and being a public transit bus operator, I'm surrounded by a lot of negativity. Now don't get me wrong—there are amazing individuals in this city who ride public transportation, people just trying to get to and from, and there are moments of beauty too. But the negativity? It often feels like it outweighs the good. Sometimes I feel like I'm constantly around people who don't aspire to do better, or worse, they're fully aware they want more out of life—but they're too worn down, too complacent, or too discouraged to chase it.

Am I wrong for saying this?

Could this be holding me back?

ESSENTIAL: Diary of a Public Transit Bus Operator Volume 1

Every day behind this wheel, someone unloads their frustration onto you. And if they're not taking it out on you, they're unloading it onto another passenger. You absorb that energy whether you want to or not. And when I look out the window, it's more of the same—constant drug use, tents up and down the boulevards, people strung out or suffering in plain sight.

When I was growing up, I don't remember homelessness and mental illness being this extreme. I know it's always been around. It's heartbreaking. And the worst part is, it starts to feel normal. That's the part that messes with your head. Being surrounded by that kind of struggle on a daily basis—it wears you down in ways you don't even notice until you sit and reflect.

Even the division I'm out of plays a part. I can't speak for everyone, but I'm surrounded by folks who want to do more but have stopped trying—caught in the comfort and stability of a paycheck. For me, one of the main reasons I've stayed a part-time operator all these years is to maintain a consistent schedule and pursue other endeavors. Contractually, I have security in the assignments I choose. As a full-time operator, that security disappears. One person with higher seniority can bump you, and that ripple effect impacts not just you but the whole division—and sometimes the whole system.

It always shocks my full-time coworkers when they see part-timers not working excessive hours just to stay afloat. Some look at you like you're crazy. Some straight up told me I was making a bad decision. I used to care. I really did. But now? Eleven years in? I don't give a shit anymore.

It appears as if this occupation has tricked people into thinking this is the best or the only thing they can do in their lives. That this is as far as they can go. But any job I've ever taken, I've taken with the sole purpose of keeping a roof over my head. Nothing more, nothing less. Because I've always understood—any job can be taken from you. I treat this one no different.

People love to remind me of "how much money" I'm missing out on or the money that they make. But deep down, I still aspire to do more. With all that being said…

Could this environment be holding me back from the true progression I seek? Time will tell

Wednesday, October 21, 2020

Today I feel bad for not requesting my wife's birthday off—which is tomorrow. Before I left for work this morning, she expressed her frustrations about it, and I completely understood where she was coming from. I just wish I had handled it better.

Working here, it feels like I've got a ton of limitations, and one of the biggest is getting days off. Now don't get me wrong—most of the time, I do get the days I ask for. But there have definitely been times where I didn't get everything I requested. With the way manpower is right now, it's been harder than usual for any of us to take time off. I try to be understanding of that, but at the same time, I feel like I'm selling myself short when it comes to doing the things I want to do for my family.

I just want to get to a place in my life where I don't have to stress about whether or not my job will let me take a day off—especially when it comes to important moments with my loved ones. Sure, I could take a sick day... but I've used quite a few already. And truth be told, I don't know how many more I've got left before it starts affecting my record or bringing on disciplinary action.

I pray for the day when someone invites me to a family gathering or celebration and I don't have to pause, check my schedule, or plan around it just because my job is holding me back. These are some of the many things we deal with as bus operators working for MTA.

As far as my wife goes, I'll find a way to make it up to her.

Thursday, October 22, 2020

Today was my wife's birthday. I wanted to schedule the day off, but I already took quite a few days earlier in the year—and I forgot to mention she wants us to have our anniversary off too. I'm trying to plan the days out right so I can at least lock that one in.

On my first trip, I picked up a lady and her son at Broadway. Her son had a noisemaker—it sounded like one of those rubber chickens kids used to play with back in the day. That shit was LOOOOUD. I wanted to walk back to where they were sitting, snatch that thing out of his hand, and toss it out the window.

When you're driving a bus, you don't just need to see—you need to be able to hear, too. Passengers tend to take that for granted. I don't mind kids playing and going about their day, but damn—I need to be able to hear what's going on around me. Some toys just need to stay at home.

Still on that same trip, I had a guy get on who wanted to get off at 43rd and Crenshaw. Only thing is, I'm not a local bus—he needed the 105.

"Driver, do you stop at McDonald's?" he asked.

"Nah bruh, I don't stop there," I replied.

"C'mon, man—look out for your boy," he said, throwing his hands up.

"Nah, you need the 105, my dude."

I picked him up at Broadway. He ran from the 105 stop near Tacos El Gavilán across the street just to catch my bus. Me being the inquisitive person I am, I threw him a question.

"Man, why you run across the street to catch my bus, dawg? The 105 was right down the block."

"Shit, I didn't see it," he replied.

Passengers always hit you with that *I didn't see it* line. The 105 was literally fifteen cars behind me before the intersection. I advised him to get off and wait for the bus he actually needed—but nah, he wasn't trying to hear that.

I kept heading down Vernon, finally got to Crenshaw, serviced the stop, and made a right turn onto Crenshaw Boulevard.

"C'mon, man—please let me off at 43rd," he begged.

I didn't pay him no mind and took his ass all the way to King Boulevard. I heard him kissing his teeth and throwing shade with his body language, but I didn't give a fuck about none of that.

I tell people all the time—pick one bus and stick to it.

Friday, October 23, 2020

Some funny shit Today.

On the trip before my last heading eastbound on Vernon Ave, I kept hearing a loud air sound coming from the rear door. I figured it could possibly be a mechanical failure—or even worse, a busted tire. I heard this sound from Figueroa all the way until I got to Central Ave. My bus was a little more crowded than usual, with a grip of people occupying the rear door area. I hit the parking brake, walked to the back door from the outside of the bus, inspecting the whole area from top to bottom. But I didn't see or hear the sound anymore.

"Did you guys hear an air sound coming from back here?" I asked one of the passengers.

A few of the passengers looked confused by what I was asking. Then one dude standing near the door spoke up.

"There was a dude standing in the doorway inhaling keyboard cleaner," he said.

I paused. I mean, I had to really take in what dude just said. I'm looking at him like I was staring at an alien explaining taxes.

"Inhaling whaaat?" I asked.

"Keyboard air. The shit you use to clean dust off electronics n shit," he replied.

I threw my hands up in the air like I just found something I'd been looking for all day—but I was laughing at the same time. I walked back to my seat and continued in service. Truth be told, I'm not surprised. Some stores even have that shit locked up now. I wasn't too aware of it being used to get high until I encountered one of my neighbors walking down the street, inhaling it like it was oxygen. Every now and then, you'll see an empty can of keyboard cleaner laying around the city—usually near a homeless encampment.

On the same trip, when I got to Santa Fe, the BNSF train held me up for fifteen minutes and I had to take a piss BADLY. My bladder was about to explode, but I made it through after they retracted back into the layover zone, allowing traffic to pass. THANK GOD! I ran into the restroom and gave myself to the Lord.

My last trip was smooth. I forgot to mention—today was my last day on Vernon Ave before I move to my new assignment next week. I don't plan to drive a bus back down Vernon ever again.

Monday, October 26, 2020

Today was my first day back on the 35/38 Line in two years. I've worked this line twice before—back in 2016 and again in 2018. The last time I did it in 2016, I had a wild-ass situation pop off on the 35 at Grand, heading westbound near the train station. Some knuckleheads tried to stab a dude over a dice game. Long story, I'll probably share that one later. Then in 2018, I had a couple accusing me of keeping their immigration paperwork after they lost it on the bus. Their paperwork went missing on a different run from the week before—but they still blamed me and held up service behind it. Shit was insane, man... two Hispanic folks, looked like they were in their late 50s. I'll share that one later too. It was some crazy-ass shit.

Only thing I hate about being back on this line is the short-ass layovers. At most, you get like eleven minutes. Just enough time to take a piss and wash your hands. That's one of the downsides of being a public transit operator—half the time you don't even have time to eat. The only ones who really get a "break" are the operators with split assignments in between shifts.

On my first trip layover after running the 35 up Washington, some old dude rolled up on me outta nowhere inside the layover on his bike, holding a can of 211. I saw him at the last stop sitting down—it was like he teleported to the front of my bus. Shit caught me off guard. I pull the bus in, and as I'm locking the front door, he rolls up on me.

"Aye man, you can't just be rolling up on niggas like that, man. What the hell wrong with you? You can't be inside this layover, dawg."

He's breathing hard, trying to catch his breath.

"I'm sorry, G. My bad, man. I'm just trying to figure my way home," he said.

He was low-key staggering, could barely keep his balance, and reeked of alcohol. I forgot to mention—his speech was slurred as hell.

"Where you trying to get to?" I asked.

"I'm tryna get to La Brea, sir."

"You just want to get to La Brea Avenue, or is there a specific boulevard you need to connect to?"

"I just want to get to La Brea."

I let him know he could catch the 35, 37, or 38—they all go to La Brea. He hopped back on his bike and rode out of the West L.A. Transit layover. Him being drunk and on a bike, I'm just glad he didn't get hit by one of the buses pulling in. He ended up back at the stop he originally came from, waiting to catch the 37 going up Adams.

The day kept rollin' smooth—until my second-to-last trip. My stomach started pop-locking like I ate something bad. It felt like I had to drop a serious deuce. Then, of course, a homeless woman with a walker gets on the bus... and she was taking FOREVER!

Time is of the essence when you gotta take a shit.

Her taking so long had me sweating like a dog. She got on at Normandie Avenue and got off at Western. Boy, was I scared—I didn't think I was going to make it. The boulevard was pretty light afterward, thank the Lord. By the grace of God, I made it to the layover just in time to handle my business.

Tuesday, October 27, 2020

Today I got mad as hell at this dude on crutches who smacked the back window of my bus like he was trying to break in.

This happened on my first trip. I was pulling into the zone at Grand while doing Line 35 right near the train station, with a DASH bus already stopped in front of me. I didn't think much of it—I just pulled in behind it, opened the doors, and started picking up passengers. Dude was walking up on crutches, but I had no idea he was trying to catch my bus. No eye contact, no wave, nothing that told me he was tryna board. So after the DASH pulled off, I went into dead throttle and started to pull off.

Then—BANG.

Something slammed into the back window, loud as fuck. So loud I damn near jumped out the seat. I thought the window broke or the bus hit something. That's how hard it sounded. I hit the parking brake and pulled back over, heart damn near pounding. I check the mirror and it's the guy with the crutches. I was HEATED.

I cracked the front door open and waited for him to get on. As soon as he stepped up, I let him have it.

"Damn man, what the fuck is you doing, dude!? Shit—you gone fuck around and break the damn window, man! Last thing I need is to be filling out a punk-ass accident report!"

He looked shook. Embarrassed, like he knew he messed up. His whole energy shifted.

"I'll wait for the next one. It's quite evident that I pissed you off. My bad, bro."

I took a breath.

"C'mon man, you can get on the bus. Just don't be hitting the window like that, my dawg."

He got on, still apologizing, and I could tell it was genuine. I let him know real calm that when it comes to catching a bus, it's all about body language.

"If you see a bus coming and you need it, just throw your hand up—let the driver know you're trying to board. Especially since you on crutches. I ain't expecting you to run, but at least give me something."

We both apologized. Squashed it. Kept it moving.

Shit, the last thing I want is to spend an extra hour after work writing up an incident report over something that could've been avoided. I got enough stress on this job—don't need no busted window adding to it.

This job will have you doing mental gymnastics on the daily. One second you're pissed, the next you're trying to explain something calmly to the same person who just had you ready to snap. It's a constant back and forth between reacting and restraining. That emotional flip-flop wears on you after a while—but that's the reality of driving in this city.

Friday, October 30, 2020

I'm back from taking two sick days off—straight. I needed it.

Today on my second trip, the biggest drop of bird shit hit my window going eastbound on Jefferson Boulevard. Looked like someone grabbed a serving spoon and dropped mayonnaise mixed with peanut butter. I don't know what the fuck these birds be eating to be dropping massive loads the way they do—especially these gangster-ass seagulls. Our division parking lot in West Hollywood is riddled with them after a certain time. I tried using the windshield wipers with fluid, but all it did was smear the mess across the glass and made visibility even worse. I was so thankful when I got to the layover. I proceeded to wash it off with paper towels and soap.

Still on that second trip heading down Jefferson, I got to 10th Ave and saw this dude bullshitting at the stop, looking at his phone. I pull into the zone, open the doors, and I'm looking in the mirror waiting on him—but he's just standing there being indecisive, still looking at his screen. After a few seconds, I closed the doors and pulled off. He throws his hands up like he's mad.

Like—dawg, ain't nobody got time to be figuring out if you want the damn bus. Either you want this muthafucka or you don't!

On my third trip, I was dropping off passengers at Vermont. As I'm sitting at the stop, some young dude comes rolling up on his fixie bike. I hate when I'm ready to roll out and here comes someone pedaling up last second. When I got to the end of the line at Broadway and Venice and switched to the 35 to continue westbound on Washington, I noticed him walking up toward the front of the bus.

It's a red light facing Venice northbound—I had just dropped off the passengers from the 38 and picked up the ones trying to head west.

"You don't go downtown?" he asked.

"Naw, dog. What was you doing? I called last stop," I replied.

"My bad, bro—I need to get off," he said.

I was heated. I called out last stop before continuing in service, and homie wasn't paying attention. I make it a point to call it because people assume I'm heading deeper into downtown—but I'm not. That's one of the curses of these damn phones, folks not being aware of their surroundings.

I wanted to press him and ask what the fuck he was doing, but from the looks of it, he was watching a YouTube video—so I let it go. I pulled the bus back over before crossing the intersection and let him off.

I wish people would pay the fuck attention!

The rest of the night went smooth. Had a few crazies, but that ain't nothing new—especially on a Friday night. I'm thankful I don't have to work Halloween, and with the coronavirus, can't nobody do shit anyway.

Tuesday, November 3, 2020

Nothing major went on yesterday—it was a pretty smooth day overall. One thing that fucked me up though, was when I was driving down Washington on my second-to-last trip, I saw this homeless dude just casually walking down the street while urinating. I mean, this man was just going about his day like there was absolutely nothing wrong with what he was doing. And the wild part? People were just walking by like that shit was normal. This is what the city has come to—an outdoor toilet. From downtown to the Westside of L.A., I've seen people urinate and defecate on sidewalks like it's just another part of city life.

I remember when people had the decency to find a restroom or, at the very least, somewhere discreet. Not no more. These days, folks will drop their pants right in the middle of the sidewalk without a second thought. The tent dwellers will even dump their sanitation buckets straight into the gutter. With as many people pissin' and shittin' on city streets freely, I'm surprised the jails ain't overcrowded with those who have been charged with indecent exposure.

Now today, my wife was worried about me going to work because it was Election Day. With the energy around everything, and the way the news media hyped it, it felt like something was bound to pop off—riots, protests, full-blown anarchy. But surprisingly, the day was real smooth. Nobody was actin' crazy, passengers were on their best behavior, and the energy wasn't anything like I expected. A handful of businesses downtown had their windows boarded up, but that was about it.

Only thing that really caught me off guard was seeing a lot of Hispanic men driving trucks through downtown waving *Trump 2020* flags. That threw me. But then again, when I used to drive Line 33 down Venice Boulevard back when he first got elected, there were already tons of supporters in that area, so I shouldn't be surprised.

I drove the whole day with no issues—low traffic, not too many passengers. It honestly felt like a major holiday out there. Hell, I'll take that. We'll see what the energy feels like in the days to come.

Thursday, November 5, 2020

On my second trip yesterday, heading down to Washington and Fairfax on the 35, I picked up this dude near the McDonald's—and right as I'm pulling into the zone, I catch him downing a tall can of 211 malt liquor with the quickness. All I could think was, *"Ooooh shit."* I was concerned about him causing a ruckus, but he ended up just crashing out. When I got to the end of the line, I couldn't even wake his ass up. That trip had a few delays, so I didn't have much layover time when I pulled into the West L.A. Transit Center. I hit the parking brake and walked to the back. Homie was slouched in the rear seats, door side, knocked the hell out.

I tried tapping the windows, panels, even kicked his shoe. Nothing. The 211 knocked him into another dimension. Since I didn't have time to deal with it, I pulled the bus through the layover and parked it over where the 780 makes its last drop at Electric Ave. Ran to the restroom, came back—and he was still in the same damn spot. So I kept it pushing.

Went on and did the next trip, lines 38 and 35. Came back to the layover again, same story—dude still sleep. I didn't feel like fighting that battle, so I repeated the same routine. Finally, on my last trip, he woke up and got off somewhere before Western. I let him sleep... fuck it.

Now today, I made relief, and the operator I was relieving let me know the A/C wasn't working.

Lord have mercy...

I don't know about anybody else, but I'm courteous as hell when I'm handing off a bus. If I've got an issue, especially something like the A/C, I'll do my best to get a new one before the next operator hops on. I learned that lesson early on back when I used to do Line 2. There was this one operator who would let me *have it* every time there was even the smallest issue with the coach I handed over. He was picky—but honestly, it taught me a lot. So first thing I did was call BOC to request a coach change. By the time I got back to the layover at Washington/Fairfax, a mechanic had already pulled up—within four minutes too. Beautiful timing. I swapped buses, and the A/C on the new one? Blowing like a dream. I gotta be comfortable when I'm behind the wheel, especially once passengers start piling on and the body heat gets going.

Later in the day, I saw someone I hadn't seen in years. Dude used to hang around when I worked as a cart attendant at the Target on La Cienega and Obama (back when it was still Rodeo Road). He'd be out in the lot joking with us just to kill time. I remember he got mad once 'cause we called him Ethiopian, but he corrected us—said he was West Indian. Back then, he looked like a king. Seriously. Real tall, healthy, full head of hair, perfect teeth, carried himself like royalty. Fast-forward to today, and I see him in a wheelchair with gray hair and teeth cracked and missing. He looked completely broken. I picked him up at Crenshaw and Jefferson—he was mad because the driver in front of me passed him up. Don't get me wrong—I remember he used to be a bit much. But damn... seeing him like that? That shit hit me hard. I remember how vibrant he used to be. But I guess after all the drug use over the years, that vibrancy has worn away, leaving only a faded version of who he was.

Same trip, going westbound on the 35 near Union Avenue, I pull into the zone and spot a dude doing all kinds of crackhead gymnastics—dancing, twitching, putting on a whole show. But a few feet away, I notice another guy slouched against the wall of an abandoned business, completely motionless. The first dude starts trying to wake him up.

I'm about to close the door, ready to pull off, when the twitchy one runs up.

"Hey man, you need to call an ambulance—he won't wake up," he said.

I panicked for a second but snapped out of it quick. I looked at him suspiciously.

"He might just be high. Is his body cold or anything? Did you check his pulse?" I asked.

"No, not at all. He's breathing," he said.

"Well, he'll be alright. He's probably drunk, high, or just tired and needs rest," I said, throwing my hands up like, *whatever*, and kept it moving.

I remember thinking, *how do I not know that you gave him some shit he couldn't handle?*

Next trip coming back—dude was gone.

I don't mean to sound insensitive, but I can't save everybody. I'm just one man. All I can do is pray that folks get better as the days go.

Friday November 6, 2020

Approaching Fridays feel like a milestone, but there are times where I feel like the universe makes me work real hard before my off days.

Today on my first trip heading eastbound on Washington at the light on Vermont, a young girl came begging me to let her off so she can catch her bus.

"Please sir, please let me off here, I need to catch my bus," she demands as she's pointing toward the front door.

I look up and down the block to see if a bus is coming in any direction and I don't see one.

"There's no bus coming, ma'am," I expressed.

She forms the prayer hands and her body language is that of an impatient kid waiting for a candy store to open.

"Please, please, I need to catch this bus—please let me off here!" she begged.

As much as I don't like letting people off in the middle of the street, I also don't like holding people hostage. I don't underestimate anybody out here on these buses. I cracked the rear door open and let her off. She didn't even say thank you —not that I was expecting her to, but me not being in the zone and taking a huge risk to let her ass off in the street... it's the least she coulda done. She ran across to the farside of the intersection and gave a fist pump of victory as the 204 pulled up heading southbound. Well, wherever she was headed I pray she made it there in a timely and safe fashion.

On my second trip when I got to the 35 side, this guy waited 'til the last minute to get off the bus at Cimarron and Washington heading westbound. I had just dropped off two people and as the door is closing, he decides to get his ass up yelling at the top of his lungs. The shit startled me.

"Hey, my stop! I'm getting off! This my stop!" he yelled.

All I could do was shake my head and take a deep-ass breath due to the sheer frustration of his bullshit.

"Dude, what the hell was you doing, bro?" I asked.

I reopened the rear door and he jumped off. Nine times outta ten, it's that damn phone distracting folks.

Then on that same trip, this lady takes it upon herself to walk up to the front of the bus while everyone else is exiting through the rear door at Arlington. It was only about four people getting off, I was pulled perfectly to the curb, everything in order. But she walks up to the front.

"Front door, please," she requested.

"Ma'am, what makes you so special that you couldn't get off the back door like everyone else?" I asked.

She hits me with a line I wasn't expecting.

"I wanted to see you, handsome."

I gave her the Ed Lover *c'mon son* face but cracked the front door open at the same time.

"Yea okay ma'am, I'll take it today—much appreciated," I said.

All I could think to myself was, *well played woman, well played.*

On my last trip, people kept jumping out in the street flagging me down along Jefferson Boulevard. I hate that shit. Like c'mon man, I'm not blind. They flagging the bus down like you're visually impaired and can't see them. Shit is annoying. *Must be a lotta blind bus operators out here,* I sarcastically thought.

On that same trip, I picked up a guy at Washington and Flower heading westbound. I've seen him before as he has rode my bus more than a dozen times. He got on and sat midsection, driver side. When I approached Union he had a question.

"Hey, is this Arlington?"

"Naw, not yet," I answered.

I get to Hoover and start servicing the stop. I was driving a New Flyer Xcelsior and the rear doors take for fuckin' ever to close. While the rear door is closing, he jumps up at the last minute trying to get off and ends up getting caught in it.

"LET ME OFF, YOU BITCH ASS NIGGA!" he yelled.

I was puzzled. I've been nothing but respectful to this dude. I've waited on him in the past when he's been running. I would have considered him to be a regular customer. And to hear him distribute that form of disrespect? Of course I felt some type of way.

As he's walking by I still apologized to him. Him getting caught in the door wasn't intentional and I didn't want no bad blood between us in the future just in case he rode again.

"My bad bro bro—you didn't have to come at me like that. It wasn't intentional," I said.

He stands a few feet away from the front door—maybe that was a bad idea because now he had more negative shit to say.

"What you gone do about it, bitch ass nigga?" he said.

I looked at him a bit confused. Surprised... but not surprised.

"I'm not trying to beef with you, sir," I said.

"Either you gone get off the bus and fight, or you gone talk shit and call the police like the rest of these bitch ass bus drivers do," he exclaimed.

I made the face of a cartoon villain plotting his next move. I had a fire burning inside me wanting to fuck this dude up for how he came at me.

"Daaaaaamn... that's how you feel bro?" I asked.

"If you ain't gone do shit then shut the fuck up," he replied.

I almost fucked around and hit the parking brake on his bitch ass. I had to take a few breaths to calm down. I really wanted to catch hands with this dude. He crossed the street, walked through the gas station parking lot and continued north on Hoover.

I should've known his priorities was fucked up when he had a clean pair of Jordan 11 Concords but the rest of his clothes looked like he rolled through the dirtiest alley in L.A. Picture a bum-ass version of Rick Gonzalez from *Coach Carter*—that's exactly who he looked like.

The disrespect that dude displayed was so sour that if I see him at a stop in the future, I'm passing him up and everyone else. Every now and then, we get cussed out by somebody—it comes with the territory—but I wish there was a system that banned muthafuckas like him from riding until they made right on their wrong.

Too many people out here are comfortable disrespecting bus operators because they know nothing is gonna happen to them. It's like the uniform protects them. It took every ounce of strength not to beat his ass into clean clothes... but then again, cats like him ain't got shit to lose so it would be wise to not even entertain the bullshit.

I just pray I don't see him anytime soon.

Fuckin' asshole...

ESSENTIAL: Diary of a Public Transit Bus Operator Volume 1

Monday, November 9, 2020

Today the weather was much colder—it was so nippy outside I almost broke out my sweater. Traffic was heavy as hell today for a Monday, especially coming out of downtown. This supposed to still be a pandemic and it's a grip of damn people out here. Somebody please make it make sense.

Something else I gotta get off my chest—there was a guy on the 38 who got on at Crenshaw going eastbound with a big-ass travel bag. Sometimes I be wondering *did I just pick up somebody with a dead body in that thing?* There's an abundance of folks riding with these oversized bags, and outside of the homeless, I'm starting to ask what the fuck do they got in there? They can barely roll 'em on or off the damn bus. A few years back, somebody on the Gold Line really did have a dead body in their bag. I wouldn't even be surprised at this point if someone rolled up on my line with something "unknown."

My day was cool—until I got into it with a road supervisor on my last trip.

I was running ten minutes late pulling into the West L.A. Transit Hub. My next trip was my last, and I didn't have time to layover because of how heavy traffic was. I was gonna just continue in service, but I made a last-minute decision to hit the restroom. I drove through the layover and parked outside, where Line 780 makes its last drop-off on Electric Avenue. Hazards on. Bus parked. I ran inside, wasn't even in there two minutes. As I'm walking back out, drying my hands, I spot a road supervisor parked in the northwest corner of the lot. It was dark, so I hadn't even noticed him before.

I got back to my bus from the breakroom where the restroom resides. I opened the front door from the driver-side window and walked around to the entrance. I stepped inside, hopped into the driver's seat, and threw on my seat belt before covering the service brake, releasing the parking brake, and easing into a dead throttle.

Then—BANG!

A loud-ass knock hits the right side of the bus. Scared the shit outta me.

I pull back into the zone thinking I done hit some shit, check the mirror—and yep, it's the supervisor from the corner. I'm thinking *damn, he must've ran over here. Ain't no way he walked from his car that fast.*

He gets to the front door. I crack it open.

"Man what's wrong with you, dude? It's dark as hell over here and I can't see shit. Why would you do that?" I snapped.

"You mind telling me why you're laying over right here?" he asked.

"It was a last-minute decision to use the restroom. My apologies," I said.

Didn't expect him to be on the bullshit he was on after that.

"So you mean to tell me, instead of parking inside, you decided to layover here?"

I kept it cool, but my annoyance was beginning to show.

"Sir, I didn't have time to layover. I was gonna continue in service but made a last-minute decision to use the restroom. My bad."

Despite my response, he kept pressing the issue.

"I'm trying to grasp why you parked here?"

Bruh looked like Van Pelt from *Jumanji*. Energy all off—like a plantation overseer catching somebody outside the field. Yeah, I went there.

He continued, "Why didn't you park inside the layover, Operator?"

Now my blood's starting to boil. It's clear as day he just came over to fuck with me.

"See, now you harassing me, sir," I shot back.

"Harassing? I'm not harassing you," he scoffed.

I shook my head with the straightest face known to man.

"You and that other supervisor in Hollywood are always harassing operators. Why is that, man?" I demanded.

He went quiet for a few seconds. I honestly couldn't believe that this shit was happening.

"I sense an attitude coming from you," he said.

"You got damn I got an attitude—because you're holding up service to ask me a question I already answered. If you don't got anything else to say, please let me go. People are waiting on me."

I started to close the door, and he sticks his right foot in it.

"Hold on, Operator. There's no rush. If it's Metro-related, I can hold up service as long as I want to."

Now I'm fully over it, but I'm still with all the smoke. I was thinking to myself *is this muthafucka serious right now?*

"Sir, if you're not gonna give me a write-up, let me get going. Hell, if what I did bothers you that fuckin' much, take me out of service so I can go home to my wife."

Now he's giving me the Stone Cold Steve Austin death stare. I'm staring back trying to burn his soul with the facial expression I was distributing.

"I'm not going to write you up," he said.

I cut him off before he could finish the rest of what he was saying.

"At this point I don't give a damn what you do—you already had motive before you came over here."

"You sure about that?" he asked.

He keeps trying to talk, and I just kept pointing at the bus radio like a play-by-play announcer.

"You holding up service. You holding up service. You holding up service."

I could tell that got under his skin, and he finally gave up afterwards.

"Bus 5804, badge 76454—you got it," he muttered, storming off back to his vehicle.

This company constantly fails to address the continuous stupid shit that some managers and Transit Operations Supervisors hit us with—and it plays a major role as to why we have a lack of manpower systemwide. What he did was totally unnecessary. It's a straight-up abuse of authority.

These are the type of folks who are habitual line-steppers. Some operators would've gone straight sick for the rest of the week behind that bullshit. Others? Stress leave. Easy.

What really pisses me off is you got operators out here passing up passengers, riding around with "Not in Service" on the sign while they're in service, violating hella rules—but these fools would rather mess with the ones out here actually doing the job. Damn, all I did was run to the restroom. What the fuck man? I didn't feel like going through the fuckin' notion of throwing on my hazards, tapping my horn and backing up a bus—I just wanted to jump into the muthafucka and keep it moving.

Somebody make it make sense please. I'm just over all this bullshit.

Tuesday, November 10, 2020

Today was much better than the day before. I guess I'll keep a lookout for an upcoming write-up. I ain't gone front, I'm still in my feelings from the day before. I'm tired of these damn jobs with people who abuse the shit out of their authority. I don't know why companies won't address this shit—it is not conducive to daily operations.

The supervisor from the day before is just one of many of them who think they are God out here in these streets. I refuse to believe some of them used to be operators—man, some of them be out here treating us like shit. Ain't no way. I should've took a sick day today because I honestly didn't feel like working. I don't feel "essential" at this moment in time.

It seems like some of those above us don't take any accountability for any wrongdoings, and I feel that's one of many reasons there is a lack of bus operators. It's funny that Metro stay giving classes to bus operators in order to protect themselves from any liabilities—but hell, do they give any classes to those who hold positions above bus operators on how to be a proper human beings to those below them? If they do I wouldn't be able to tell.

This here is one of many reasons why I got one foot in and one foot out. This is an issue with plenty of jobs—hell, even my last two jobs I've dealt with the same shit involving superiors. What is the psychology behind those with higher positions treating those below them like peasants? I'm sure this is a rhetorical question. Something is going to have to give.

All day today I seen some clowns juggling bowling pins in traffic at the intersection of Washington Boulevard and Normandie Avenue. Every time I got to this intersection, I stared at these guys thinking about my personal life. That's what my life feels like right now. I'm an employee juggling between staying an employee with this company that really don't give a fuck about me and moving on and pursuing something different in my life.

At times, I feel like a spouse who's staying in an abusive relationship.

Thursday, November 12, 2020

How could I forget to give a shout out to all the veterans? Yesterday was Veterans Day, right? Every year at our division there is a board that has pictures and shows appreciation to bus operators who served in the military. You never know how many people served this country.

I've been told by a handful of other vets who have ridden my bus throughout the years that those who panhandle are drug users making excuses. Whatever the case is, you should have a home, and you should have enough money coming in monthly to sustain a very nice living until your dying days. I feel this should be equal across the board for all vets—but hey, I'm no politician or anyone of that nature. Hell, what do I know?

I had a great day on the bus side of things, just wanted to get that off my chest. Today was a day of people being all up in the damn layover. On my first layover there was a guy walking around in the layover and he almost got backed into. I had to blow my horn to inform the operator of the bus he was behind to stop. He hit the brakes, saw the guy in his mirror view, and gave me a thanks wave. The passenger had a question but came into the layover to ask—passengers are not allowed in layovers.

Then prior to my last trip, there was a dude pacing back and forth going from bus to bus. He looked real suspicious and it raised my antennas. I had a pocket knife in my left front shirt pocket and I saw him approaching the operator who was doing the 780 at the layover. The operator had his front door open but his back was turned as he was checking the aisle and seats for lost items. This man appeared to look mentally ill and I wasn't too sure what he had up his sleeve. Plenty of my co-workers have been attacked out here by crazy-ass people, so I started walking toward the bus with my hand in my pocket. He stepped on the bus and I saw some dialogue exchanged, then he got off and walked toward the exit of the layover. The operator stepped off his bus as I was approaching.

"Damn dawg, what was that all about?" I asked.

"Oh, he wanted a lighter," the operator said.

I breathed a sigh of relief afterwards.

"Oh okay cool. I thought he was about to be on some bullshit—homie didn't look sane at all."

We both laughed about the situation and conversed as we walked to the restroom, sharing our sentiments about the crazies in the city that ride the bus. We all have stories—some worse than others. The layover is dark as hell when nighttime falls. I don't put anything past anybody out here. Lord forbid anything happens to any of my co-workers, but I refuse to sit back and watch them suffer an attack at the hands of one of these "zombies." We all we got.

On my last trip heading southbound, La Cienega had traffic at a standstill. It took me thirty minutes to get from Jefferson and La Cienega to La Brea. While heading southbound, there was a fire truck blocking the southbound side of the intersection. It was my last trip, and I got exhausted just sitting in that traffic. I bogarted the turning lane all the way down, but when I got to Jefferson to go eastbound, there was traffic there too. Once I got past La Brea Avenue, I was able to roll.

The traffic that makes a right turn onto La Brea had cars backed all the way up past Hauser—which is about a mile up the road. Sitting in traffic will have your ass worn out at the end of the day.

Friday, November 13, 2020

On my first trip coming out of downtown transitioning from the 38 to 35, I serviced the northbound stop at Broadway and Venice. There were a handful of passengers there, but a young couple grabbed my attention when they boarded. They had a grip of bags, their clothing was a bit dirty, and they appeared to be under the influence of something. Although they were the youngest amongst the passengers, they moved the slowest. They moved like they were walking underwater—and the boyfriend had a damn bike. The girlfriend got on, but man... the boyfriend made me miss two light cycles as he was getting his bike on. All I remember thinking was, *man if you don't hurry yo ass up!!!*

I continued in service, heading westbound on Washington. I pull into the bus zone on the far side next to the Burger King, servicing the stop. Right when I'm about to leave, I hear somebody in the back yelling.

"Wait driver, wait! Right here! Right here—we getting off!"

I look my ass in the mirror—it's the boyfriend. All I could think was, *Got dammit!* I throw my hands up in frustration and hit the parking brake because I already knew how long it was gonna take them to get off. Between how slow they were moving and the stuff they had, it took them almost three minutes to exit. When they finally got off, they walked in front of the bus, jaywalking toward the south side of Washington Boulevard. I felt like I was looking at two sloths crossing from one side of a forest to the other. It's a sad sight to see anyone on drugs. Judging from their movement's it's evident they were high off something.

Driving a bus, every week somewhere in the city, I always come across young couples strung out on drugs. It's nothing new, but I see it so much now.

On my second trip, I picked up a wheelchair patron. But he wasn't just any wheelchair patron—he knew a lot about driving for MTA. He knew the names of some of our coworkers, the lines, and everything else. When I got a good look at him in the mirror, I realized he was an operator who used to be out of my division. Last time I saw him was back in 2011–2012. Even though he was still big back then, he was able-bodied—but it sucks seeing him in a wheelchair now.

He talked about how much stress the job caused him, which led to his health deteriorating. And he's not the only one. I know plenty of coworkers who were once able-bodied, and now their physical condition isn't all that great. As he was talking to me, I started thinking to myself, *damn, I don't want this to be me.* It seems as if you work here long enough, you're going to encounter some type of health issue that results from driving public transit. He rode all the way to Jefferson and Grand—he wanted to go to the downtown L.A. Department of Motor Vehicles.

I'm looking forward to this weekend. I'll be celebrating being married for two years, and I've got a much-needed three-day weekend.

Tuesday, November 17, 2020

I'm back feeling good and thankful after a three-day weekend.

On my second trip heading down Jefferson Boulevard, there was a guy standing in the street with his bike at the stop near the old liquor store on 12th Ave. I don't have time to be taking chances on people standing in the street. He was flagging me down as I was approaching the stop, but his ass wouldn't step on the curb. It irritates the fuck out of me when people are standing in the street trying to catch the bus. I tried to pull into the zone, I'm waving at him to get on the curb—he refused to do so. I got tired of his shenanigans and kept it rollin'. Besides, with the way he was acting, ain't no telling what kind of bullshit he would've started doing once he got on.

What people don't understand is that standing in the street like that is a liability. If I hit him, even by accident, they'll throw me under the bus. It's always the driver who ends up blamed, suspended, or filling out a stack of paperwork. I'm not risking my license or my peace of mind for someone who won't do the bare minimum and get on the damn curb.

Then on my last trip, I picked up a brother who went by the last name Miles at La Brea Ave heading westbound on Washington Boulevard. He was a real cool dude. He was struggling to get on the bus because he had a walker with groceries on both sides. I helped him to board by pulling his walker up the ramp. I hit the parking brake, reached out, and grabbed it—which allowed him to free himself to safely board. His gratitude was beyond measurable, and I was extremely grateful for that.

Moments like that go a long way. This job will have you jaded as hell, but every now and then, someone reminds you that not everybody is on bullshit. Mr. Miles was one of those people. Respectful, patient, appreciative—just a solid rider.

I know it seem like I'm writing bad things all the time, but I do have my good moments. This was one of many. There are plenty of passengers that help to make your shift smooth, and he was one of a few.

Shout out to all the passengers that help to make the days better. You might not even realize it but y'all make a major difference.

Wednesday, November 18, 2020

An absolute great day! Nothing to report here! It was smooth sailing and I'm very grateful.

One thing I do want to give props to is not having to collect bus fare. It feels good just pulling into a bus zone and picking up passengers. I don't know how long this will go on, but I love it. It is such a relief not to hear the excuses people give for not being able to pay their bus fare.

I done heard all kinds of stories—*"I lost my wallet," "I had to pay a bill," "I had to get groceries"*—or the usual *"I just don't have it today."* And then you got people that just don't give a fuck. You got people that will walk right past your ass as if you're a light pole on a city street. You got people that get on with brand new Nike and Air Jordan shoes that just came out that day—with no money for bus fare. You'll have people get on the bus with food from their favorite fast food restaurants saying they don't have money.

Even if you quote the fare like the rulebook says, you run the risk of an altercation from an unruly passenger—which Metro can flip the script on and say *you* provoked the attack. Just the blatant lack of priorities people display on public transportation alone is enough to make you blow a fuse internally.

One thing I don't miss is people standing at the farebox doing the "hokey pokey," acting like they're looking for money knowing full damn well they don't have it. Women sitting their purses on the dashboard or the farebox, digging through it like they're on a treasure hunt—when they could've done it *before* getting on.

I don't miss the damn farebox getting jammed with coins from passengers carelessly dumping everything in the slot. You got people that would throw the coins in all at once and then swish them with their finger back and forth until the majority went down. And a lot of the time, coins got stuck.

Another thing I'm also happy about is not having to load TAP cards. I remember when they started issuing us TAP cards to sell to the public—there were times when someone would put five dollars in the machine, and it would show as one dollar. Then you'd have to load the card using the short fare button. I got called to the office a few times for that mechanical failure—having to explain to management and write miscellaneous reports as to why I sold two TAP cards but a value of $11 and some change was missing. So to avoid that, I stopped selling them altogether. These niggas called me to the office over a mechanical failure.

I don't miss any of those discrepancies involving bus fare. *It feels good to just pick up and go.*

Thursday, November 19, 2020

Today on my third trip heading eastbound on Jefferson Boulevard, I seen the most unusual shit at Figueroa. I saw a guy driving a 4th generation Cadillac Deville with its hood missing. On the portion where the carburetor would be, there was a shiny disco ball. *What the fuck?* L.A. never lets you down when you think you've seen it all.

Today I was bothered by people constantly hitting stop requests and not getting off. Doing Line 35 between Normandie and Vermont, I've found myself getting frustrated with passengers hitting the request and not getting off. This happened on multiple trips... I remember thinking, *fuckin' with me I'll turn into a dick and stop at every stop until the end of my line.*

On my trip before the last, I was heading down Washington Boulevard westbound and right at 6th Ave, there was a girl that jumped out toward the curb, throwing both her arms up in a "what the fuck?" gesture. I pulled the bus over and picked her up. What irritated the fuck out of me was that this girl was standing damn near 50 feet from the bus zone—and it was dark as fuck.

Not to mention, she didn't make it any better rocking all black clothing.

I tell people all the time, *if you're going to be in the dark, wear reflective gear so that a driver can see you.* I open the door and she boards through the rear.

"I'm sorry, I didn't see you. You need to be under the light—that stop in particular is very dark," I said.

She initially didn't hear me at first because she was listening to music, but she took her headphones off.

"I didn't hear you, sir," she said.

"I was saying I didn't see you because the stop was dark and you were waiting far."

"Oh I'm sorry, sir. There were some guys driving around the block staring at me and I didn't trust it."

"Oh okay, I understand—but for future reference, keep your head on a swivel," I replied.

I don't blame her at all. It's some predators out here on and off the bus. People circling the blocks, people out here committing human trafficking—it's all kinds of shit going on out here that the average everyday person is not aware of.

On my last trip heading down Washington as the 38, I was sitting in the intersection at Grand waiting to make a left turn. Traffic heading eastbound came to a standstill because the far side of the light was a traffic jam. The light turned red and I began to proceed to make my turn when the green arrow showed up for me—a punk-ass Toyota Prius came to a complete stop then ran the light, which forced me to slam on my brakes. I blew the shit out of my horn at that knucklehead. Boy, I tell you about a lot of these Prius drivers—they live up to their stereotypes regularly. I can't speak for those who live in other cities, but it is terrible out here in L.A. It just seems like there's a mechanism to make you a douchebag if you end up owning and driving one of those cars.

Friday, November 20, 2020

On my first trip heading westbound on the 35, it was crazy. I picked up a guy at Washington and New England who was blind. The trippy part about it was, when I pulled into the zone I yelled the line and the direction. He just stood there. I gave him a little bit of time and he didn't move at all. *Could he be hearing impaired as well?* I thought.

I started to close the door. I figured, *maybe he's waiting on someone else?* As I started to close it, he abruptly stepped onto the bus. Shit threw me off guard. I'm guessing he finally figured out that the bus was there. He got on, and I was trying to tell him where the seats were—but he couldn't hear either—so I got out the seat and guided him. With a straight face, he gave me a thumbs up and chunked up a deuce. I was worried which stop he would need. It wasn't like I could ask him or write it. But he knew exactly what stop he had to get off. He hit the stop request for Catalina Street, and when he got off, he gave me a thumbs up. *Damn, for someone to not have both hearing and vision—I can only imagine.*

The day went swell up until my last trip on the 38 at Arlington. Every time I get to Arlington, there are a handful of knuckleheads that hang out at the bus stop near the liquor store and the Louisiana Fried Chicken. As I'm picking up people, a young crackhead-appearing woman crossed the street, almost getting hit in traffic to catch my bus. At the same time, a dude coming from the eastbound side—running past the church—ran across the street to get on. He sat next to her as soon as he boarded.

As I'm continuing eastbound past Western, the lady that jaywalked started fussing and cussing at the guy that ran from the eastbound side.

"You're a fuckin' user and abuser! Fuck you! I can't stand your ass!" she said.

She was real, real loud. I wasn't expecting that, especially with how decent the day had been. All I could think to myself was, *aww shit, here we go.*

The guy really didn't say much—he just let her argue. They rode all the way to the end of the line. The guy waved at me to tell me thanks as they both made an exit at Broadway and Venice. I was so happy when they got off. I swore up and down something would pop off between them.

Well, the day went good. Looking forward to my weekend.

Monday, November 23, 2020

On my first trip on Line 38, I picked up a lady at Crenshaw Boulevard who was visually impaired. She got on and immediately yelled out her request.

"Operator, I wanna get off at Vermont, okay!?"

"Okay ma'am, cool—will do!" I replied.

Driving down Jefferson Boulevard, she literally kept yelling at me every two minutes inquiring about her stop.

"Driver, I need Vermont please! Driver, I need Vermont please!" is all I heard.

I kept it cool, and I was very conscious of her disability. I understand that you don't want to miss your stop, ma'am—but calling out the stop every damn few minutes is annoying. Also, we have damn annunciators calling out the stops. Prior to me approaching Vermont, I yelled that shit out so loud I damn near blew my own eardrum out.

On that same trip doing the 35, I had a few lazy passengers. What do I mean by lazy passengers? The ones who are too lazy to walk further up into the stop and get on. This always occurs when I get to my last stop downtown on Venice and Broadway before doing the 38. They don't want to walk up like everyone else when I'm sitting in the zone behind another bus—I'm talking about able-bodied people. The shit grinds my gears when people start flagging me down as I'm leaving the zone after I done serviced the stop. Everybody else was alert and moving, ready to board—what's the deal with the others? Bet they asses will be ready for the next one.

On my last trip coming out of downtown on the 35, I had an older guy fall while getting on the bus at Figueroa. He had some fast food—either Jack in the Box or Burger King—I couldn't really tell. He slipped after missing the step, spilling his drink and everything. Anytime someone falls on your bus, you're supposed to report it to the company and fill out an accident report at the end of the day to cover your backside. But I've got to the point where I'm not reporting shit—they're gonna have to prove it. There's always the fear that later on someone will come and try to pursue legal action due to a lack of care being distributed from an operator. At this point in the game, I'm not worried about that. I don't feel like filling out no accident report or incriminating myself so the powers up above can get their egotistical jollies off.

The man was okay. He got up and went on about his evening. He rode to Crenshaw Boulevard.

Tuesday, November 24, 2020

On my first trip doing Line 38, there was a guy that got on at Crenshaw Boulevard asking a TON of questions. From the time he boarded to the time he got off, it was non-stop. He asked things like, "How do I get downtown? How far do you go? If I take this bus what side of town will it lead me to? How often this bus run?" etc.

I don't mind questions, but got damn—to be asking me the same set of questions in different forms from the time you board to the time you get off is a straight-up headache. What made matters worse is that he got off at 10th Ave. With the questions he was asking, you would've thought he was heading in the direction of the lines he inquired about.

You don't mind answering a few questions to help passengers get to where they gotta go—but for all the other questions? You can Google that or call customer service.

Chillin' at the layover for that last trip, I'm standing outside my bus. I park closer to the Washington side at the West L.A. Transit layover. I hear and feel something hit the ground—I thought I was trippin', because it sounded like a body. I look behind me and there's a guy laying on the ground, wincing in pain. He's trying to get into the CalTrans yard that's next to our layover. I was confused as to why he was laid out like that. Then he got back up and attempted to hop the fence on the side closest to the layover.

That's when it dawned on me—he fell from trying to climb the gate.

"Bro, what is you doing?" I asked, looking confused as hell.

He's a short dude wearing what looks like construction gear. He had a heavy Hispanic accent, but based on how he was talking, you could tell he'd been drinking.

"They got my bike," he said, pointing toward the CalTrans lot.

"Dawg, the gate on the other side is open—just walk in," I said. "Hopping the fence is not your best attribute at this moment in time."

He gives me the cut-throat gesture and continues trying to hop the fence. I threw my hands up, indicating I wasn't a witness to shit.

"Aight man, I ain't see shit dawg," I said.

I turned my back and went on with my day. He eventually made it over the fence, and once he landed inside the CalTrans yard, I heard a few dudes yelling at him, asking what he was doing. I minded my business and kept it pushin'. I stepped outside the layover on Fairfax Ave to talk on the phone with my wife.

On my second trip doing Line 35, I had two dudes who got on downtown. They were both handicapped—one walked with an extreme limp and the other had a cane. I was sitting at the red light at Broadway and Venice, ready to continue in service. If it wasn't for that red light, I would've never picked their asses up. But me still being near the curb, I allowed them to board.

They both needed 17th Street near Union Ave. I informed them I would call the stop when I got close.

The part that was so annoying about them is that they kept asking how close they were. I get to Washington and Grand—

"How close are we, Operator?"

I get to Figueroa and Washington—

"How close are we, Operator?"

Heading down Washington, passing all the dealerships—

"How close are we, Operator?"

Like got damn man, how many times you gone ask? I had to constantly remind them that I hadn't forgotten about them. When I got near the post office, I called that shit out real loud so they could be ready to get off.

What a relief it was when I got to their stop.

I don't mean to bitch, but my God. I don't mind helping passengers get to where they gotta go—but the lack of patience they had is what gets me the most.

Outside of all that, the day went okay.

Wednesday, November 25, 2020

Today something happened that I would've never imagined—something that very seldom happens within this company. The supervisor that I bumped heads with not too long ago actually apologized to me for what occurred on that day.

I was shocked.

A road supervisor apologizing for their fuck-up? It seems like it's almost a sin for those above bus operators to take accountability for anything.

I was walking to the restroom after doing my first trip at the West L.A. Transit Center layover. I saw one of my co-workers talking to him on the way. When I came out and greeted her, she was getting her bus started and informed me that he felt bad for everything that went down. I didn't believe her at first, but she wasn't lying. I told her I'd believe it when I see it.

After my second trip, I made another restroom run. As I came out and walked to my bus, that's when he rolled up on me.

"How's it going, Operator? I just want to take the time to apologize for what happened a few weeks back. I've been meaning to apologize, but I haven't been working this area these past few weeks. I was wrong for that."

Man... the element of surprise is a muthafucka. I was extremely surprised—but I was also appreciative. I honestly thought I was having a dream. I had to take a second to recollect myself and respond to what was just bestowed upon me.

"Man, thank you so much. I truly appreciate that. You didn't have to do that, but hearing those words come out your mouth—it means a lot. And trust and believe, I'm beyond appreciative. Thank you so much," I said.

"You got it, Operator. Enjoy your Thanksgiving," he said.

"You do the same. Be safe out here. Happy holidays."

He drove off out of the layover, and I walked back to my bus—shocked, but happy at the same time. Out of all the road supervisors I've encountered throughout the company that have committed any wrongs, he's the first I've seen take accountability. That was a first for me. And truth be told, that made my day a whole lot better. I know things ain't perfect and never will be, but I'm not trying to make enemies out here—especially amongst my co-workers.

On my last trip heading down Jefferson eastbound, a man started cussin' and fussin' because he missed his stop at Vermont. I didn't make the stop because no one wanted it. As I was approaching the zone, I looked up in the mirror to gauge body language, to see if anyone was preparing to get off—but I didn't get any hints. I had slowed down, but once I got past the intersection, I floored it to continue up the street.

Then, outta nowhere, I start hearing someone screaming with a heavy Asian accent—

"FUCK! GOT DAMMIT! FUCK! FUCK!"

He spooked the shit outta me blurting out like that. With how loud he was yelling and how frustrated he seemed, I didn't know what was about to happen next. Shit sent my anxiety through the roof.

I've had people give off the energy like they were about to attack me over missing a stop. When he was standing at the rear door, he was still looking down at his phone, so I'm guessing he was distracted and missed it. He ended up getting off at McClintock near USC and walked back.

I wish people would just keep their heads on a swivel.

Friday, November 27, 2020

Yesterday was Thanksgiving, and due to the holiday, my part-time assignment, and MTA being on a Sunday schedule, I only had to work three hours. I usually don't like working holidays, yea the pay is cool, but I don't care about any of that. I'd rather be off.

Full time drivers get double time and a half. What's so funny is that's the only time you'll see damn near all of them at work, they ain't tryna miss that pay.

My day was going smooth. On the trip coming back from Jefferson, some chick who was texting almost merged into my bus heading down Washington Boulevard approaching 6th Ave. When we got to the light, I laid on my horn, opened my window, and yelled at her.

"PUT THAT GOT DAMN PHONE DOWN!" I shouted.

Of course, she acted like she didn't hear me, but I know damn well she did. She was driving a burgundy Mercedes SUV. People with the nicest cars are hella reckless out here, especially on the Westside of L.A. It don't make no damn sense.

After my trip, I pulled my bus in—but I didn't use the original route. I continued up Fairfax and made a left on Venice. What fucked me up was the tent I saw on the northwest corner. There was a woman and two dudes outside, all conversing with each other. The woman was barefoot, had on a wool green sweater, a beanie, and just underwear. Yes—underwear. She had on them same big-ass draws that Brenda from the movie *Cooley High* was wearing. Just walking around outdoors like she was at home alone. I was surprised, but not surprised—if that makes any sense.

I'm just happy I worked a short day. Couldn't wait to get home and relax afterwards.

Today, I relieved an operator that I had run-ins with earlier this year, the same one that threatened to write me up for *passing people up*. When I got to the layover and saw him, all I could think was, *muthafucka*. I used to see him on the 14 every Monday before the coronavirus hit. He was trying to have small talk, and all I did was hit him with the "unhun, yea" response. I'm thinking *nigga I ain't forgot about that bullshit you did.*

On my second trip, I picked up a younger man who was with a much older woman at the first stop for Line 38 going up Jefferson. Throughout the week you'll see younger people helping out elderly folks on the bus—being caretakers and whatnot.

But there was a plot twist.

He wasn't her caregiver—they were actually dating. She was old enough to be his grandmother.

They both got on through the front. Her being elderly, I understood, but the young man greeted me and immediately started talking about some mental health issues he had been dealing with. We were conversing as I drove, and he said he was thankful for his girlfriend helping him through tough times. Then he pointed her out.

"Wait a minute... that's your girlfriend?" I asked.

"Yea," he replied, nonchalantly.

I was quiet for a moment. Then me being me, the questions kicked in. I worked my way to La Cienega from Fairfax, heading southbound after making a left turn.

"How old are you?" I asked.

"Twenty-five," he said.

I looked in the mirror with a look of concern.

"How old is she?" I asked.

"She's in her mid-sixties."

"Mid-sixties!?" I repeated, surprised.

"Yea," he said again.

He didn't specify her exact age, just the bracket. I know opposites attract but damn—I wasn't expecting that at all. This dude looked like comedian Craig Robinson, and the lady he was with was a short, older Asian woman. A bit frail, but not much. The whole thing reminded me of when Maury Povich would have those "odd couple" episodes—people explaining their romances to the audience, saying how they "hit it off." These two were prime candidates for one of those episodes.

Very seldom do I question why people choose their mates, but I remember thinking, *man, that woman must be doing some amazing things.* But hey, that's none of my business. They rode all the way to the train station on Jefferson.

Smooth day nonetheless.

Monday, November 30, 2020

I was heading eastbound on my first trip on Jefferson Boulevard when I got to Normandie and serviced the stop. All the customers boarded and exited the bus, but there was one passenger who had just gotten off who started whispering through the rubber seal of the rear door. I'm sitting at the red light waiting to continue up the boulevard, and I see him with his whole mouth pressed up against the rear door, slightly prying the rubber in the middle open—whispering to a younger lady who was sitting on the far side of the exit. I started blowing my horn at him to back away, but he refused to move. The light turned green and I hit the gas as hard as I could, getting outta that zone quick. What the fuck is wrong with muthafuckas out here, man? Dude looked like a life-size Goomba from the *Mario* video game.

As I was continuing up Jefferson, it dawned on me—I've had issues with this dude before. He usually rides between Vermont and Arlington. He always waits until he gets off the bus, then starts doing dumb shit outside—trying to get the attention of some female passenger he finds attractive. These dudes be something else out here.

On my second trip, I picked up a drunk dude at Western who was stumbling his ass off. I appreciate picking up drunk people because I'm thankful they're not out here driving. But the flip side is they might fall on the bus, pass out and not wake up at the end of the line, or act belligerent from liquid courage—causing a disturbance for me and everybody else onboard.

I ain't gone lie—I tried to avoid picking him up, but as I was boarding other passengers, he took the time to catch up to the rear door and slid right on. When I got to Denker heading eastbound, he slipped into the gutter hard as hell trying to get off—but he didn't fall or bust his ass. Thank God for that. Lord knows I'm not filling out no damn accident report. He was so intoxicated that as soon as he got to the grass near the apartment building, he just flopped down like he'd just got home from a long day of work.

Then on my second-to-last trip while doing the 35 portion of the line, this girl who had put her bike on the rack got pissed because I didn't wait for her when she got off. Real talk—I forgot it was her bike. She didn't let me know she was grabbing it. You're supposed to notify the operator before you get off that you'll be retrieving your bike. She didn't do that and had the nerve to cop an attitude.

This was at Washington and Norton. As she's unloading her bike from the rack, I opened the window.

"You're supposed to let us know you're getting your bike, ma'am! Thank you!" I sarcastically yelled out.

Then I slammed the window shut. She hit me with the "crazy" gesture—twirling her hand around her ear like *I* was the one trippin'.

Whatever, woman, I thought. *Next time, I'll take off with your shit and leave it at the layover. How 'bout that? Matter of fact, hop yo remedial ass on that muthafucka next time and ride it to your destination.*

ESSENTIAL: Diary of a Public Transit Bus Operator Volume 1

Tuesday, December 1, 2020

On my second trip heading eastbound on Jefferson Boulevard, I began slowing down to enter the bus zone at Normandie Avenue, and I seen an elderly blonde-haired woman walking toward the curb. She appeared to be homeless. You could tell she hadn't bathed in a while—with how dirty her skin was and the dress she had on looking just as filthy. I didn't know what to expect, so I slowed down a little bit more so I could be prepared just in case she did something out of the ordinary.

I didn't expect her to do what she did next.

She pulled down her underwear, lifted up her dress, and started urinating on the curb right before the bus zone. *Uggggh* is all I could think. All I could do was shake my head. I mean damn, people really don't give a fuck out here anymore. I serviced the bus zone at Normandie and rushed all the passengers to get on, because she started walking in my direction. I didn't want to run the risk of her hopping on the bus. As soon as the light turned green, I floored the shit out of the gas pedal and pulled out of the zone.

These people nowadays don't give a shit where they use the restroom. With as many homeless and mentally ill people pissin' and shittin' everywhere, it's safe to say that starting a business power washing surfaces wouldn't be a bad investment. What's wild is how stuff like this doesn't even shock me like it used to. I just hit the gas and kept it moving. That's how much this job will desensitize you.

The streets are a different kind of wild now. You see people in full psychosis one minute, then watch them walk into traffic or relieve themselves like they in their own backyard. The mental illness and homelessness crisis out here is out of control, and those of us behind the wheel—we see it all, up close, every single damn day. And the cold part? Ain't no training for this. No manual prepares you for watching someone use the sidewalk as a toilet before your first break. It's just another shift. I stay looking on the ground as I walk anywhere outside the bus. I've had moments where I've almost stepped in human waste—whether it's urine or straight-up fecal matter. Especially at layovers.

One layover that's notorious for human waste is the Maple Lot downtown off 5th and Wall Street. There isn't a week that goes by where you don't see a pile of shit either inside or outside the lot. Now that I'm mentioning it, I'm thinking back to the time I seen human waste inside the Maple Lot the length and width of a footlong Subway sandwich—no bullshit. A few years back, there used to be a convenience store around the corner that drivers would walk to. On the way there, a few of my coworkers weren't even trippin' about the fact someone dropped a deuce—it was the size of the damn thing that had everybody stuck.

We were standing there like, *what the fuck did this individual eat to drop off such a massive load?*

What made it even funnier was the fact that a road supervisor came through and put construction cones around it—with a sign that said, CAUTION: HUMAN WASTE. It reminded me of that movie *Mimic*, when Charles S. Dutton's character was describing the shit smeared on the wall. Yeah... I had that exact same reaction. I didn't mean to get sidetracked, just reminicisng on some of the crazy shit I've witnessed during my tenure with the MTA. Let me get on with the rest of my night.

Friday, December 4, 2020

Sometimes as an operator, I always have these random thoughts. On my second trip driving down Jefferson, I picked up a few dudes who were in the back of the bus talking to each other. These muthafuckas sounded like Bootsy Collins talking to Parliament or some shit. You know them niggas that never left the '70s?

"Eyy baby! What's goin' on baby!"—you know, that 70s blaxploitation lingo. That shit makes me laugh. Anyway, they were talking about COVID.

On that same trip, I picked up a homeless woman. She took a long ass time to put her bike on the rack. I was so frustrated I hit the parking brake and looked at the timer on the ATMS—it took her about three light cycles just to get her bike on.

My last trip I was irritated because somebody was playing loud ass music on the 38. For the life of me, why can't people just do right by others and wear some damn headphones? I just don't understand it.

On the same trip, some dude riding his fixie bike was moving like a bat outta hell down Jefferson as I was going eastbound. He was weaving in and out of both lanes. Annoying as shit. He almost got hit at 10th Ave by a car trying to pass him, but he was out here "owning" the road like he had it to himself. He threw his hands up in frustration like the driver was the one in the wrong. I can't stand bicyclists like him.

He rode all the way to 4th Ave and then boarded the bus to head toward Figueroa. As fast as he was riding, it didn't make no sense for him to get on the bus—he would've got to his destination quicker. But then again, people always tell me, *"Man, I'm tired. I been riding all day."*

Friday, December 11, 2020

Today I linked up with a passenger I haven't seen in a long ass time. His name is Paul, and I used to see him on Line 35 a few years back. We would talk all the time. I forgot how we initially met, but brother was real cool. Since this shakeup, everybody I see all look the same—we all rockin' masks. You know the saying: *"Everyone fits the description."* It's been hard to recognize people lately, so when someone familiar pops up, it kinda snaps you outta the routine for a second.

I picked him up at Hauser. After he boarded through the rear door, he starts walking up the aisle toward the front.

"What's up, brother? It's been a long time," he said in a muffled tone from under his mask.

I'm lookin' in the mirror trying to figure out who it is, then it finally hits me.

"PAUL!? Damn dawg, what's good with you bruh? It's been a long ass time!" I said.

We chopped it up for a bit, catching up on how life's been the last couple years. It felt good to have that kind of exchange—genuine energy, not just surface-level convo. Folks like Paul remind you that this job ain't all crazy. There's still people out there who show love, respect, and keep it real. When I got to the end of the line, I dropped him off and pulled into the layover. Stepped outside to holler at him for a minute. Told him that when the next shakeup kicks in, I'd be working Line 37 down Adams. He said he rides that line sometimes, so who knows—we might cross paths again.

Moments like that really do help balance out the madness. Because on the trip afterwards? Man, fuck that trip.

I was heading eastbound on Jefferson when some young dude used the bike rack just to ride from St. Andrews to Western. That's literally the next stop. He could've pedaled that in under a minute, but nope—had to throw his bike on the rack like it was a damn road trip. What pissed me off even more was the way he looked at me when he got off. Smirked like he knew he was being lazy and just didn't give a shit. One of them smug little "yeah I know I'm on bullshit" type of looks. He knew damn well I was heated.

It's stuff like that that chips away at you throughout the day. Not enough to cause a blow-up, but just enough to wear on your nerves.

When I rode public transit as a younger kid, I always thought to myself, *"I'll walk,"* if the distance was close. I just felt it was rude to get on a driver's bus and only go one block or one stop. In my old neighborhood where I stayed, Line 40 that went down King Boulevard would stop at St. Andrews. If I was going to any of the spots in the shopping centers that were catty-corner from each other on King Boulevard and Western Avenue, I wouldn't be wasting a driver's time unless I was going past Denker or some shit.

People, I tell you.

Tuesday, December 15, 2020

Driving down Beverly on my second trip, I blew a fuse at a young man for still sitting down when I approached the stop. I was heading westbound approaching Highland, and this kid was still sitting. I was going to pass the stop up, but he jumped up at the very last minute and flagged me down.

Normally I pass up stops, but the light had just hit red, so I came to a stop and opened the door.

"Got damn man, you see me coming—stand your ass up!" I yelled as he boarded.

The young man was looking at me the whole time while he was sitting down. I didn't understand why he was still posted up as I'm approaching—an able-bodied young man at that. I'll give a pass to an elderly or disabled person who can't stand that long or appears to be visually impaired, but that didn't seem to be the case with him. If it was, then hey—I'll apologize for that. But outside of that, he needs to be ready and standing.

This ain't Uber. I'm not slowing down for somebody still deciding if they want to ride or not. If you see a 40-foot bus coming up the block, you should already be up on your feet, ready to go—not sitting there chillin' like you at a damn bus museum. That kinda stuff adds to the stress. It's like, damn, do I gotta do everything? Drive, protect, read minds, and coach you on how to catch the bus too?

Last but not least, a pompous-ass Jennifer Lawrence-looking woman took it upon herself to step into the street right before Stanley Ave—on the same trip with the young man that boarded.

I was approaching the intersection, and this girl abruptly walks into the street, standing dead center in the number two lane. I know they tell us to "expect the unexpected," but I honestly wasn't expecting *that* shit.

I hit my horn and everything—it didn't faze her one bit. She stood right there in the middle of the lane, ignoring my honks, finishing up a text message like I wasn't operating a whole-ass bus coming right at her. And she's only a few feet from her car door.

I'm frowning like, *Ain't this a bitch? What the fuck kind of shit is this?* Boy, I was pissed.

Once she finished her text, she got in the car and bounced like it was nothing.

That's the part that gets me—it's not just the actions, it's the attitude that comes with it. No awareness, no urgency, just that "I do what I want" energy. And it's always worse on this side of town. The entitlement over here is different. Folks walk into the street like they're invincible, It's draining. Dealing with people who don't have a single ounce of situational awareness, while you're the one responsible for everything that goes down. One wrong move, one incident, and guess who's doing the paperwork or sitting in the office explaining shit? Me.

This is why I say over and over: the hardest part of this job ain't the driving—it's everything else. It's the people, the attitudes, the chaos, the unpredictability. The constant back-and-forth between being calm and wanting to lose it. Sometimes, when I get home, I gotta sit in the car for five or ten minutes just to mentally clock out. Can't take this shit inside. Can't carry that Beverly Boulevard energy into the house with me.

Friday, December 18, 2020

Well, what's new—there's more confirmed COVID cases at our division. Now they have operators sitting in their cars. They also removed all the furniture and taken away all of the recreational materials like pool tables, sticks, foosball tables, etc. Each table can only have one person sitting at it.

The operator lobby use to have some life to it, now it feels like the waiting room to a doctors office that treats terminally ill patients. We used to at least have some comfort—some normalcy between trips. That's gone. And the worst part is, nobody even says much anymore. Man...the times we are living in.

On my first trip heading southbound on Grand approaching 5th Street, there was a Silver Line bus sitting in the zone. The Silver Line takes you from downtown all the way to the San Pedro/Harbor City area of Los Angeles. I don't know how often they run, but when they are running, they pick up a ton of people.

There was a lady running for the bus who decided to jump into the street as I was pulling into the zone. I'm constantly honking my horn at her so I can pull into the bus stop, but she's so adamant about catching the bus that she's being negligent to everything else. People were yelling at her to step onto the curb, but she didn't give a fuck about none of that. She finally hops on the curb when she got close and made her bus. People sacrifice their lives for these buses, and I don't understand it. You really putting your life on the line... for public transit? That's the part that blows my mind. Like this is a $1.75 ride, not the last helicopter leaving the roof in an apocalypse. I've seen people run out into traffic, damn near get clipped, cuss out other drivers, bang on windows—all for a bus that another one is probably ten minutes behind. It's not that deep.

On my first layover at Washington and Fairfax, there was a couple walking through the layover taking pictures. Out of all the places you could take pictures, they chose the damn layover—where buses are backing out and pulling in. Jesus...

Outside of bus operators or authorized personnel, no one is supposed to be in the layover zone. They're in the area where the buses start to turn after pulling into the driveway. Buses are trying to pull in and these fools were all in the fuckin' way.

I gave them heads up after seeing that bullshit.

"Aye man, y'all can't be in here!"

The boyfriend looks like a skateboarder from the '90s and the girlfriend looks like a hillbilly who finally traveled miles away from her trailer park to go on vacation. They neglect the words I tell them, and the boyfriend continues to take pictures of the girlfriend. They were also obstructing a few buses from turning.

I start to honk my horn and give them the cut-throat gesture. They keep ignoring me—then the guy finally replies to my honks in frustration.

"OKAY YOU FUCKING ASSHOLE!" he yelled.

I frowned up and responded, still looking out the window.

"What part of y'all can't be in here don't y'all fuckin' understand!? And you smoking a cigarette in a layover zone where buses are powered by CNG fuel, what's wrong with you man?" I asked.

They start to leave out the entrance, and I see the girlfriend give me the middle finger as they're walking out of the layover. I walk out the front door, manually closing it so I can begin heading to the restroom, but I got some final words for her.

"Fuck you too, bitch! As a matter of fact—fuck the both of y'all!"

They continue walking southbound on Fairfax Ave. They'll be the same people that try to pursue legal action because they fucked around and got hurt while doing some stupid shit. Hell, that's if they were to survive.

It's always the folks that got no business being somewhere that wanna act the boldest. It's like people forget that we're driving 30,000-pound vehicles that don't stop on a dime. This ain't no damn photo op—this is an active traffic zone.

Every day it's something different. Whether it's people risking their lives over a missed bus or walking through restricted areas like it's a public park. And when shit goes wrong, guess who gets blamed? Us. The operators. The ones who are just trying to do our jobs and go home in one piece.

But anyway—rest of my day went smooth.

Tuesday, December 22, 2020

On my second trip coming out of downtown, I hit a tree branch at 1st and Hope Street. On our New Flyer buses, there's a cover to the CNG pipes that's about three feet tall, and depending on where you drive, you can hit a few branches. But what had me puzzled was the fact that I been pulling into this zone for years in the same manner and have never hit the tree.

Could the branch be hanging a little lower? I thought.

I hit the parking brake, put the gear in neutral, and stepped outside to take a look. I hit the rear top portion of the cover and left a crack at the top of the bus. I didn't say shit about it. I never incriminate myself over something like that. They would need to provide proof of it. If someone goes to the company and says something, they just gone have to find out for themselves— because I'm not saying shit. Although... I could use a suspension. But hey, that's a story for another day.

On my last trip, on the 37 portion of the line heading toward Washington and Fairfax, I almost collided with a reckless-ass bicyclist. I'm glad I only go a certain speed downtown, because if you're going any faster than residential speed, there is a possibility that you can make contact with one of them.

A lot of the ones who ride downtown—man, they have no regards for their own personal life. So what makes you think they give a fuck about anyone else's? A lot of the bikes they ride don't even have brakes, and they're coming at speeds going almost 30 to 40 mph. This bicyclist in particular was heading eastbound on 7th Street as I'm heading southbound on Grand Ave with ten seconds left to cross the intersection. As I get closer, here this dude come flying fast as shit—dude was moving at lightning speed. I had to slam on my brake to keep from hitting him.

Luckily, nobody fell out of their seats from me committing this panic stop. I wanted to give him a middle finger so bad, but I just kept driving.

On the same trip, when I got to Adams and Grand, there was a younger Hispanic couple that wanted Line 38 going down Jefferson westbound. The boyfriend was arguing with the girlfriend, and it seemed like he was having demonic movements. I couldn't tell if he was high or having withdrawals.

From down the street I could gauge their body language and tell they were arguing about something. The boyfriend's body language alone kept me from wanting to make the stop. There were people there flagging me down though, so I pulled into the bus zone.

She comes to the front door as I'm picking up a few elder passengers.

"Excuse me sir, do you know where the 38 is at?" she asks.

"I have no idea—one usually pulls up when I do," I replied.

The boyfriend is in the background yelling and screaming, acting like a gremlin with water thrown on it, and she's doing everything possible to keep him calm—but her efforts are minimal. Seeing this, I'm thinking, *Man I hope they don't ride my bus.*

Some people will ride Line 37 going down Adams if the 38 going down Jefferson takes too long.

"We been waiting on this bus for a long time and it hasn't showed up."

I looked at the time on the radio to show some form of gratification, as if I knew exactly when the bus was coming—but in all honesty, I didn't know shit.

"You shouldn't have to wait too long. It should be coming soon," I said.

"Okay, thank you, sir," she replied.

She tended back to her boyfriend, who was still acting belligerent. I closed the door, and as I'm leaving, the boyfriend runs to the curb abruptly and starts yelling at the bus real loud— at the top of his lungs. I got scared because I thought he was going to start hitting the bus or doing some other stupid shit, but with the help of his girlfriend temporarily pulling him away, I was able to safely make my turn and continue up Adams.

I went the rest of the night with no issues. I'm glad that I didn't have to deal with them riding, but I also recognize that at some point I'm going to encounter a situation similar in the near future— as a bus operator you just can't avoid it.

Tuesday, December 29, 2020

On my first trip, while waiting to go into service, there was a guy that jaywalked across San Vicente Boulevard to wait on my bus at the layover. He was staring at me the whole time. I got irritated by it and hopped my ass off the bus and walked away toward 3rd Street. It's annoying as fuck when someone comes to your layover and just stares at you like Sonic the Hedgehog with no movement from whoever is playing the game. I came my ass back fifteen minutes later—he was gone, thank God.

On my second trip at Crenshaw heading eastbound on Adams, I picked up a couple who took their sweet time getting on the bus, and they both had bikes. I hate when I pull into a bus zone and after I've picked up all my passengers, a muthafucka makes a last-minute decision to board. The girlfriend had a beach cruiser and the boyfriend left it up to her to put both bikes on. It was taking her so long to get it on the rack that I ended up hitting the parking brake and began daydreaming. The parking brake is a nightmare to passengers because when they hear that, they know you're going to be there for a long time. Once the boyfriend heard the parking brake hiss, he got off and helped her. I was thinking to myself like, *dude, you should have been helping her in the first place.* They rode to Grand near the county building, and at least this time he helped her get both bikes off.

On the same trip heading westbound on Beverly, there was a guy dicking around at Gardner. I picked up a few passengers—he waited until the door was closing to jump on at the last minute. I hate that shit with a passion. And you know what made matters worse? He had the audacity to ride the bus one stop up. This that bullshit. He could've walked his ass to the next stop. I wish people would stop wasting our damn time.

On my last trip, there was a guy doing road gymnastics at San Vicente—I mean, this dude was all in the street. Now, if you ever drive up Beverly Boulevard before San Vicente Boulevard heading eastbound, you can't see the stop until you get close to the intersection due to parked cars and how the right turning lane is set up. I could see him standing in the street, and I'm trying to pull into the zone while he's walking into the street toward the bus. I start to give the arm gesture, telling him to get back on the sidewalk. So he hops back near the curb and I open the door for him.

"I see you bossman—I can't hit the parked cars," I said.

"I got passed up by the last driver. I didn't wanna get passed up, shit—*even if you didn't pick me up, I was gon' ride the back of this muthafucka,*" he said.

We both laughed and I let him know it was all good.

The rest of the night went great. At the last stop, there was a homeless guy who got on at Beverly and Alvarado and fell asleep. He rode all the way to the last stop at Washington and Fairfax. It took some time to get him to wake up, and when he did, he asked me a question.

"Driver, you going back the other way?" he asked as he was still waking from his slumber.

I'm standing out the seat in the middle of the aisle, in the process of checking for lost items and sleeping patrons.

"Nah man, I'm done for the night. But wait at this stop—you can catch the same line going back," I said.

He had the look of defeat on his face. I thought he was going to be a problem, but he got off with no issues—thank God. I deadheaded to the division afterward, ending the workday.

Wednesday, December 30, 2020

On my second trip today going through downtown, there was a dude at 9th Street and Olive trying to ride my back bumper. I seen him in the right-side mirror—every time I began to leave out the bus zone, he would jump onto the rear right bumper. Then when I'd hit the brakes, he'd hop off. He was laughing at me in the mirror while doing it.

I began making another attempt to leave and he did the same shit again. I missed the light due to his shenanigans and was pissed off. I hit the parking brake and opened the door—he ran into the nearby parking lot. I wasn't going to do anything to him; I was just going to inform him to cut the bullshit. People love trying to go viral with this bullshit. I continued in service afterwards.

When I got to Reno, I picked up a lady who had a wheelchair where the front wheels were going in separate directions. Because of that, it was taking a long time for her to get on. She either needed to get the wheels fixed or a brand-new wheelchair altogether.

It took her so long that some of the passengers began getting impatient. Some Nate Dogg-looking ass dude copped an attitude and started kissing his teeth. I turned around and looked directly at him.

"Hold tight, sir. You're gonna get to your destination—we're almost done."

The lady had to be real cautious with how she rolled her chair back and forth because the front wheels would lock up and prevent her from going forward. I hate when people treat public transportation like it's their own personal vehicle—it's annoying as fuck. You don't have that luxury to bitch and complain. Take a taxi, Uber, or Lyft if you're under a time constraint. Public transportation most definitely ain't for you if elderly and disabled people getting on the bus gets on your nerves.

I continued in service and she rode all the way to Western. Rest of my day went good.

Thursday, December 31, 2020

#newyearseve

Happy New Year to all.

I got the next three days off—much needed, thank God. I don't even got big plans, but just knowing I don't have to deal with traffic, schedules, passengers, or none of that bullshit for a few days is lovely.

This year been exhausting in ways I can't even fully describe. Mentally, physically, emotionally. Between COVID, wild passengers, constant rule changes, and just trying to stay healthy and sane—it's been a hell of a ride. I'm thankful I made it through in one piece.

I ain't trying to get all deep or write some big motivational speech n shit, but real talk—if you survived this year with your peace of mind even halfway intact, you already did enough.

I'm looking forward to just resting, maybe catching up on some sleep, resetting my head a bit. I already know the bullshit will be waiting on me when I clock back in, so imma enjoy this little stretch while I got it.

Here's to 2021. I don't expect miracles—but I do expect to keep pushing, keep surviving, and keep doing me regardless.

Wednesday, January 6, 2021

On my last trip, there was a lady with a young man at Figueroa while I was doing Line 37. I don't know if he was her son, lil' brother, nephew—hell, I don't know. They had just rushed out of the Popeyes on the corner that was adjacent to the stop. The bike that the young man had was a BMX-style bike with pegs on both the front and back tires.

I had just finished servicing the zone as they came running down the ramp. The woman was aggressively waving and yelling prior to me closing the door.

"Aye waaaait! Waiiiit!"

The light was still red, so I cracked the door for them to get on. She got on, but the young man she was with was having a problem putting his bike on the rack. She goes back outside to assist him. As I'm looking at the wheels, I see that it's his pegs that's preventing the tires from going into the rack slot.

"Take the pegs off, you should be straight!" I yelled as the front door was open.

They're now both struggling to get the bike mounted. The woman is becoming frustrated, and she shakes her head in a "no" gesture with a frown on her face.

"The pegs is what's keeping his wheels attached to the frame," she said.

I shrug my shoulders with my hands to each side.

"Well, I'm sorry—I don't know what to tell you. But his bike has to be secure in the frame," I said.

She kisses her teeth and takes her frustration out on the young man.

"C'mon, take your damn bike off. Let's go!"

He still hasn't given up—he's still trying to find a way to get his bike on the rack. The young man was determined. I wasn't mad at him at all. Her anger grows, and she raises her voice at him again.

"Take your damn bike off the rack and let's goooooo!"

He finally gives in to what she's saying and slowly takes his bike off the rack. After she yelled at him, his whole demeanor changed. It was like she sucked the life out of him. I ain't gon' front—I felt kind of bad seeing that reaction from him. I damn near started to tell him to bring his bike on the bus, but per rule, the only time a bike can come inside is if it's the last run of the night and the rack is full.

They began walking westbound on Adams. As I crossed the intersection, you could see she was still talking to the young man in a frustrated manner, and his body language was equivalent to Eeyore from the cartoon *Winnie the Pooh*. Her approach made it seem like it was his fault they were unable to board the bus.

Man, I often don't feel bad about certain things, but for some reason, that hit me hard. Kids just be trying to get through the day, and adults be taking their anger out on them like they're a burden. That shit don't sit well with me.

ESSENTIAL: Diary of a Public Transit Bus Operator Volume 1

Thursday, January 7, 2021

Today I signed on and saw a picture of one of my co-workers who died. I forgot his name, but I would always find myself doing the same lines as him. I predominantly saw him on Washington, Adams, and Jefferson. He was a much older gentleman—give or take, he had to have more than twenty-five years with the company, I might be wrong. Judging by his appearance, he had to be in his early to mid-60s.

Every time I get to work and see a picture of a co-worker who's passed, it gets the best of me. I've been here for eleven years and I can't even keep count how many times I've seen one of my co-workers' badge photos taped to the sign-on window. What's even sadder is that even though the company puts a 5-gallon water jug out for people to donate toward funeral expenses, they just continue on with daily operations like nothing happened.

You could drop dead in the lobby with all your co-workers witnessing your demise, and management will still tell you to report to your bus for rollout—disregarding any trauma that might've caused the ones who saw that. (I heard that this actually happened a few years back out of one of the bus devisions.)

Looking around the division, it's sad to say—but everyone you come across, there's a possibility that you'll see one of their pictures on that window as the year continues. Our job is deemed the "silent killer" because of how many illnesses and physical injuries a lot of my co-workers have suffered due to the nature of this work. On average, I've seen about one to two pictures a month—whether it's a co-worker at your division or at another. Even if it's a retiree, you're going to be seeing one.

On a lighter—and funnier—note, something happened to me today that hasn't happened in a long time: I fuckin' fell going up some stairs!

After I got off, I went to grab a bite to eat at The Halal Guys on the corner of Santa Monica and San Vicente. I used the stairwell near the sheriff's station at the division, and that was a bad idea. As I was walking up the stairs to my car, a mouse bolted past me so fast it caught me off guard. I lost my footing and fell right at the top of the stairs. Damn... I was just happy I didn't drop my food.

That grassy area between the sheriff's station and the bus stop on the corner has a ton of mice. It's so many, you can hear them and see them out the corner of your eye. Shit is wild.

Well—thankfully I didn't suffer any injury. Just my pride. And I'm thankful no one saw that!

ESSENTIAL: Diary of a Public Transit Bus Operator Volume 1

To be continued in Volume 2

ESSENTIAL: Diary of a Public Transit Bus Operator Volume 1

www.newgreeneera.com

Instagram: @switchinlanes2022
TikTok: switchinlanes2022
X (formerly Twitter): switchinlanes22

www.ingramcontent.com/pod-product-compliance
Lightning Source LLC
Chambersburg PA
CBHW030450100526
44580CB00002B/63